Korea and the World

Lexington Studies on Korea's Place in International Relations

Series Editor: Jongwoo Han, Syracuse University

This series publishes trailblazing research by pioneering scholars on contemporary Korean issues. Transformative events in the early twenty-first century have marked a watershed for South and North Korea in many areas, including political economy, democracy, international power politics and security, ongoing disputes over the past with China and Japan, and North Korea's nuclear and missile programs, to name a few. Furthermore, post-modern cultural influences and the global advent of digital technology have led to the diversification of Korea's culture, religion, sports, diasporic community, and inter-Korean linguistic differences, as well as the Korean Wave. This series aims to explore and dissect these issues to further understanding of contemporary Korean life and politics.

Recent Titles in This Series

Korea and the World: New Frontiers in Korean Studies
Edited by Gregg A. Brazinsky

Korea and the World

New Frontiers in Korean Studies

Edited by Gregg A. Brazinsky

LEXINGTON BOOKS
Lanham • Boulder • New York • London

Published by Lexington Books
An imprint of The Rowman & Littlefield Publishing Group, Inc.
4501 Forbes Boulevard, Suite 200, Lanham, Maryland 20706
www.rowman.com

6 Tinworth Street, London SE11 5AL, United Kingdom

Copyright © 2019 The Rowman & Littlefield Publishing Group, Inc.

All rights reserved. No part of this book may be reproduced in any form or by any electronic or mechanical means, including information storage and retrieval systems, without written permission from the publisher, except by a reviewer who may quote passages in a review.

British Library Cataloguing in Publication Information Available

Library of Congress Cataloging-in-Publication Data

ISBN: 978-1-4985-9112-6 (cloth)
ISBN: 978-1-4985-9113-3 (electronic)
ISBN: 978-1-4985-9114-0 (paper)

This book is dedicated to Professor Young-Key Kim-Renaud, whose passion for Korean Studies has greatly strengthened the field and laid the foundation for our Korea programs at The George Washington University.

Contents

Acknowledgments ix

A Note on Romanization xi

Introduction 1
Gregg A. Brazinsky

Chapter 1 From Supply Lines to Supply Chains: Busan, the Korean War, and the Rise of Global Logistics 13
Patrick Chung

Chapter 2 From Dependency to Self-Sufficiency: American Relief Food in the Korean Peripheries in the 1960s 39
Dajeong Chung

Chapter 3 "The Carter Zeal" versus "The Carter Chill": U.S. Policy Towards the Korean Peninsula in the Carter Era 69
Khue Dieu Do

Chapter 4 Armed with Notebooks and Pencils: North and South Korean Students at the Tehran Foreign School, 1983 93
Benjamin R. Young

Chapter 5	North Korea's Changing Policy Toward the United Nations *Jie Dong*	111
Chapter 6	Explaining Economic Order in North Korea *Sheena Chestnut Greitens*	129
Chapter 7	Multiculturalism as State Developmental Policy in Global Korea *Darcie Draudt*	157
Chapter 8	Democratic Support and Generational Change in South Korea *Steven Denney*	179
	Index	203
	About the Author and Contributors	207

Acknowledgments

The majority of the essays in this volume and the idea for the volume itself came about as a result of a signature conference hosted by the GW Institute for Korean Studies in May 2017. I would like to thank the other core faculty and staff of the institute most especially Jisoo M. Kim, Young-key Kim-Renaud, Ann Yang, Celeste Arrington, Miok Pak, and Richard Grinker.

The conference, the institute, and this volume were all supported by the Core University Program for Korean Studies through the Ministry of Education of the Republic of the Korea and Korean Studies Promotion Service of the Academy of Korean Studies (AKS-2016-OLU-2250009). Chapter 6 "Explaining Economic Order in North Korea" was supported by the Laboratory Program for Korean Studies through the Ministry of Education of the Republic of Korea and the Korean Studies Promotion Service of the Academy of Korean Studies (AKS-2016-LAB-2250001).

Several distinguished Korea experts from both GW and elsewhere served as commentators during the 2017 signature conference and helped the authors to sharpen their ideas. These included: Arissa Oh, Mitch Lerner, James F. Person, Jiyoung Lee, and Harris Mylonas. I would also like to thank several conference participants who had already agreed to publish their papers elsewhere: Jeongmin Kim, Jooeun Kim, Peter Banseok Kwon, and Thomas Stock.

It has been a great pleasure to work with the series editor, Jongwoo Han. His dedication to promoting Korean history and enthusiasm for the volume have been a great source of encouragement. The editors and staff at Lexington Press have also been highly efficient, extremely patient, and congenial throughout the acquisition and production process.

As always, I would like to thank my mother and stepfather, who have eagerly awaited this and everything else that I am working on, as well as my many excellent colleagues in the History Department and the Elliott School of International Affairs at The George Washington University.

A Note on Romanization

Korean words and names have mostly been rendered according to the revised romanization system. A full description of this system can be found at the National Institute for Korean Language website: https://www.korean.go.kr/front_eng/roman/roman_01.do. Exceptions have been made, however, for widely known popular romanizations such as Park Chung Hee. All Chinese words and names have been rendered according to the pinyin system.

Introduction
Gregg A. Brazinsky

During the winter of 2014–2015 the melodrama *Gukjesijang* dominated the box office in South Korea becoming the country's second highest grossing film of all time.[1] The film's distributor, CJ Entertainment, released it internationally under the English title *Ode to My Father*—a reference to the main character's long quest to honor his father's wishes—but *Gukjesijang* could more literally be translated as "International Market." The film sets the story of its main character, Yun Deoksu, against the background of recent Korean history, especially South Korea's rapid economic and political transformation during the decades after the Korean War. It uses the protagonist's life story to retrace South Korea's journey as a nation within the maelstrom of global forces during the twentieth century.

Gukjesijang begins with Deoksu, his mother, and two siblings being separated from his father and younger sister, Maksun, during the December 1950 Heungnam Evacuation, a rescue operation that brought thousands of refugees from North Korea to the South Korean port city of Busan. In subsequent years, Deoksu goes to great lengths to support his family. As a young man he participates in the Gastarbeiter program, through which several thousand Koreans traveled to West Germany to work as miners and nurses. During the 1970s, again in need of money for his family, Deoksu takes a technician job supporting the ROK military units who fought alongside U.S. forces in Vietnam. The film reaches its tear-jerking climax when Deoksu manages—with the help of a 1983 KBS television program that connected South Koreans to lost missing family members—to reunite with his long-lost sister Maksun, who, it is learned, had been adopted by an American family as a small child. The historical narrative in *Gukjesijang* is interspersed by scenes from the present day that focus on Deoksu's family and his grudging decision to finally sell his modest family-owned imported goods store.

The film's title and story can be read in several different ways. At the most literal level the "international market" refers to the small marketplace where Deoksu's family ekes out a modest living by operating a store selling imported goods. Yet the experiences of Deoksu's family are in many ways an allegory for the turbulent historical era that all South Koreans lived through. During the Cold War, South Korea was forcefully incorporated into the U.S. led economic order by an authoritarian government determined to achieve rapid economic growth. Initially, the country's poor but disciplined workforce produced low cost goods such as textiles, wigs, and garments for export.[2] The sale of Deoksu's labor abroad into unfamiliar contexts is symbolic of how South Korea itself was compelled into a new role in the global division of labor by external forces that it had little ability to control. The protagonist is, in this sense, an almost powerless subject of an authoritarian state forced to shoulder the costs of his country's modernization.

At the same time, the film can be read in another more optimistic way. Even while sweeping and uncontrollable global forces pull Deoksu out into the world and force him into dangerous circumstances, he is also, in some ways, an opportunistic buyer in the international marketplace. Never completely surrendering his own agency, Deoksu constantly finds new ways to support his family, earn money, and survive under challenging circumstances. In this sense, the protagonist's journey mirrors how South Korea itself seized the opportunities provided by the Cold War international system to transform its economy and achieve prosperity. Moreover, by reuniting his family at the end and fulfilling his promise to his father, Deoksu symbolically overcomes the legacy of wartime trauma.

This tension in *Gukjesijang*'s representation of Korean history mirrors debates inside and outside of Korea about the country's last seven decades of engagement with the world. Were Koreans passive victims in processes of integration and globalization that enabled foreign ideas, cultures, and institutions to gain influence and even dominance in Korean society? Or did Koreans make strategic choices about how to participate in international society and adapt to global trends? How much did the Great Powers shape decision making in both Koreas and how much did Seoul and Pyongyang use what leverage they had to preserve their autonomy? These questions have gained prominence because, at the most basic level, they speak to broader issues of Korean identity. How they are answered determines how Koreans see themselves in relation to the rest of the world.

The essays in this volume seek to address these questions by examining different dimensions of Korea's global engagement during and after the Cold War. By global engagement, I mean something slightly different from globalization, which has been a popular buzzword in the field of Korean Studies in recent years.[3] Globalization is most often defined in terms of the creation of new networks and the diffusion of ideas, culture, goods, and knowledge in a transnational setting.[4] Global engagement encompasses these non-official and often informal processes but it also includes more formal diplomatic and state to state relations. Indeed, several of the essays in this volume highlight the interconnections between Korea's international relations and its integration into global economic and cultural networks.

These essays explore Korea's global engagement during and after the Cold War through a variety of methodological and thematic frameworks including diplomacy, migration, development, and social change. They seek to shed light on the dramatic changes that have occurred both north and south of the 38th parallel since the demise of Japanese colonialism in 1945 led to the massive influx of new forms of global influence. Some of the essays focus on specific historical periods while others examine contemporary problems and issues. The essays offer different understandings of how both of the two Korean states and their citizens influenced and were influenced by global circumstances. At the same time, they do not find any consistent pattern for how Korea's negotiation with the global occurred. In certain times and circumstances, Koreans exercised a surprising measure of agency while in others they struggled to gain even a modest degree of control over their own destinies.

All of these essays are written by promising young scholars in the field of Korean Studies and, in different ways, push the boundaries of their subfields. Several of the historical essays break new ground by introducing new archival materials that reveal important details about the past diplomacy of the two Korea's. Others consider dimensions of U.S.-Korean relations that have been ignored by more standard accounts of the subject such as America's impact on urban development and food consumption. The essays on contemporary Korean politics and society make sense of some of the most recent developments in North and South Korea, which have thus far received limited attention from other scholars. They also present intriguing new interpretive frameworks for investigating these developments.

The first three essays in this volume by Patrick Chung, Dajeong Chung, and Khue Dieu Do focus on U.S.-Korean relations during the Cold War. In my own previous book, *Nation Building in South Korea*, I examined American efforts to promote economic development and democracy in South Korea in the three decades after the Korean War.[5] Yet I focused primarily on very deliberate U.S. efforts to encourage modernizing change in the ROK and how South Koreans in turn adapted to and resisted these efforts. I argued that Korean agency played a critical role in South Korea's rise to a prosperous democracy. These essays have somewhat different takes on the centrality of Koreans as historical actors, however. They sometimes emphasize how Koreans reshaped American influence but in other instances they depict the United States as the real driving force behind important changes. Their view of how the United States influenced South Korea and what aspects of American influence were most important also differs in some ways from the one that informed my work. Rather than emphasizing the intended consequences of American military and economic aid, these essays highlight the incidental impact of American power on the Korean peninsula. Change sometimes occurred in ways that defied the expectations of Koreans and Americans alike.

Patrick Chung's essay on the U.S. military's role in the development of transportation infrastructure in the port city of Busan provides an especially compelling example of this phenomenon. While there is now a significant literature on the social and economic impact of the American military on South Korea, Chung explores a dimension that has thus far received little attention.[6] The presence of large numbers of U.S. forces on the peninsula during and after the Korean War not only spurred the creation of camp towns and black markets but also reshaped the urban landscape and exerted an important impact on the environment. Chung focuses on the critical role played by the Korean War in Busan's emergence as a global entrepôt during the late twentieth century. Although U.S. logistical officers took over the city's highways, railroads, and telecommunications they did not initially have a plan for the city's development. Instead, the demands of the war often forced them to swiftly pave roads and build bridges with whatever materials were available to them. Especially during the first ten months of the war (June 1950–April 1951), the city's infrastructure grew in a rapid but haphazard fashion that was not planned by either the ROK government or UN forces. In Chung's account, South Koreans exercised relative control over the transformation of Busan. American military planners designed and expanded the facilities needed to enhance the city's connections to both Korea's interior and the rest of the world. As he sees it, "American soldiers remade southeastern Korean into one of the most advanced logistics centers in the Pacific, if not the entire world."

Dajeong Chung's essay shares several common themes with the preceding one but strikes a slightly different balance between Korean agency and American influence. Based on deep research in the records of the U.S. Agency for International Development and new South Korean materials, her essay tells the story of American food relief programs in Korea during the 1960s. Through the Food-for-Peace Program, the United States used its agricultural surplus to provide food for Korean villagers who were expected to participate in "self-help" projects in exchange for the food. These projects included: land reclamations, paving roads, and building dams to control irrigation. Like Patrick Chung, she demonstrates that the United States had a transformative influence on the South Korean landscape through its aid programs. Upland reclamation projects, the development of marine cultivation fields, and other initiatives brought about changes in even some of the country's most remote villages. And yet, Chung ascribes a far greater role to South Koreans in shaping how American programs ultimately played out. The United States Operations Mission (USOM) often partnered with local governments that played significant roles in implementing the programs. Ultimately, Chung's essay explains, the Park Chung Hee government completely took over these community development programs from the USOM and incorporated them into its New Village Movement (Saemaul Undong). Thus, even if community development programs were originally the brainchild of American development experts, over time they incorporated more and more Korean input.

Chung's essay also pushes the boundaries of Korean Studies in another important way. Much of the previous literature on South Korean economic development has focused on the state's role in the country's industrialization and the policies of the central government.[7] Building on Daniel Immerwahr's recent study of Cold War development policy, Chung finds that "thinking small" played an important role in both American aid programs and the ROK government's approach to modernization.[8] Large scale projects such as laying a network of highways received a great deal of emphasis but so too did more local campaigns to promote development from the bottom up. In this sense, the essay expands our view of how both American assistance programs and state-led development programs transformed the nation.

Khue Dieu Do's essay offers a more traditional diplomatic history and casts its lens primarily on state to state relations. She examines the parallel efforts of the Carter administration to engage North Korea and withdraw American units for South Korea. Although American policy occupies center stage in Khue's narrative, it is nonetheless easy to see how the two Korean states shaped both the outcomes of Carter's policy and the global orientation of the Korean peninsula. As Khue notes, Carter wanted to encourage the resumption of talks between Seoul and Pyongyang because he thought it would facilitate American troop withdrawals. But the Park Chung Hee government in South Korea initially refused to accede to America's wishes. Ultimately, Seoul's skillful maneuvering on this issue contributed to Carter's decision to abandon his efforts to reduce the number of American troops stationed in South Korea. Khue's emphasis on South Korean agency poses an interesting counterpoint to much of the existing literature on this subject, which has emphasized disagreements between the administration and the Pentagon or the general disarray of Carter's foreign policy as the main factor behind the failed troop withdrawal policy.[9] She also describes a similar dynamic at work in Sino-North Korean relations with Beijing unable to get Pyongyang to shift its behavior. The North Koreans were "inflexible and disobedient" and at times played the Soviets and Chinese off against each other to get their way. Above all, Khue's essay seems to point out that, at least in the realm of international diplomacy, the two Korea's were acting with increasing autonomy by the mid 1970s.

The next two historical essays in the volume shift the focus more completely to North Korea's foreign relations and its competition for legitimacy with South Korea. Benjamin Young expands what is to date a very limited literature on North Korean activities in Afro-Asian countries during the late Cold War in his essay on competition between North and South Korea in Iran. Rather than looking at the realm of diplomats and policymakers, however, Young explores the interaction between North and South Korean students at the Tehran Foreign School during the 1980s. Tehran maintained normal diplomatic relations with both Seoul and Pyongyang in the years after the Shah was overthrown and personnel from both Korean states were stationed in Iran and sent their children to the same school. Although the number of Korean students studying at the school was small (eleven South Koreans and seven North Koreans) Young sees their interactions as a microcosm of the wider competition between the two Koreas in Afro-Asian countries. Drawing on a fascinating cache of documents that he discovered in the ROK Diplomatic Archives, he shows how the lives of private citizens from both Koreas were governed by the political demands of the Cold War. At the same time, some of the intriguing details about the students' interactions that Young uncovers suggest that the lives of these students could not be completely reduced to the binary international order. The North Korean students befriended Taiwanese classmates at the school even while they did not speak to their South Korean and sometimes embraced a "reckless and materialistic" lifestyle that made them imperfect exponents of North Korean socialism abroad. Yet ultimately when the students deviated from the geopolitical narratives that were imposed on them it seemed to be in relatively limited ways.

If anything, Dong Jie's essay on North Korea's entry into the United Nations ascribes even less agency to the DPRK although Pyongyang was not without some capacity to influence events. One of the leading young scholars of North Korea and the Cold War in the PRC, Dong bases her analysis on Chinese materials, many of which have only recently become available. Dong asks why Pyongyang suddenly changed its policy toward Korean representation at the UN in 1991. After insisting for decades that only the DPRK should be admitted to the organization, Pyongyang finally agreed to a formula for the simultaneous admission of both Koreas. Dong finds that the change was far more a result of Chinese pressure than of the internal deliberations of the North Korean leadership. The early 1990s were a difficult period for both China and North Korea. Beijing was still seeking to recoup some of the trust and legitimacy that it had lost in the aftermath of the 1989 Tiananmen protests while both countries had kept a nervous eye on the collapse of communist governments in Eastern and Central Europe. Hoping to recapture its lost standing in the UN, Beijing wanted to be part of a constructive solution to the Korea question and pressured its erstwhile ally to accept dual admission. Nonetheless, North Korea was not completely without agency in this process. Through acceding to Chinese pressures on the UN issue, Pyongyang was able to obtain assurances from Beijing that it would not recognize Seoul. Although, of course, the PRC and the ROK normalized relations just a year later, Dong Jie argues that this process unfolded more slowly than Beijing wanted because it had to placate North Korea. These insights offer some historical context for China's current inability to dictate North Korea's behavior despite the latter's dependence on Chinese aid.

Sheena Greitens's essay in chapter 6 on the evolution of North Korea's dual economy picks up where Dong Jie's piece leaves off. Like Dong Jie, Greitens analyzes how the demise of the Communist Bloc during the early 1990s inevitably made its influence felt on North Korea. The DPRK had long relied on fraternal communist countries, especially China and the Soviet Union, as critical sources of trade and economic assistance. Once socialist internationalism collapsed in Eastern Europe and the Soviet Union, North Koreans had little choice but to adapt to changing circumstances. Greitens argues that different groups of North Koreans struggled to survive by creating two distinctive economic orders. Elites centered in Pyongyang used their privileged position in North Korean society to launch new illicit business operations including currency counterfeiting and narcotics production that generated revenues for themselves and the regime. Ordinary citizens faced an even more arduous struggle for survival. They adapted in part by establishing a parallel economic order centered around the DPRK's northeastern border with the PRC. They created cross border smuggling networks through familial and other connections while engaging in a variety of other black-market activities. Greitens's essay thus strikes a balance between the impact of irresistible global forces and Korean agency. On the one hand, neither the North Korean state nor it subjects could do much to stop the geostrategic foundations that had long supported the DPRK economy from crumbling during the 1990s and throwing their country into poverty. On the other hand, North Koreans still have capacity to act in the difficult circumstances they inherited. While their activities—especially those of party elites in Pyongyang—might not seem admirable, they give North Koreans in both the elite stratum and the lowest echelons of society a means of both surviving and defying the expectations of the rest of the world.

The final two essays move us closer to the present day and more directly discuss the evolution of contemporary Korean politics. Darcie Draudt's chapter examines the South Korean government's use of multiculturalism (damunhwajuui) as a development strategy during the twenty-first century. She focuses in particular on how this strategy relates to the government's efforts to achieve "Global Korea." The very premise of her paper makes clear that South Korea is now actively seeking to control the terms of its global engagement rather than simply letting international forces dictate its choices. The government chose to encourage greater immigration and a measure of multiculturalism because it believed that doing so would bolster the nation's economy. It recognized that offering long-term status for skilled and highly educated laborers could mitigate potential problems created by the country's aging population. South Korea has, in this sense, been able to channel the transnational movement of peoples to its own purposes. And yet, Draudt notes that even as immigration policy served national economic needs it was also a product of necessities created by South Korea's demanding and competitive global environment. Indeed, South Korea had long been one of the countries that were most resistant to immigration but needed to change its policy as its demographics and international position shifted.

Finally, Steven Denney's essay looks at how South Korea's democratic transition and consolidation influenced the political opinions of its citizens by placing the country's experiences in a comparative context. He examines how South Korean attitudes toward democracy can be compared to both those in the other newly consolidated democracies in East Asia and those of the older democracies in American and Western Europe. He finds some interesting parallels and disparities. In both South Korea and the Western democracies, it is the younger generation that exhibits ideas that are most critical of living in a democracy. In this sense, South Korea's political values seem to be situated within a broader global trend toward growing skepticism of all institutions. At the same time, South Korea does not completely resemble other democracies in Asia and the West. One interesting phenomenon which Denney points to is the relatively high priority that older Koreans from what he terms the "authoritarian generation" attach to living in a democracy. This generation's experiences with state-led violence and oppression ultimately left it with unusually strong convictions about the value of democratic institutions. Thus, even though some of the same political and generational trends that have been in play throughout the democratic world made their impact felt in South Korea, some sectors of Korean society did not conform to them. In essence, Denney's is a study of the degree to which structural factors shape democratic beliefs in South Korea and structure is, of course, often considered to be the very antonym human agency. Yet the author's analysis is perspicacious enough to acknowledge that South Koreans have had some measure of choice in the political ideals and values they have chosen to embrace.

Taken together, the essays in this volume point to the complexity and diversity of Korea's engagement with the global during the late twentieth and twenty-first century. These forms of global engagement included formal diplomacy, migration, cultural exchange, and trade (both licit and illicit) among others. At the same time, these essays do not propose any single or conclusive answer to the question of how much agency Koreans ultimately exerted during these global interactions. Some of the authors represent the transformative power of global forces as far more potent and irresistible than others. Nonetheless, they do make it clear that global and transnational phenomena never completely determined the course of events or shaped cultural and economic developments in Korea. Instead, many of the most significant changes that occurred on the Korean peninsula during and after the Cold War were part of a dialectical process that Koreans influenced even if they could never control it.

Finally, these essays make it clear that Korea's global engagement is still an evolving process that will continue to reshape Korean society. Shifting trends in geopolitics, transnational migration, and the world economy will no doubt make their influence felt on the peninsula. They bring to mind one particular moment in *Gukjesijiang*—the film I began this essay discussing. In one of the scenes taking place in contemporary Seoul, a young South Asian couple is seen sitting and talking at a café when a group of South Korean teenagers begins taunting them. The young man confronts his tormenters by yelling: "If you live in Korea then you are Korean!" Before a fight can break out, Deoksu intervenes grabbing one of the young South Koreans and scolding them for their behavior. The scene suggests how South Korea's continuing global engagement has precipitated the ongoing contestation of Korean identity and will likely continue to do so in the future. By the same token, the essays in this volume collectively anticipate that Korea's interplay with transnational and international forces will continue to defy expectations and that there will be no easy resolution to debates over agency and subjectivity in defining Korea's world role.

Notes

1. "A Korean Forrest Gump," *South China Morning Post*, 7 April 2015.
2. There is a substantial literature on this. See, for instance, Woo, *Race to the Swift*; Lie, *Han Unbound*.
3. See among others: Kim ed., *Korea's Globalization*; Chang, et al., eds., *Korea Confronts Globalization*; Marinescu ed., *The Global Impact of South Korean Popular Culture*.
4. There is a vast literature on the topic but some of the most important definitions of the term are derived from Giddens, *The Consequences of Modernity* and Harvey, *The Condition of Postmodernity*.
5. Brazinsky, *Nation Building in South Korea*.
6. Scholars have looked at the social and economic impact of the U.S. military from a variety of different perspectives ranging from black markets to military prostitution. Among others see Moon, *Sex Among Allies*, Yeo, *Activists Alliances, and Anti-U.S. Base Protests*; Cheng, *On the Move for Love*.
7. See for instance, Cole and Lyman, *Korean Development*; Amsden, *Asia's Next Giant*.
8. Immerwahr, *Thinking Small*.
9. See for instance, Oberdorfer and Carlin, *The Two Koreas*; Gleysteen Jr., *Massive Entanglement, Marginal Influence*.

Bibliography

Amsden, Alice. *Asia's Next Giant: South Korea and Late Industrialization* (New York: Oxford University Press, 1992).

Brazinsky, Gregg. *Nation Building in South Korea: Koreans, Americans, and the Making of a Democracy* (Chapel Hill: The University of North Carolina Press, 2007).

Chang, Yun-Shik, et al. eds., *Korea Confronts Globalization* (New York: Routledge, 2009).

Cheng, Sealing. *On the Move for Love: Migrant Encounters and the U.S. Military in South Korea* (Philadelphia: The University of Pennsylvania Press, 2010).

Cole, David C. and Lyman, Princeton. *Korean Development: The Interplay of Politics and Economics* (Cambridge: Harvard University Press).

Giddens, Anthony. *The Consequences of Modernity* (Stanford: Stanford University Press, 1990)

Gleysteen Jr., William H. *Massive Entanglement, Marginal Influence: Carter and Korea in Crisis* (Washington D.C.: Brookings, 1999).

Harvey, David. *The Condition of Postmodernity: An Enquiry into the Origins of Social Change* (Malden: Blackwell, 1990).

Immerwahr, Daniel. *Thinking Small: The United States and the Lure of Community Development* (Cambridge: Harvard University Press, 2015).

Kim Samuel S. ed., *Korea's Globalization* (Cambridge: Cambridge University Press, 2000).

Lie, John. *Han Unbound: The Political Economy of South Korea* (Palo Alto: Stanford University Press, 2000).

Marinescu, Valentina ed., *The Global Impact of South Korean Popular Culture: Hallyu Unbound* (Lanham: Lexington Books, 2014).

Moon, Katharine H.S. *Sex Among Allies: Military Prostitution in U.S.-Korea Relations* (New York: Columbia University Press, 1997).

Oberdorfer, Don and Carlin, Robert. *The Two Koreas: A Contemporary History* (New York: Basic Books, 2014).

Woo, Jung-En. *Race to the Swift: State and Finance in Korean Industrialization* (New York: Columbia University Press, 1991).

Yeo, Andrew. *Activists Alliances, and Anti-U.S. Base Protests* (New York: Cambridge University Press, 2011).

CHAPTER ONE

From Supply Lines to Supply Chains

Busan, the Korean War, and the Rise of Global Logistics[1]

Patrick Chung

> Although warfare in itself is strictly an unbusinesslike venture, getting supplies to the front can be put on a business basis.
>
> —Lt. Robert Fulton, US Army, 1952[2]

On any given day, thousands of ships, trains, and trucks transport 26 million metric tons of goods around the world.[3] Almost everything we consume—from the food we eat to the cars we drive to the phones we cannot put down—travel through a vast network of roads, railways, wharves, and warehouses. While often overlooked, these physical structures play a critical role in today's global economy—without their existence, the seemingly frictionless flow of goods would come to a grinding halt.[4]

The postwar history of South Korea highlights the importance of transportation infrastructure. While among the poorest countries in the world following World War II, South Korea has become the world's most technologically advanced and prosperous nations. Despite its relatively small size and population, it has become one of a leading exporter of goods.[5] The country's emergence as a global economic power occurred in lockstep with the development of the country's primary seaport, Busan.[6] The vast majority of South Korean products—whether LG televisions, Samsung phones, or Hyundai cars—pass through Busan's various roads, warehouses, and piers. And as a result, the city has become one of the busiest ports in the world.

14 ～ Patrick Chung

Figure 1.1 Port of Busan, 2013.
Photo by Patrick Chung

This chapter examines the evolution of Busan. Specifically, it focuses on the US military's development of the port during the Korean War. Situated at a key point in the flow of goods in East Asia, the city became a global entrepôt through the efforts of foreign imperial powers as well as Koreans. The first step Busan's rise as a global seaport occurred during the Japanese colonial period. The Japanese modernized the city's harbor to facilitate the flow of rice from Korea to Japan and other points in its Pacific empire. Though the contribution of the Japanese should not be overlooked, it was under US aegis, starting with the Korean War, that Busan emerged as a center of global rather than East Asian trade. Crucial to this process was the US military.

During the Korean War, US soldiers oversaw the recreation of Busan's transportation systems to conform to US standards. At the onset of the war, massive quantities of men and supplies flowed into Busan. To facilitate the entry and distribution of matériel, US Army engineers made concentrated efforts to make the city's transportation and shipping facilities compatible with US vehicles and equipment. They initiated a wide-range of construction projects, including the expansion of piers and wharfs, updates of road and rail lines, and the construction of storage facilities and oil pipelines. These investments integrated the port, and by extension South Korea, into the US military's global supply network.[7] The standardization of Busan's transportation infrastructure would play a vital role in linking South Korea to the rest of the US-led "Free world" following the Korean War.

The wartime construction of Korea's transportation systems was part of a larger expansion of the US military's presence around the world.[8] As historian Bruce Cumings has observed, the Korean War inaugurated the construction of a worldwide network of military outposts, which he called an "archipelago of empire." The United States spent billions of dollars on the construction of not only overseas bases but the transportation systems needed to link them.[9] Through this process, US specifications for harbors, roads, and rail lines were adopted throughout the non-communist world. In other words, US transportation standards become global ones. And, as a result, the US military's standardization of Korea's transportation infrastructure provided the physical facilities necessary to receive and send goods to nations and markets around the globe.

In tracing Busan's development, this chapter argues US military logistics during the Korean War played a key role in South Korea's postwar economic development. Scholars of postwar South Korea have attributed the country's economic success to the large scale of US foreign assistance to the country and the efficacy of the Korean state's developmental policies, particularly during the Park Chung Hee era.[10] In addition to these studies, scholars of Japanese colonial period have emphasized the contributions that Japanese investment and developmental efforts during the colonial period in explaining the success of postwar South Korean capitalism.[11] In focusing on the war, this chapter seeks to bridge these two strands of scholarship by showing the role of the US military in the country's transition from Japanese colonial rule and in laying the groundwork for the industrialization that would occur during the Park era.[12]

More broadly, the history of Busan highlights the role that US military construction projects played in shaping the postwar global economy. Scholars have demonstrated the importance of military logistics and transportation systems in the spread of empire. From the time of the Roman Empire, roads and sea routes served to move the troops, goods, and information necessary to control and administer foreign lands.[13] The military played a similar role for the consolidation of postwar US empire.[14] The United States was just as dependent on the construction and standardization of transportation systems.[15] Overseas military bases served as critical nodes for the consolidation of US power during the Cold War, and South Korea's strategic import made it one of the centerpieces of the US military's base network. Though the scale and purpose of US troop deployments varied by location, US soldiers needed supplies wherever they went. As a result, transportation systems around much of the world were expanded and standardized by the US military. In doing so, it built much of critical transportation, communication, and logistical infrastructure upon which corporate supply chains depend on today.[16] And Busan, as the starting point of the US military's Cold War infrastructural development efforts, demands the attention of those seeking to understand not only South Korean industrialization but also the spread of global capitalism after World War II.

The Geography of Busan

The history of Busan, like that of Korea itself, cannot be understood apart from geography. The city dates back to at least the first century AD when it served as an oceanfront fortress for the Silla Dynasty (57 BC—935 AD).[17] Busan developed into a trading center due to its proximity to major waterways. It is located next to the Nakdong River, which links the city to agricultural regions along Korea's eastern coast and southwest plains, and straddles a deep, well-sheltered ocean bay.[18] While a combination of oceanic currents and submarine land features make most of the waters around Korea dangerous to navigate, those outside of Busan are calm and easy to travel.[19]

As a result of its geography, Busan served as a gateway between the Asian mainland and Japan. After a long period of relative isolation following Toyotomi Hideyoshi's invasion at the end of the sixteenth century, Busan reemerged as a center of regional commerce after the forced opening of Korea by Japan in 1876.[20] The military defeat forced the Korean government to sign the Ganghwa Treaty, which opened Korea to Japanese influence in the way that Commodore Perry's "gunboat diplomacy" had opened Japan to Western influence two decades prior.[21] The treaty was effectively the first step toward Japan's 1910 Annexation of Korea. The resulting influx of Japanese commercial activity transformed the political economy of the Korean peninsula.[22]

The treaty forced Korea's main ports open to foreign commerce. Port cities saw the first large-scale flow of Japanese people and goods following the Ganghwa Treaty.[23] Between 1895 and 1905, the Japanese extended nearly 7.9 million won in loans and direct investments for the improvement communications and transportation systems in Korea.[24] With the backing of the Japanese state, Japanese companies invested heavily in the development of shipping routes—among the most active participants was the Mitsubishi *zaibatsu*. Due to such efforts, ocean shipments between the two nations increased from around 10,000 tons in 1884 to nearly 300,000 tons in 1907.[25]

Busan received the lion's share of Japanese capital and investment because it was the Korean terminus of many of the new shipping routes. British geographer Isabella Bird saw the extent of Busan's transformation first-hand during her visit to Korea in 1894. She observed upon her first arrival, "It is not Korea but Japan which meets one on anchoring." Her account described a city overrun with Japanese-run business and Japanese-made products—everything, from administrative buildings to lighters, were Japanese. In sum, she concluded, Busan was a "fairly good-looking Japanese town."[26]

The Imposition of Japanese Standards

Under Japanese rule, Busan became an important node in Japan's growing Pacific empire.[27] Japanese colonial policy was designed to remake Korea into an agricultural colony, serving as the breadbasket for Japan's growing industrial, urban workforce.[28] Busan was particularly important in this regard due to its proximity to Japan. It became the principal trans-shipment point for Korean rice shipments. In making Busan the sorting and shipping center of the growing rice trade, the Japanese built up a large number of administrative and transportation-related structures. Additionally, Japanese merchants and administrators formed over a hundred different social and commercial organizations in the city during the colonial period.[29]

Japanese capital and corporations brought about a significant change in the pattern of Korea's infrastructural development—a rise in private investment and administration of railroads.[30] Following annexation, Korean entrepreneurs worked in tandem with Japanese settlers to establish local industrial and production facilities.[31] Korean and Japanese entrepreneurs not only took part in small scale manufacturing operations but also in large-scale infrastructural projects. Jun Uchida has shown that the rapid expansion of Korea's railway network was in part due to the prevalence of private Korean and Japanese rail operators throughout the country.[32] The breadth of rail operators led to greater penetration of the country's interior and resulted in the country's first integrated overland transportation network. Over the course of the colonial era, Uchida notes, successive waves of Japanese "established nodes of settler power at key cities such as [Busan], [Incheon], and Seoul, and gradually penetrated the interior to develop new cities such as [Daejeon]."[33]

The development of inland transport augmented rather than diminished the importance of port cities like Busan. The expanded rail network made more of the peninsula accessible, but it did not change the primary purpose of the country's transportation networks—the funneling of grains and raw materials from Korea to Japan. For this purpose, the colonial state expanded Busan's port facilities and improved the city's access to the interior by augmenting the rail network into and out of the city.[34] These rail lines linked the city to the rest of Korea and, eventually, Manchuria. As a result of these efforts, Busan emerged as a key logistical error in Japan's growing colonial empire, which would eventually come to encompass large portions of China, Southeast Asia, and the Pacific Islands.[35] This role became particularly critical with the start of the Pacific War (1931–1945) as Japan expanded its empire throughout Asia and the Pacific in search of raw materials to fuel its war efforts.

The Pacific War not only increased Japanese demand for Korean rice and agricultural products, but also for war matériel. The mobilization efforts led the Japanese imperial state to streamline industrial production throughout the empire.[36] Within this new system, Korea became a staging ground for Japanese military operations in Manchuria.[37] Strategically located Korean cities became sites for the manufacture of products for soldiers like clothing, cigarettes, and tools.[38] Busan, already a transportation hub, became a center for the shipbuilding industry during the late 1930s. Large-scale shipyards were built around the city to build and repair ships for the Japanese Navy.[39] The creation of the shipbuilding industry made Busan among the most highly industrialized regions not only in Korea but also within the Japanese Empire.[40]

Though highly developed by Japanese standards, Korean infrastructure was ill-suited to US military needs. Starting in the 1920s, the Japanese engineers and manufacturers became increasingly isolated from their US and Western European counterparts. As a result, Japanese standards for the construction of transportation systems (and for a wide range of goods, facilities, and processes) diverged from those of allied nations. While the differences were most often not monumental, they would become a factor for US military logisticians during the Korean War. Roads, for instance, illustrate this point. Built to Japanese imperial standards, Korean roads were often too narrow for US jeeps and trucks while bridges were too weak to support any form of motorized transport. A US Army engineer later noted that Japan had missed out on critical developments in road constructions that had occurred in the years preceding the World War II.[41] The decades following the passage of 1916 Federal Aid Road Act saw the rapid expansion of highway planning and construction in the United States. In the years leading up to its entry into World War II (1937–1941), the United States saw the construction of 29,360 miles of highway per year.[42] Cut off from these advances, Japanese roads lacked many of the paving and surfacing technologies deployed in the West—this was especially true in colonies like Korea where road development was not a priority.[43]

With Korea's liberation in 1945, the movement of refugees superseded the flow of goods through Busan. The city served as the focal point of the repatriation of Japanese colonists and Koreans who had been dispersed throughout the Japanese Empire. The influx of refugees overtook the shipment of war goods into Busan during the five years after the end of World War II. With the start of the Korean War, however, Busan would resume its leading role in the movement of soldiers and weapons.

Supplying the UN War Effort

On the grey dawn of June 25, 1950, mortar and artillery fire fell along with the rain on the 38th parallel. In quick succession, 90,000 North Korean troops swept across enemy lines and overwhelmed South Korean defenders. North Korean troops captured Seoul within days of the initial attack.[44] While hostilities began at the 38th parallel, the heart of UN war efforts would develop hundreds of miles southeast, in Busan. The city received the initial deployment of UN troops and, over the next three years, became the center of all logistical activities for UN forces during the war.

Combat dictated the infrastructural development in Korea during the war. US military leaders deployed engineers and construction crews in response to the needs of soldiers on the front line. Initial construction efforts were largely improvised, because of the chaotic nature of combat. It was not until the second half of the war that US logistical troops began to build permanent structures or consider the postwar needs of South Korea.[45] Throughout the war, US logistical officers focused primarily on repairing existing or standardizing infrastructure incompatible with US vehicles and equipment. Despite the incomplete nature of their efforts, the US military's wartime improvements would serve as the foundation for postwar Korea's transportation systems.

The two most salient features of the war's chronology for Busan's development are the unexpected nature of the initial North Korean invasion and the duration of the stalemate that ensued over the next two years. The war's first phase saw the haphazard construction of roads, railways, and bridges around Busan and the rest of the country in response to immediate combat needs. While this initiated Busan's wartime transformation, it was not until the second phase of the war that US logistical troops remade Busan into a world-class transportation center. The war, therefore, will be discussed as unfolding in two phases—the "chaotic" first ten months and the subsequent "reconstructive" two years.

Chaos—June 1950–April 1951

On June 30th, Douglas MacArthur, Commander-in-Chief of the Far East Command headquartered in Tokyo, received authorization to send US combat forces to Korea. At MacArthur's command, the US Eighth Army entered Korea through Busan, the closest port to its headquarters in Tokyo-Yokoyama. Luckily for UN forces, Busan was the best port in Korea at the outset of the war—endowed with harbor facilities that could accommodate deep-water vessels, as well as pier and stevedoring facilities to unload 12–15 ships at once.[46] Its warehousing and storage facilities by far exceeded those of other ports or cities, with the exception of Incheon, which was much farther away on the western half of the peninsula.[47] In all, Busan's harbor could handle an estimated 40,000 to 45,000 tons of matériel a day.[48]

Despite being Korea's most developed port, Busan was ill-equipped for a massive deployment of troops and provisions at the start of UN operations.[49] During the first week alone, 52 vessels carrying over 10,000 troops, 1,300 vehicles, 7,600 tons of ammunition, and 3,200 tons of other cargo entered the harbor.[50] Logistical officers had to oversee the tidal wave of supplies that began flowing into the country. Undermanned throughout the war, they were responsible for moving, feeding, and equipping hundreds of thousands of men from twenty different countries.[51] This massive undertaking would force logistical troops to do everything but engage in combat. They were even responsible for accommodating the dietary needs of the various national units.[52]

US logistical troops struggled most to establish supply lines during the initial months of the war. The bulk of UN supplies were imported from either the United States or Japan. The initial transportation of matériel to the Korean peninsula proceeded without much difficulty due to the well-developed state of US and Japanese facilities.[53] The smooth flow of matériel was abruptly halted once it landed in Busan, however. Moving matériel required both transportation and communication facilities, both which Korea lacked. Over the following months, logistical units had to oversee the building, expansion, and maintenance of a "massive supply pipeline" that stretched from the western United States across the Pacific Ocean to Japan and then finally to Korea.[54]

US logistical troops immediately took control of the entire country's telecommunication lines, highways, and railroads upon arrival. However, none of these systems could fully support UN operations. The existing communication network, for instance, included only three direct lines between Seoul and Tokyo—one landline, one radiotelephone, and one Teletype.[55] The road and rail networks were a little better. The lack of suitable rail lines forced US transportation officers to rely on trucks to transport goods across dubious roads. A member of the 377th Transportation Company ruefully recalled driving food, arms, and gas on a one-lane road "over a mountain that was 11 miles uphill and 9 miles downhill (going north)."[56] Many US drivers no doubt endured similarly nerve-wracking experiences as UN forces made their way northward from Busan.[57]

The road conditions faced by US Army drivers were a legacy of the Japanese colonial period. The colonial state's uneven developmental policies left Korea with few roads outside of major urban centers. Where roads existed, they were not on par with US standards. At the time, US Army specifications called for roads to have gravel or crushed rock (if not paved) surfaces, to be at least 22 feet wide, have 1.5 or 2 lanes, and have grades below 10%.[58] Even the best Korean roads failed to meet these minimum requirements. Built for oxcarts, Korea's roads, US engineers found, were unpaved, 18 feet wide (often narrowed at points to 11 feet), single-laned, poorly drained, and often had sharp curves and grades up to 15%.[59] As a result, US Army engineers had to continuously improve and construct roads during the first year of the war.[60] During the UN advance from Daegu and Seoul in the fall of 1950, they oversaw the construction of 22 railway bridge crossings.[61]

The efforts of US logistical troops were hampered by the difficulty of obtaining necessary supplies. According to Richard McAdoo, 65th Engineer Combat Battalion, construction materials like lumber and steel bracings were rarely available. Still, his battalion managed to build thirty-five bridges in the first nine months of the conflict. Decades later, amazed by the scale of their accomplishment, he recalled, "We built eight timber bridges, three from 120 to 180 feet long, in one week!"[62] Yet, another logistical officer recollected with frustration, "Every advance in Korea created new problems of supply. The inadequacies of the transportation facilities thwarted attempts to increase the scope of supply from existing bases."[63]

Supply shortages forced military engineers to improvise all sorts of ways to keep troops and supplies moving. For example, the 1st Cavalry Division took extreme, seemingly absurd, measures to cross the Geum-ho River, roughly 90 km northwest of Busan, in September 1950. After several failed attempts to ford the river using sandbags, engineers had to "borrow" a bridge from the 24th Cavalry Division, which had set up a 300-foot-long bridge nearly 50 km away on the Nakdong River. 1st Cavalry Division troops were sent to the Nakdong to disassemble, transport, and reassemble the bridge on the

Geum-ho, and then had to repeat the process in order to return it the Nakdong River by the next morning, when the 24th was scheduled to cross the river.[64] While an extreme example, the Geum-ho River crossing highlights the extent of the challenges facing US logistical forces, and the inventive ways they overcame them.

Logistical troops played a large role in one of the war's most critical events—the Incheon Invasion. Often seen as a stroke of MacArthur's strategic genius, the invasion could not have taken place without the ingenuity of logistical officers.[65] In preparation for the invasion, logisticians had to carefully coordinate the flow of supplies through Busan to Incheon from several points in Japan and the United States. Despite the complexity of the operation, the invasion was a stunning success, and by the end of 1950, UN forces had crossed the 38th parallel and pushed all the way up to Korea's border with China.

Ironically, the Incheon Invasion's overwhelming success made life even more difficult for US logistical units. The subsequent advance of troops extended already strained supply lines. The rapid advance of UN troops made it impossible for engineers to build intermediate supply points and depots.[66] Therefore, supplies continued to be routed primarily through Busan even as combat moved hundreds of miles north.[67] The difficult logistical situation became an outright disaster with the entry of Chinese forces into Korea in December 1950. The unexpected counterattack halted the UN advance, and their subsequent retreat undid much of the work engineers and logisticians completed following the Incheon landing. Logistical troops tried desperately to reverse the flow of supplies southward, but the hasty retreat led to heavy losses of equipment, as the engineers were forced to destroy some of the roads, rail lines, and structures that they had just built.[68]

Reconstruction—April 1951–July 1953

The war's dramatic first act came to a close by the spring of 1951. Between January and June of the next year, intermittent fighting occurred along the border. By the summer of 1951, each army held fast to their side of the 38th parallel.[69] UN troop levels stabilized by April, and the influx of supplies regularized.[70] The shift must have been a welcome change for logistical operators, who no longer had to struggle to keep up with rapid troop movements and unpredictable tactical shifts. For the duration of the war, US Army engineers and transportation officers worked to rehabilitate their side of the Korean peninsula.[71] By the middle of 1951, the Eighth Army was granted control of

$150 million in civilian relief funds, a large portion of which was earmarked for infrastructure projects by army planners.[72]

The Army Corps of Engineers spearheaded a construction program meant to improve supply flows. As discussed above, supply problems did not stem purely from the lack of infrastructure, but also from the incompatibility of existing transportation systems with those that were being constructed by American troops. Korean roads, rails, and harbor facilities were not designed to the specifications required by the US military. Even the infrastructural upgrades made by the Japanese did not meet muster, and US engineers rebuilt existing structures using materials produced in the United States. Upgrading South Korea's transportation infrastructure to meet US standards necessitated a four-fold increase in the importation of building materials and equipment between April and September of 1951.

Construction cannot occur without building materials, and for this reason, the initial focus of the US military's construction program was on improving the "throughput" of Busan and other Korean ports. A port's throughput capacity is the average quantity of cargo and passengers processed on a daily basis.[73] During the war's second phase, the US Army invested in the construction of docking, stevedoring, and loading facilities in Busan and the satellite ports of Gimhae, Masan, Pohang, and Ulsan.[74] All within 100 km of Busan, these ports would receive and process the bulk of supplies which were flooding the country at a pace of 12,500 tons per day in 1951—an increase of over 2,000 tons per day from the previous year.[75]

In addition to improving its port, military planners determined that Busan needed improvements in three areas: storage, inland transportation, and labor capacity. While engineers could do little about the availability of labor, they began to address storage and inland transportation in the spring of 1951. Tasked with housing the majority of UN supplies, Busan existing warehouses and storage facilities proved inadequate from the outset of the war. Eighth Army engineers were immediately charged with building additional warehouses and depots. In August 1950, the pressing need for ammunition bunkers emerged as ships full of weaponry were literally stuck, anchored offshore because there was nowhere to place their cargo onshore. The man in charge of the project, Captain James McClure, recalled being hounded by superiors to complete the project as quickly as possible. Lacking manpower, McClure had to employ Korean laborers. His complaints about Koreans' lack of experience fell on deaf ears. He recalled being told, "You're a maintenance officer; it's up to you to keep the trucks rolling."[76]

Storage issues became even more critical as reconstruction and relief efforts ramped up during the second half of the war. In addition to combat supplies, the city was flooded with construction and engineering materials, food, medicine, and fuel by the middle of 1951.[77] While general materials could be stored in existing warehouses, hazardous materials like ammunition and petroleum, required specialized facilities. In fact, the concentration of storage facilities became a source of endless concern for US planners. Noting that the rest of Korea housed two weeks' worth of supplies at most, one report proclaimed that an aerial attack on Busan would cripple the UN war effort.[78] Despite concerns over the concentration of matériel, construction efforts greatly expanded Busan's storage capability. By war's end, the city was capable of housing the bulk of UN supplies.[79]

In addition to building storage facilities, engineers also worked to improve Busan's access to the country's interior. Supply stockpiles are of little use if materials do not reach troops and, as documented in initial battle reports, equipment was susceptible to both shortages and pile-ups on the front.[80] Because of unstable supply lines, those in charge of shipments tended to "overload equipment and overwork men."[81] This practice met immediate needs but was not sustainable. Thus, logistical units set about expanding road, rail, and communication networks. Better communication would facilitate the efficient programming of supply procurement and dispensation, while improved road and railways would increase the reach and speed of supply transport.

The expansion of the railroads would become the focus of the US military's development of inland transportation systems. Despite its limitations, Korea's rail network became the backbone of UN supply lines because it was the most efficient means of moving large amounts of material. In fact, a military historian contended that US forces relied more heavily on rail transport in Korea than in any other conflict.[82] There was an initial scramble to repair the damage done during the North Korean offensive, but the bulk of the war was spent expanding and standardizing the rail network. Under the Japanese, the primary function of railroads was to funnel materials into Busan for export to Japan.[83] The Japanese invested heavily in three principal lines: a direct line from Busan and Seoul; an east coast line linking Busan to Seoul through Ulsan and Yongcheon; and a line between Incheon and Seoul. The UN side employed these lines extensively even though they did not cover much area laterally. US troops oversaw the laying of standard-gauge rails compatible with US-made railcars.[84] Through these efforts, the available rail capacity multiplied from a low of 250 miles to 1,500 miles.[85]

The improvement of the rail network slashed the time it took for goods to reach the battlefront and, more importantly, ensured their regular arrival.[86] No longer concerned with if and when goods would arrive, supply officers could freely program and schedule deliveries.[87]

While trains were the primary means of bulk transport, trucks continued to play a critical role in carrying supplies the "last mile." Combat was rarely isolated to the area immediately surrounding rail lines. Thus, trucks were necessary to complete the final leg of supply missions.[88] As mentioned, Korean roads were quite poor and for the most part unable to support motorized transport. Unpaved roads were particularly problematic during the rainy season when heavy rain literally washed away dirt and gravel roads. In June 1951, the army began an extensive national road construction program that made Korea suitable for motorized transport. High-traffic routes between major cities were paved with asphalt, while secondary dirt and gravel roads were widened and compacted.[89] With the improvement of roads, supply trucks were no longer delayed or prevented from reaching troops on the front lines, no matter where in the country combat broke out.

By the end of the Korean War, US soldiers had remade southeastern Korea into one of the most advanced logistics centers in the Pacific, if not the entire world. In stark contrast with the start of the war, US military leaders had an integrated communication system and some 6,400 miles of standardized rail and highways at their disposal.[90] They were able to gauge supply requirement accurately, respond to changing conditions on the ground, and promptly send necessary materials to the correct locations. As Table 1 shows, Korean ports overall throughput rate increased by 8,850 metric tons per day as a result of the improvements made during the war. In addition to Busan,

Table 1.1. Improvement of Throughput Capacity in SE Korean Ports (Tons/20-Hour Day), 1950–1953

	Jun-50	Jun-51	Jun-52	Dec-53	Total Change
Busan + Satellite Ports	16,000	21,920	21,800	24,850	plus 8,850
Busan	16,000	29,000	25,800	15,800	minus 200
Busan's Satellite Ports					
Pohang	N/A	974	1,500	3,500	plus 3,500
Masan	N/A	3,320	3,500	2,800	plus 2,800
Gimhae	N/A	N/A	N/A	1,400	plus 1,400
Ulsan	N/A	1,370	1,000	1,350	plus 1,350

Source: Logistics in Korean Operations III.

nearby satellite ports were developed to receive overflow from Busan or to house specialized facilities (e.g., petroleum and ammunition depots, vehicle and ship maintenance).[91]

Busan remained the central entry point of goods into the country, and it processed more materials than all other Korean ports combined. In fact, Busan was the busiest military port in not only Korea but also the entire world by the second year of the conflict. The city processed two times more material than its closest competitor, New York.[92] Following the war, Busan and New York became increasingly intertwined within a single supply chain that fueled US military deployments around the world.

Conclusion

The Korean War ended on July 27, 1953 with the signing of an armistice that ended active combat. Continuing tensions with North Korea led to the permanent deployment of the US Eighth Army in South Korea. Though troops were concentrated along the 38th parallel, Busan continued to handle the majority of matériel that entered the country. As a result of this troop deployment and the start of postwar reconstruction efforts, the flood of supplies into Busan did not abate with the end of active combat. Over time, however, exports would take the place of imports as Busan's primary cargo. Whereas goods flowed into Korea during the war and its immediate aftermath, they would eventually flow outward as South Korean companies set their sights on foreign markets during the 1970s.

The long-term impact of US military operations during the war was two-fold. First, the concentration of military projects and technical expertise that flowed into the country sparked the development of the South Korea's heavy industrial sector. The US military spent over $150 million on construction during the Korean War, of this sum over $117 million went toward transportation systems.[93] In providing transportation and construction services for these projects, Korean industrial firms gained access to US technology and administrative techniques. Among the most successful examples is the Hyundai Corporation.

While known as an automobile company today, Hyundai started as a construction company working for the US Eighth Army during the war. Among the most important benefits of working as a US military contractor, according to company founder Chung Ju-Yung, was the ability to learn US construction processes and to gain access to US equipment.[94] The US Eighth Army's postwar road construction program first introduced the company to US road paving and bridge construction techniques.[95] During the 1960s and 1970s, Hyundai would use this experience in road construction to win larger and more lucrative contracts—including construction contracts from the US military in Southeast Asia during the Vietnam War and infrastructure contracts with the Saudi Arabian government during the 1970s.[96]

Second, the US military's standardization of Busan's transportation facilities laid the foundations for its postwar emergence as a leading container port. Following the war, US military assistance funds went toward the further rehabilitation and standardization of the city's harbor and transportation systems. These improvements would be expanded upon by the Park Chung Hee government, which focused its efforts on the further development of country's southeastern region.[97] Park's Second Five-Year Development Plan prioritized the further expansion transportation systems. As a part of this effort, Park used the deployment of troops to Vietnam to secure developmental assistance funds and developmental grants from USAID and the World Bank. A 1973 World Bank-funded project specifically sought to build up the ability of Busan and other area ports to handle container cargo.[98] These investments paid spectacular dividends starting in the late 1970s when container shipping became the global standard. Fueled by the rapid expansion of the country's export industry, Busan would become one of the world's leading by the end of the 1980s. According to the World Shipping Council, it was the sixth busiest container port in the world in 2015.[99]

Busan's emergence as a leading container port dovetailed with the growth of the Hanjin Corporation. The company established ties with the US military during the 1960s. It got its first big break during the Vietnam War, when it formed a partnership with the SeaLand Corporation (the pioneer of standardized container technology) to transport supplies for the US military in Vietnam. As a military contractor, the company gained the experience and technological expertise necessary to begin container-shipping operations from Busan during the early 1970s.[100] During the following decades, Hanjin grew into one of the largest shipping companies in the world.[101]

By considering the impact of the US military operations during the Korean War, this chapter demonstrated that the US military was responsible for creating much of the physical infrastructure necessary to facilitate Korea's industrialization. More broadly, it used Busan's development as a case study for understanding the central role of the US military logistics to postwar US empire. Over the course of the Cold War, the US military would spearhead the construction and standardization of shipping, communication, and storage systems around the world. These facilities would come to serve the transnational supply chains of multinational corporations.[102] Thus, the evolution of Busan demonstrates how US soldiers were as essential to globalization as economists and policymakers.

Notes

1. "Pusan" is the McCune-Reischauer romanization of "Busan." For Korean names and words, this chapter employs the Revised Romanization of Korean. Discrepancies will be noted below.

2. Lt. Robert Fulton, "Supplying UN Troops in Korea," 02 August 1952; History-Opns Interchange to Newspaper Clippings; Supplying UN Troops in Korea; Box 80; Records of HQ, US Army, Pacific Military Historian's Office Organizational History Files [OHF]; Record Group 550: Records of the U.S. Army, Pacific, 1945—1984 [RG 550]; National Archives and Records Administration, College Park, MD [NARACP]: 1.

3. This figure only includes goods transported by ship, which makes up about 90% of global trade. UNCTAD, *Review of Maritime Transport, 2014*, 5.

4. For a discussion of the "frictionless flow" of world trade, see Orenstein, "Free Trade Zones and the Cultural Logic of Frictionless Production," 36–61.

5. South Korea was the world's 6th largest exporter in 2015, shipping out $527 billion worth of goods. World Trade Organization, "Leading exporters and importers in world merchandise trade, 2015," https://www.wto.org/english/res_e/statis_e/wts2016_e/wts16_chap9_e.htm, accessed May 7, 2017.

6. I define a "modern port" as one with infrastructure and facilites compatible with those of hegemonic powers.

7. For a discussion of the impact of US military contracts on Korean economic development during the Vietnam War, see Glassman and Choi, "The *Chaebols* and the US Military Industrial Complex: Cold War Geopolitical Economy and South Korean Industrialization,": 1160–1180.

8. Cumings, *Dominion from Sea to Sea*: Chpt. 15.

9. Between 1950 and 1979, the United States provided South Korea with $9.4 billion worth of Military Assistance Program (MAP) grants and related programs. Arson and Klare, *Supplying Repression*: Appendix II, 112–119. During the same period, the overall sum of these programs for all foreign nations was $101.9 billion. Ibid., 117.

10. Woo-Cumings, *Race to the Swift*; Amsden, *Asia's Next Giant*; Chang, "The Political Economy of Industrial Policy in Korea,"; Kim, and Chang Jae Baik, "Taming and Tamed by the United States," in *The Park Chung Hee Era*, eds. Byung-kook Kim and Ezra Vogel (Cambridge, MA: Harvard University Press, 2011): 85–111. While such studies were prominent during the period of rapid economic growth in East Asia during the 1980s and early 1990s, the subsequent economic stagnation of Japan and other the "Tiger Economies" during the late 1990s, as well as the 1997 Asian financial crisis, led scholars to place a greater emphasis on non-state actors, particularly the *chaebols*. Kim & Park, "The Chaebol" in *The Park Chung Hee Era*,

265–294. See also, Kim, *Big Business, Strong State: Collusion and Conflict in South Korean Development, 1960–1990.*

11. The impact of Japan's colonization Korea is still a highly contentious subject among scholars. Much of this debate centers on how large a role Japan played in the "origins" of Korean capitalism and postwar economic success. For a representative work; see Eckert, *Offspring of Empire*; Shin and Robinson, ed., *Colonial Modernity in Korea.*

12. Sociologist Gong Jae-uk has observed many studies of South Korea's economic development have underplayed the importance of the Korean War and 1950s. Gong, "Hangukjeonjaenggwa Jaebeoolui Hyeongseong [The Korean War and the Development of Chaebols]," in *Hangukjeonjaenggwa Gangukjabonjuui* [The Korean War and Korean Capitalism]: 59–60. Gong's work is part of a collection that explores the relationship between the Korean War and South Korean capitalism. Gong argues that the decade laid the foundation for the emergence of *chaebols* through the Syngman Rhee government's dispossession of former Japanese industries and businesses, while others emphasize other aspects including the establishment of capitalist social relations, the growth of the permanent military economy, or the creation of the national security state. See essays by Jeong Jin-sang, Jeong Seong-jin, and Jang Sang-hwan.

13. Geographer Erica Schoenberger has noted the tendency of states to foster the development of new markets as part of its efforts to expand and maintain territory throughout history. Using the example of European history, she argued that state promoted the development of markets as a "mechanism for managing resources over time and space rather than as a way of facilitating exchange per se." Schoenberger, "The Origins of the Market Economy: State Power, Territorial Control, and Modes of War Fighting,": 666. For a discussion of British military forces and road construction, see Jo Guldi, *Roads to Power: Britain Invents the Infrastructure State* (Harvard University Press, 2012). Recent work by China historian Masato Hasegawa has explored the impact of Ming military logistics in northern Korea, Hasegawa, "War, Supply Lines, and Society in the Sino-Korea Borderland of the Late Sixteenth Century," *Late Imperial China* 37:1 (2016): 109–152.

14. For a discussion in the de-territorialized nature of postwar US empire, see Daniel Immerwahr, "The Greater United States: Territory and Empire in U.S. History,": 373–391.

15. Cowen, *The Deadly Life of Logistics.*

16. The close tie between military logistics and commercial development was one of the central insights of Cowen's *The Deadly Life of Logistics.*

17. For a discussion of the archeological sites around Busan; see Nelson, *The Archaeology of Korea*: 70–73, 95–96, 239–242.

18. For further discussion of Korean geography, see McCune, *Views of Geography of Korea.*

19. National Geographic Information Institute, *The National Atlas of Korea*: 85.

20. During Korea's isolationist period, Korea continued to part of the Chinese tributary system. For a discussion of Sino-Korea tributary relation during the pre-Joseon

period, see Clark, "Sino-Korean Tributary Relations Under the Ming," in Twitchett and Mote, ed. *Cambridge History of China*, vol. 8 (Cambridge: Cambridge University Press, 1998): 272–300. For a discussion of the subsequent period, see Lee Hun-chang, *Hangukgyeongjetongsa* [*The Economic History of Korea*]: 105.

21. Eckert, *Offspring of Empire*, 9.

22. Much has been written about Japan's role in the decline of the Yi state. For example, see Duus, *The Abacus and the Sword*.

23. Busan was opened in 1876, Wonsan in 1880, Incheon in 1883, Mokpo in 1897, and Gunsan in 1899.

24. Lee, *The Economic History of Korea*, 269.

25. Ibid.

26. Bird, *Korea and Her Neighbors*, 16–20.

27. See Note 11.

28. Eckert, *Offspring of Empire*, 10.

29. For pictures of colonial-era Japanese structures in Busan and a compilation of Japanese organizations in the city, see Hong, *Iljesigi Jaebusanilboninsahoe Shhoedanche Josabogo* [Report on Japanese Society and Social Organization in Colonial Era Busan].

30. This pattern of development began before the actual annexation of Korea, when a slew of private railway companies were founded at the turn of the twentieth century—starting with the construction of a rail line between Seoul and Incheon by a US and Korean joint venture in 1896. An attempt was made by Pak Ki-jong to build a railway around Busan in 1896, but the venture failed due to a lack of capital. Eckert, et al., *Korea Old and New*: 269.

31. Eckert, *Offspring of Empire*.

32. Uchida, "A Scramble for Freight": The Politics of Collaboration along and across the Railway Tracks of Korea under Japanese Rule,": 117–150.

33. Ibid., 123.

34. "Proposed Briefing on the Port of Pusan," 1 June 1958; Port of PUSAN; Container 7; USAID, Mission to Korea/Industry Division; Entry# P 585: Records Relating to Ports, Harbors, and Water Systems, 1955–1965 [Entry# P 585]; Record Group 286: Records of Agency for International Development [RG 286]; US National Archives at College Park [NARACP], 1.

35. "Proposed Briefing on the Port of Pusan," 1959; Port of PUSAN; Container 7; Entry# P 585; RG 286; NARACP, 1.

36. For a discussion of war mobilization and its impact on Manchuria and Japan, see Young, *Japan's Total Empire*.

37. Cumings, *Korea's Place in the Sun*: 173–183.

38. During this time, nonagricultural employment increased nearly 10%, and urbanization nearly doubled. These shifts were driven by the concentration of new mining and manufacturing facilities in select regions. Soon-won Park, "Colonial Industrial Growth and the Emergence of the Korean Working Class," in *Colonial Modernity in Korea*, 128–160.

39. Nam, *Building Ships, Building a Nation*: 18–20.

40. It is significant that shipbuilding emerged in Busan. In contrast to purely extractive industries like mining or light industries like food processing, shipbuilding has served as a catalyst for industrialization because it requires a high-level of technical expertise and sparks the creation of supporting industries like iron and steel production. Scholars argue that shipbuilding is a "generative sector" of the capitalist world economy, because it stimulates the growth of related industries and state policies favorable for industrialization. Shin and Ciccantell, "The Steel and Shipbuilding Industries of South Korea: Rising East Asia and Globalization": 171–173.

41. Special Report on Highway Transportation, 21 December 1961; 895B.261/2-661; BOX 2909; Central Decimal File 1960–63; Record Group 59: General Records of the Department of State [RG 59], NARACP, 1–2.

42. US Federal Works Agency, *Highway Statistics, 1946*: 65.

43. Similarly, the Japanese railroad industry was isolated from major developments during this period. While no doubt among the most advanced in the non-Western world, the Japanese lagged in the construction of railroads. Testifying to the gap in productivity of Western vs. Japanese railroad construction, the entire continent of Asia (excluding India) contained only 4.3% of the world's railroad mileage (40,800 miles) at the end of World War II while North America had 46.8% (440,600 miles) and Europe had 30.3% (284,900 miles). Topik and Wells, "Commodity Chains in a Global Economy" in Emily S. Rosenberg, Akira Iriye, and Charles Mair, eds., *A World Connecting: 1870–1945* (Cambridge, MA: Belknap Press, 2012), 626. Geography no doubt contributed to this difference, as Japan was an island nation with a much smaller landmass than the United States.

44. While a large number of UN nations sent troops to Korea, the United States dominated the planning and administration of the UN war effort. In this chapter, "UN" will be applied to combat forces and "US" will be applied to various support troops and divisions.

45. During the war, US military leaders operated under the assumption that Korea would be unified by war's end. Therefore, the construction of permanent transportation systems was not fully undertaken even as fighting stalled at the 38th parallel.

46. The only other South Korean port that could provide deep-water berthing was Masan, but it could only unload two ships at a time. Gough, *U.S. Army Mobilization and Logistics in the Korean War*: 71.

47. HUAFFEEUSA, *Logistics in the Korean Operations*, Vol. II; 1 December 1955; Logistics in the Korean Operations, SUPPLY, APPENDIX A; Box 71; OHF; RG 550; NARACP [hereafter Logistics in the Korean Operations II], Figure 21.

48. Gough, *U.S. Army Mobilization and Logistics in the Korean War*, 71.

49. At the start of the war, only ten officers comprised the entirety of US military personnel in Busan. Just two days before Douglas MacArthur received official authorization to begin deployment, these ten men were notified to begin preparations for the arrival of US forces.

50. Logistics in the Korean Operations I, Chpt. II, 6.

51. Troop levels fluctuated throughout the war. At no point did non-combat troops make up over 44% of this total.

52. For instance, logistical units prepared rations that had extra rice and curry powder for Indian troops who could not consume beef for religious reasons. James A. Huston, "Time & Space Vol. 1—Chapter VII: Friends and Foes," 28 October 1953; Time and Space Chapter 7; Box 21; Center of Military History; TIME AND SPACE; Record Group 319: Records of the Army Staff; NARACP, 23–30.

53. The western United States had undergone rapid development in response to World War II mobilization efforts and had several excellent ports including San Francisco and Seattle. Hooks and Bloomquist, "The Legacy of World War II for Regional Growth and Decline: The Wartime Investments on U.S. Manufacturing, 1947–1972,": esp. 306–310. Similarly, Japan possessed several excellent harbors with US Army facilities concentrated in Yokohama, Kobe, and Moji. Gough, *U.S. Army Mobilization and Logistics in the Korean War*, 70.

54. One military historian described the supply chain as "two mammoth supply pipelines" from the US and Japan that empty into Busan port. 8086 Army Unit (AFFE) Military History Detachment, "Offshore Procurement in Korea—Problems and their Solutions," 21 May 1955; Offshore Procurement in Korea—Problems and their Solution Folder I; Box 76; OHF; RG 550; NARACP, i.

55. HUAFFEEUSA, *Logistics in the Korean Operations*, Vol. IV, 1 December 1955; Logistics in the Korean Operations, TECH. SERVICE & SPEC. LOG. ACTIVITIES, Vol. IV; Box 71; OHF; RG 550; NARACP [hereafter Logistics in the Korean Operations IV], Chpt. VII. 70.

56. Quoted in Westover, *Combat Support in Korea*: 53.

57. During the first year of the war, it is estimated that over 200 truck runs were made daily. Appleman, *South to the Naktong, North to the Yalu (June–November 1950)*: 489.

58. These specifications were designed to accommodate the dimensions of standard army transports, the Willys MB and Ford GPW jeeps. Both vehicles were standardized during World War II. Their basic dimensions were 11ft × 5.2 ft × 5.8 ft. Its weight with a full load of cargo was 2,453 pounds. Thus, the minimum width requirements of roads were designed to allow for at least two jeeps to travel at a time and withstand the minimum weight of a fully loaded jeep. For more on the standardization of army Jeeps, see US War Department, *1/4-Ton 4X4 Truck (Willys-Overland Model Mb and Ford Model GPW)*: 10–12.

59. Appleman, *South to the Naktong, North to the Yalu*, 102–103.

60. Engineers sought to construct "class 50" roads, which is defined by the US Army field manual as capable of sustaining "average traffic." For a discussion of military road classification, see US Army, FM 3-34.170/MCWP 3-17.4—"Engineer Reconnaissance," March 2008, https://rdl.train.army.mil/catalog-ws/view/100.ATSC/408C0E5B-80A2-4255-99A8-C73EA71C81D9-1308730109242/3-34.170/toc.htm#toc; accessed August 1, 2015.

61. Logistics in the Korean Operations IV, Chpt. VII, 18.
62. Quoted in Westover, *Combat Support in Korea*, 11.
63. Logistics in the Korean Operations II, Chpt. IV, 17.
64. Westover, *Combat Support in Korea*, 231.
65. For details of the UN counteroffensive; see Appleman, *South to the Naktong, North to the Yalu*, Chpt. 25–38.
66. According to standard US military doctrine, the extension of combat lines required the creation of intermediate supply points and depots in order to ensure the steady flow of supplies to all points along battlefront. Logistics in the Korean Operations I, Chpt. II, 12.
67. The situation might not have been as dire had Incheon had a more suitable port. In contrast to Busan, Incheon's port was not only surrounded by turbulent waters, but also lacked the facilities to receive deep-water vessels.

A certain amount of supplies were sent directly to Incheon. However, this often caused accounting problems because the same supplies were often sent to both Incheon and Busan. Logistics in the Korean Operations II, Chpt. IV, 18.
68. Logistics in the Korean Operations II, Chpt. III, 20. In fact, the mass destruction of materials during the retreat would spark criticism in the United States from members of Congress and the public.
69. For the devastating consequences of these operations and its long-lasting impact on North Koreans, see Bruce Cumings, *The Korean War*: Chpt. 6.
70. Troop levels reached 70% of the peak levels by 1951. Logistics in the Korean Operations II, Chpt. III, 2.
71. Initial efforts were started by the Provisional Government of Korea established by the US military in 1945 following Korea's liberation from Japan. While celebrated among Koreans, independence disrupted the flow of essential goods and services. The US military addressed this situation by establishing distribution systems for necessities like food, fertilizer, clothing, and fuel. The Economic Cooperation Administration (ECA) expanded these efforts in 1948 when the military occupation ended and the State Department took over US assistance efforts from the US Army. In the hopes of promoting long-term economic development, ECA planners initiated plans to rehabilitate the country's roads, rails, and industrial facilities. The outbreak of the war put reconstruction efforts on hold.
72. A Repair and Utilities Division of the Eighth Army was established in August 1950. Repairs of power and water plants were made throughout the conflict. Logistics in the Korean Operations IV, Chpt. VII, 30–31.
73. For a discussion of throughput, see HUSAFFEEUSA, *Logistics in the Korean Operations*, Vol. III, 1 December 1955; Logistics in the Korean Operations, EVAC. HOSPITALIZ., TRANSPORTATION; Box 71; OHF; RG 550; NARACP [hereafter Logistics in the Korean Operations III], Chpt. VI, 25–30.
74. With the exception of Pohang, they all fall within the Busan Perimeter established at the outset of the war.

75. The daily inflow of supplies increased every year of the conflict. Logistics in the Korean Operations IV, Chpt. VIII, 28. The US military most often reported weights using the "standard" or "short" ton, which is equal to 2,000 kg and is most commonly used in the United States.

76. Quoted in Westover, *Combat Support in Korea*, 44.

77. Logistics in the Korean Operations II, Chpt. IV, 23.

78. Fortunately for the UN-side, North Korea did not have sufficient aerial capabilities to carry out such an attack. Nevertheless, starting in the summer of 1952, efforts were made to disperse supplies outside of Busan. These efforts were largely unsuccessful and the situation was "little improved" by war's end. Logistics in the Korean Operations II, Chpt. IV, 145–148.

79. Logistics in the Korean Operations II, Chpt. IV, 147.

80. Gough, *U.S. Army Mobilization and Logistics in the Korean War*, 71–75.

81. Westover, *Combat Support in Korea*, 151.

82. Logistics in the Korean Operations III, Chpt. VI, 7.

83. Logistics in the Korean Operations IV, Chpt. VII, 24.

84. Railroad gauges are the distance between iron tracks. Standard gauge rail lines are 4 ft., 8.5 in while narrow-gauge lines were 2 ft. 6 in. Narrow gauges are cheaper to lay and are often employed when bulk transport is the primary goal. Both of these aligned with Japanese goals for the Korean railways and explain why the country had a large amount of narrow-gauge lines before the war. There were approximately 3,500 miles of standard-gauge rail lines in Korea at the start of the war. For the exact capabilities of prewar railway lines, see Logistics in the Korean Operations III, Chpt. VI, Figure 7.

85. Logistics in the Korean Operations III, 7.

86. For changes to turnaround time, see Logistics in the Korean Operations III, Chpt. VI, Figure 8.

87. This is demonstrated by the increase in the volume of goods transported by rail. For exact figures, see Logistics in the Korean Operations III, Chpt. VI, Figure 17.

88. Some frontline areas were too mountainous for even motor vehicles, so the US Army forced Korean soldiers and civilians to transport supplies by foot.

89. The majority of new construction focused on highways and bridges. In January 1952 alone, nearly 13 different highway bridges were completed and over 4,300 feet of high bridges were under construction and repair. Logistics in the Korean Operations IV, Chpt. VII, 22.

90. Logistics Briefing for Mr. John Thurston, May 1953; Logistics Briefing for Mr. John Thurston, May 53; Box 68; RHQUSAPMHO; OHF; NARACP, 5.

91. The growth of these ports led to a slight decline in traffic into Busan itself. By the end of the war, Busan's throughput capacity declined largely due to the withdrawal of UN forces following the end of hostilities. However, at its height, the port throughput capacity reached nearly 30,000 tons per day.

92. Logistics in the Korean Operations III, Chpt. 6, 34.

93. US Congress; House; Committee on Government Operations; *Relief and Rehabilitation in Korea*; July 29, 1954; 83d Cong., 2d Sess.; H. Report 2574, 71.

94. Chung noted that the lack of equipment was a major challenge to overcome during the 1950s. However, through his connections to the US Eighth Army, he was able to buy military surplus road paving equipment. Chung, *I ttangeseo taeeonaseo* [Born in this land: my life story]: 70.

95. Between the period between 1953 and 1963, the US Eighth Army oversaw the construction of an additional 15,000 miles of roads. Memo from Chief, Public Works Division, Term End Report, 25 July 1960; TERM-END REPORT; Container 2; Entry#P 588; RG 286; NARACP, 2.

96. Hyundai's first overseas project was the construction of the Pattanni Naratiwat highway in Thailand. Glassman, Choi, "The *Chaebols* and the US Military Industrial Complex," 1170–1173; Woo, *Race to the Swift*: 94–97.

97. O recalled that the development of the Ulsan Industrial Complex commenced almost immediately after Park took power during the summer of 1962, O, *Hangukhyeong Gyeongjegeonseol Je 1 Won* [Korean-style Economic Development Vol. 1]: 25–27.

98. As a result of this project, container traffic to and from Busan more than tripled. World Bank, "Appraisal of A First Port Project, Korea," 29 May 1973; The World Bank, www.worldbank.com, accessed 3 May 2015, table 19. Additional World Bank ports projects started in 1977 and 1986 further expand Busan's container handling capabilities.

99. World Shipping Council, "Top 50 World Container Ports," http://www.worldshipping.org/, accessed May 1, 2017.

100. Hanjin directly contributed to the expansion of Busan's container facilities by obtaining a container crane for the Korean government in 1977. Letter to Harold Young, 14 October 1977; Port Project—Korea, Republic of—Loan 0917—P004053—Correspondence—Volume 9, Folder ID: 30213959, ISAD(G) Reference Code: WB IBRD/IDA 06; Records of the East Asia and Pacific Regional Office; World Bank Archives, Washington, DC, 1.

101. Pak, *Han'guk ui 50 tae chaebol* [Korea's 50 Biggest Corporations]: 82–84; Hanjin Group, History—"Challenges 1966–1974," http://www.hanjin.net/english/about/history_1.html, accessed 26 May 2016.

102. For a discussion of the evolution of corporate supply chains, see Lichtenstein, *The Retail Revolution* and Hart-Landsberg, *Capitalist Globalization*.

Bibliography

Archival Sources

National Archives and Records Administration, College Park, MD
Record Group 59
Record Group 286

Record Group 319
Record Group 550
World Bank Archives, Washington, DC

Other Sources

Amsden, Alice. *Asia's Next Giant: South Korea and Late Industrialization* (New York: Oxford University Press, 1992).

Appleman, Roy. *South to the Naktong, North to the Yalu (June–November 1950)* (Washington, D.C.: U.S. Army Center of Military History, 1992).

Arson, Cynthia, and Michael T. Klare. *Supplying Repression* (Washington, D.C: Institute for Policy Studies, 1981).

Chang, Ha-joon. "The Political Economy of Industrial Policy in Korea," *Cambridge Journal of Economics* 17:2 (1993): 131–157.

Chung, Ju Yung. *I ttangeseo taeeonaseo* [Born in this land: my life story] (Seoul: Sol, 1998).

Clark, Donald N. "Sino-Korean Tributary Relations Under the Ming," in Twitchett and Mote, ed. *Cambridge History of China*, vol. 8 (Cambridge: Cambridge University Press, 1998).

Cowen, Deborah. *The Deadly Life of Logistics: Mapping Violence in Global Trade* (Minneapolis, MN: University Of Minnesota Press, 2014).

Cumings, Bruce. *Dominion from Sea to Sea: Pacific Ascendancy and American Power* (New Haven, CT: Yale University Press, 2009).

——. *Korea's Place in the Sun: A Modern History* (New York: W. W. Norton, 2005).

——. *The Korean War* (New York: Random House, 2010).

Duus, Peter. *The Abacus and the Sword: The Japanese Penetration of Korea, 1895–1910* (Berkeley, C.A.: University of California Press, 1998).

Eckert, Carter. *Offspring of Empire: The Koch'ang Kims and the Colonial Origins of Korean Capitalism, 1876–1945* (Seattle, WA: University of Washington Press, 1996).

——, et al. *Korea Old and New: A History* (Seoul: Ilchokak Publishers, 1991).

Glassman, Jim, and Young-jin Choi. "The *Chaebols* and the US Military Industrial Complex: Cold War Geopolitical Economy and South Korean Industrialization," *Environment and Planning A* Vol. 46 (2014): 1160–1180.

Gong, Jae-uk. "*Hangukjeonjaenggwa Jaebeoolui Hyeongseong* [The Korean War and the Development of *Chaebols*]," in *Hangukjeonjaenggwa Gangukjabonjuui* [The Korean War and Korean Capitalism] Gyeongsang University Sociology Research Center (Seoul: Hanul, 2000).

Gough, Terrence J. *U.S. Army Mobilization and Logistics in the Korean War: A Research Approach* (Washington, D.C.: U.S. Army Center of Military History, 1987).

Hart-Landsberg, Martin. *Capitalist Globalization: Consequences, Resistance, and Alternatives* (New York: Monthly Review Press, 2013).

Hooks Gregory, and Leonard Bloomquist. "The Legacy of World War II for Regional Growth and Decline: The Wartime Investments on U.S. Manufacturing, 1947–1972," *Social Forces* 71:2 (1992): 303–337.

Hong, Sun-swon. *Iljesigi Jaebusanilboninsahoe Shhoedanche Josabogo* [Report on Japanese Society and Social Organization in Colonial Era Busan] (Seoul: Sonin, 2005).

Immerwahr, Daniel. "The Greater United States: Territory and Empire in U.S. History," *Diplomatic History* Vol. 40 No. 3 (2016): 373–391.

Kim, Taehyun, and Chang Jae Baik. "Taming and Tamed by the United States," in *The Park Chung Hee Era*, eds. Byung-kook Kim and Ezra Vogel (Cambridge, MA: Harvard University Press, 2011): 85–111.

Kim, Eun Mee, & Gil-Sung Park. "The Chaebol" in *The Park Chung Hee Era*, 265–294.

Lee Hun-chang. *Hangukgyeongjetongsa* [The Economic History of Korea] (Seoul: Haenam, 2014).

Lichtenstein, Nelson. *The Retail Revolution: How Wal-Mart Created a Brave New World of Business* (New York: Picador, 2010).

McCune, Shannon. *Views of Geography of Korea* (Seoul: The Korean Research Center, 1980).

Nam, Hwasook. *Building Ships, Building a Nation: Korea's Democratic Unionism Under Park Chung Hee* (Seattle: University of Washington Press, 2009).

National Geographic Information Institute. *The National Atlas of Korea* (Suwon, South Korea: ROK Ministry of Land, Transport and Maritime Affairs, 2009).

Nelson, Sarah M. *The Archaeology of Korea* (New York: Cambridge University Press, 1993).

O, Won-cheol. *Hangukhyeong Gyeongjegeonseol Je 1 Won* [Korean-style Economic Development Vol. 1] (Seoul: KIA Economic Research Center, 1995).

Orenstein, Dara. "Free Trade Zones and the Cultural Logic of Frictionless Production," *Radical History* 109 (Winter 2011): 36–61.

Pak, Pyong-un. *Han'guk ui 50 tae chaebol* [Korea's 50 Biggest Corporations] (Seoul: Management Efficiency Research Institute: 1986).

Schoenberger, Erica. "The Origins of the Market Economy: State Power, Territorial Control, and Modes of War Fighting," *Comparative Studies in Society and History* 50: 3 (2008).

Shin, Gi-wook, and Michael Robinson, ed. *Colonial Modernity in Korea*, (Cambridge: Harvard University Asia Center, 2000).

Shin, Kyoung-ho, and Paul S. Ciccantell. "The Steel and Shipbuilding Industries of South Korea: Rising East Asia and Globalization," *Journal of World-Systems Research* Vol. 15, No. 2 (2009): 171–173.

Topik, Steven, and Allen Wells. "Commodity Chains in a Global Economy," in Emily S. Rosenberg, Akira Iriye, and Charles Mair, eds., *A World Connecting: 1870–1945* (Cambridge: Belknap Press, 2012).

Uchida, Jun. "A Scramble for Freight": The Politics of Collaboration along and across the Railway Tracks of Korea under Japanese Rule," *Comparative Studies in Society and History* Vol. 51, No. 1 (2009): 117–150.

UNCTAD. *Review of Maritime Transport, 2014* (New York: United Nations Publications, 2014).

US Federal Works Agency. *Highway Statistics, 1946* (Washington, D.C., US Government Printing Office, 1947).

US War Department. *1/4-Ton 4X4 Truck (Willys-Overland Model Mb and Ford Model GPW)*, (Washington, D.C.: US Government Printing Office, 1944).

Westover, John G. *Combat Support in Korea* (Washington: D.C.: US Army Center of Military History, 1990).

Woo-Cumings, Meredith. *Race to the Swift: State and Finance in Korean Industrialization* (New York: Columbia University Press, 1991).

CHAPTER TWO

From Dependency to Self-Sufficiency

American Relief Food in the Korean Peripheries in the 1960s

Dajeong Chung

In November 1966, villagers of Wondang-ri in Gangweon Province wrote a letter of appeal to Joel Bernstein, the Director of United States Operations Mission (USOM) in Seoul, requesting relief grain to feed their community of 128 people.[1] The villagers were historically fire-fallow (slash-and-burn) farmers, but they had been resettled in a new village, Wondang-ri. In the previous year, USOM's Food for Peace (Pyeonghwa reul wihan singryang) program had provided them with grain to feed their families while they reclaimed farmland and built houses to resettle. However, as the villagers pleaded, despite their hard work, the year's harvest had not been plentiful and they would need relief grain to sustain them through the next harvest season in June. USOM-Seoul suggested that the villagers should consult their local government for the matter. The villagers' appeal to USOM was not an isolated incident. Between 1961 and 1968, USOM Korea received numerous petitions and letters from village communities asking for grain and other support.[2]

The grain that the villagers from Wondang-ri hoped to attain from USOM was made available under a rural self-help program (Title II, Section 202) of the Food for Peace Act.[3] The enabling legislation for the Food for Peace Act was the Agricultural Assistance and Trade Act of 1954, also known as U.S. Public Law 480 (PL 480). It was a global food aid program using U.S. agricultural surpluses. Under Public Law 480, U.S. government disbursed agricultural surpluses, especially wheat flour, to foreign nations through various commercial and aid channels, and promoted its foreign policy aims in the Cold War.[4]

Inaugurated in 1964 as part of the U.S. Food for Peace Program, the official name for rural self-help programs was the Provincial Comprehensive Development Program. In the mid-1960s, the planners decided that for these programs, the only major investment coming from outside the community was to be grain paid as wages, and that grain was given out for the direct consumption of workers and their families. Villagers exchanged their labor for food, and performed simple projects such as land reclamation for farming, reforestation, building fishing villages, flood control, irrigation, soil erosion control, water impoundment, and marine product cultivation.

The self-help programs put forward an alternative picture of modernization and development to the one espoused in large-scale industrialization.[5] Self-help programs under the U.S. Food for Peace Act combined poor relief and village development, and significantly, from the mid-1960s precluded the use of sophisticated machines, advanced technological expertise, and intensive capital investment. The programmers selected development projects to be completed by unskilled laborers doing dirt work, and cutting trees and rough stones. Some projects looked similar to the ones of Mao Zedong's Great Leap Forward in the late 1950s in the People's Republic of China and of Kim Il-Sung's Cheollima (1958–ongoing) in North Korea.[6]

In South Korea, U.S. supported self-help programs in the 1960s transformed the furthest peripheries of South Korean landscape in rural and fishing villages, small islands, and forest settlements. Not only USOM-Korea and South Korean provincial governments, but also U.S. voluntary agencies participated in village self-help programs. Thus, U.S. aid grain reached the people on the villages as CARE took community development to Ulleungdo, the second furthest island in the East Sea after Dok-do, and to Mountain Taegi, atop a 4,100-foot village in Hoengseong gun, Gangwondo.[7] To the west, Seventh-Day Adventists implemented tideland reclamation projects in Anmyeon Island in South Chungcheong Province.[8]

While this model of self-help village development presented a contrasting picture to the one of large-scale industrial projects, both development models co-existed in South Korea in the 1960s. While Food for Peace development program veered towards small-scale village self-help projects, some international organizations such as the World Food Programme (WFP) and the South Korean government carried out large-scale river projects and highway construction programs. Just as in India the Etawah model of decentralized community development co-existed with large-scale programs like the construction of the Rihand Dam,[9] self-help programs in South Korea operated in tandem with other developmental programs.

The large-scale infrastructural constructions had their theoretical bases on Walt W. Rostow's modernization theory. According to Rostow and his colleagues, (economic) development was aimed to close the gap between developing and developed countries. In seeking efficiency to achieve the goal, modernization theory promoted implementing large-scale infrastructural projects, such as hydraulic dams, highways, and ports that would provide the economic infrastructure to catch up with industrially advanced countries. These projects required technologically advanced machines and expertise as well as large-scale capital investment. In the 1960s, modernization theory and its idea of convergence garnered much support among South Korean intellectuals, as is evident from the Park Chung Hee regime's build-up of heavy industries in subsequent Five-Year Plans (1962–1989).[10]

In contrast, the self-help programs were much smaller in scale compared to other developmental programs. However, it is important to present this history in order to understand that modernization theory alone is not sufficient to understand South Korea's development. In addition to academic exchanges and technological transfer of modernization theory to South Korea, small-scale village development programs in the 1960s bore more direct U.S. imprint than previously acknowledged. Food was especially a crucial part of the story: U.S. wheat flour was the medium that made direct connection with the people on the ground possible and transformed their diets. Food was the medium that linked U.S. domestic politics of agricultural surpluses to the South Korean village self-help programs.

The hallmark of USOM sponsored village self-help programs in the 1960s was that it combined providing relief to the poor and helping them help themselves through small-scale projects. Prior to the implementation of self-help programs in the 1960s, U.S. PL 480 regulations had prohibited aid agencies from distributing grain as compensation for work. Aid food had to be given out based on the need. However, now for self-help programs, only people who had the ability to work and at the same time were unemployed or poor could work in projects. By providing U.S. wheat flour and cornmeal as wages-in-kind, self-help programs supported local villagers build their own houses, drinking water wells, and increase agricultural productivity. Allowing an exchange of labor for food showed the focus of U.S. food aid was moving from humanitarian aid to development.[11] It was important to gradually decrease the need for food assistance, especially when U.S. food surplus was not as abundant as before. In 1966, only cotton and tobacco were in surplus.[12] After development, U.S. aid would not be necessary.

Food Aid as Anti-Communist Policy

In South Korea, the focus of U.S. food aid changed over time from providing emergency relief in the post-Liberation and the Korean War period, to humanitarian assistance in the 1950s, to sponsoring development in the 1960s in search for more effective anti-communist strategies.[13] Numerous scholarly works discuss the topic of development as part of U.S. strategy in the Cold War: Rockefeller Foundation's rural reform programs in China in the 1930s and in Mexico in the 1940s; community development and the Green Revolution in India and the Philippines; and population control in various Asian countries.[14] This paper is informed by those works.

U.S. food relief to Korean civilians began in 1946 with the purpose of stabilizing the highly volatile population after the demise of the Japanese empire and the following national division. However, U.S. military's food aid in the late 1940s failed to garner sufficient popular support for a U.S.-led democracy in the south. Giving out foreign food such as wheat flour in insufficient amounts failed to give a message that the South was preferable to the North, where land reform had initial success.[15] In order to present U.S. food aid as a more desirable alternative, the U.S. State Department began to channel more of its food aid through voluntary agencies and international organizations, which adopted the language of humanitarian relief.[16]

That the U.S. government instigated foreign humanitarian aid as a political tool for the Cold War was apparent by the time the American Korean Foundation sent the Help Korea Train around U.S. cities in 1954.[17] The American Korean Foundation planned the train event to take place shortly before the International Conference on Far Eastern Problems during the Geneva Convention. Behind the veneer of a private organization, the America Korea Foundation acted with strong backing from the U.S. Information Agency and President Eisenhower.

As Charles Armstrong shows, after the Korean War (1950–1953), the Soviet and East German "fraternal" aid to North Korea helped the reconstruction of the North.[18] U.S. aid to South Korea competed against this socialist aid. In the letter circulated to the USOMs (U.S. Operations Missions), Henry C. Alexander, National Campaign Director of the American Korean Foundation used the American Korean Foundation's train project as an example to disparage the socialist aid. Alexander emphasized that not only AKF's ambitious program of raising 500 carloads of relief donation was overwhelmingly larger than the 60 carloads of relief train sent from East Germany to North Korea, but also that American aid gave a distinctly humanitarian message to South Koreans.[19]

Alexander claimed that individual U.S. citizens spontaneously donated help to South Koreans, while the East Berlin train was sent by the "Communist Government of East Germany" at the expense of its own people. This decentralized and democratic channels of giving was to distinguish American aid from that of the Soviet Union and East Germany.[20] The slogan for the American Korean Train was "Help Koreans Help Themselves," and the train came with freights called "The Freedom Express."

In the same year, U.S. Congress passed the Agricultural Trade Development and Assistance Act of 1954, also known as U.S. Public Law 480 (PL 480). PL 480 was a surplus food program which enabled the U.S. government to allocate surplus agricultural commodities to "friendly" nations for the relief of hunger and tacitly for the fight against communism. By disbursing surplus agricultural commodities piled up in warehouses, the U.S. government could link its domestic agenda to its foreign policy goals and win on both fronts.

Under U.S. Public Law 480, the U.S. government ran several aid programs in foreign countries: the concessional sales program (Title I) sold grain to the South Korean government at around one tenth of the world market price. Title II was the emergency aid that later became the self-help program in the 1960s. Title III was the voluntary agency program. The U.S. Department of State donated grain to voluntary agencies, and the voluntary agencies ran their aid programs in South Korea, promoting an image of humanitarian assistance from private U.S. citizens.[21] U.S. voluntary agencies such as the National Catholic Welfare Council, C.A.R.E., Church World Service, and Seventh-Day Adventist ran community self-help programs using Food for Peace grain.

The term Food for Peace Act was first used by Eisenhower in 1959 to promote using U.S. agricultural surpluses "for the relief of human hunger, and for promoting economic and social development in less developed countries."[22] However, the phrase "Food for Peace" became more widely known during the Kennedy administration, which established a Food for Peace Office in the White House in 1961, and honed its institutional focus on self-help and development.[23] The establishment of the Peace Corps was in line with this change of policy.

In South Korea, the U.S. Operations Mission in Seoul put the Work-Relief (Geullo-Guho) Program into practice in 1961 to order to prevent social discontent from exploding in pro-communist unrest. As Immerwahr showed, by this time, the U.S. government had gained experience in using community development as a counter-insurgency method in the Philippines in the 1950s.²⁴ In fact, plans for the South Korean program were being discussed well before the events in 1960. The two governments of South Korea and the United States discussed the National Reconstruction Service (NSC) in 1959 in which the South Korean government would mobilize unemployed workers for public works and pay them with U.S. aid grain. The events that prompted the USOM-Korea to direct humanitarian relief to the Work-Relief Program came in 1960.²⁵

For the U.S. Operations Mission in Korea, the April Revolution of 1960 provided an urgent context to instigate the Work-Relief Program in South Korea as an anti-Communist measure. In April 1960, student-led demonstrations against the series of political and economic corruption scandals put pressure on Syngman Rhee's regime, and Syngman Rhee resigned from Presidency.²⁶ The priority cablegram sent from Raymond T. Moyer, Director of USOM-Korea in the Far East Program, to the U.S. International Cooperation Administration (ICA) in Washington showed that the events brought to the fore the decade-long Cold War anxiety about popular demands being exploited by communists.²⁷ From Seoul, Moyer assessed that poverty and the distress of the unemployed fed to the "communist propaganda (which produced) increasing dissatisfaction and social unrest" and that "this problem (was) greatly increased by the events of April 1960 permitting freer expression and criticism."²⁸ In the same cablegram, Moyer warned that this might result in a "potentially explosive situation." To check the danger, he requested emergency relief grain for food-for-work programs that would absorb large numbers of unemployed people in the cities.²⁹

Unanticipated, by the time USOM Korea received funds for the National Construction Program in 1961, the interim government after the April Revolution was overthrown by Park Chung Hee's coup, and Park's Revolutionary Committee was in charge of the affairs of the state. As a result, Food for Peace grain ended up buttressing Park's military junta.

For the United States, anti-communism was a major reason for supporting community development all over Asia. Rural reconstruction programs in Taiwan, which was also called "Free China" to discredit the communist People's Republic of China, was also part of the anti-communist strategy. Following the model of rural development, the Taiwan program gave work to underemployed farmers and paid them with U.S. surplus grain. On that account, USOM's official gazette, the JCRR (Joint Commission on Rural Reconstruction) Newsreel, introduced the Wu Chieh dyke project in Taiwan as a project requiring "109,125 kilograms of flour, a similar amount of rice and 25,317 lbs. of edible oil." The nature of these projects was similar to those in South Korea: building small dams for flood control, irrigation, drainage canals, wells, and cisterns; building rural-to-market roads; reforestation; and soil protection and restoration.[30]

The Far Eastern Bureau of the United States ICA was instituting an already proven method of community development that had been tested in the Latin American Bureau of USOMs. By 1963, the food-for-wages model was reaching 3 million people globally. The Food for Peace Committee proudly announced that its food aid was altering the climate of the Algerian part of the Mediterranean through reforestation, and reaching out to children in small villages of Bolivia and Peru through school lunch programs.[31]

The anti-communist agenda of Food for Peace aid was repeated at the National Conference on Food for Peace on September 30, 1963.[32] The conference pamphlet noted that food aid "is a program which gets past governments to people" and thus was a suitable medium through which to form direct relationship with the people. At the time, Food for Peace sent food to the United Arab Republic (1958–1971) in Egypt where "Food for Peace program is now an extraordinarily important part of the Egyptian's everyday diet" and to Yugoslavia, albeit in much smaller amount. That the Food for Peace planners chose to send food to the areas which were "Communist by their own proclamation or are tending or moving in that direction" showed their belief that the society was separate from the state. The same pamphlet also claimed that "Against the Communist notion of a monolithic society, organized under a single, centralized authority," U.S. Food for Peace helped local societies to make their own decisions for the future.[33] This strategy was incorporated to the amendment to Public Law 480 in 1966 to "include assistance to friendly peoples without regard to the friendliness of their government" in non-governmental programs.[34]

In the early 1960s, Food for Peace focused on supporting large-scale industrial projects in its global development programs. The Rihand Dam, which was constructed between 1954 and 1962, was an example of its Indian program. The Rihand Dam was largely financed by local (Indian) currency generated through the sale of U.S. PL 480 grain.[35] During this time, Food for Peace committees financed large-scale infrastructural projects by selling U.S. agricultural surpluses in the recipient country. They used the local currency generated through the sales in order to purchase raw materials, machines and skilled workers to carry out the projects.

However, in the mid-1960s, Food for Peace planners under Lyndon Johnson's administration made an important conceptual shift in favor of small-scale community self-help programs. The food program was still an anti-communist strategy, but now with small community development programs, it presented an alternative picture of modernization and development to the ones espoused by the followers of modernization theory. From the mid-1960s on, Food for Peace development programs in South Korea avoided using advanced technology and capital investment, but turned to much smaller-scale community projects that relied on unskilled labor mostly performing dirt works. Food for Peace committees no longer sold PL 480 grain to generate local currency. They allocated grain only for the direct consumption of workers and their families. Workers who participated in small village community projects received PL 480 grain.

In the 1960s, this vision of community development co-existed with the large-scale industrial developmental programs of the South Korean government and other international organizations. At times, however, there were clashes of opinions. The World Food Program (WFP) did not shun large-scale developmental schemes in South Korea. The World Food Program (WFP) was an international organization jointly established by the United Nations and the Food and Agriculture Organization (FAO) in Rome, Italy, in April 1962.[36] Through the World Food Program (WFP), the United States planned to move away from foreign food aid programs that were negotiated bilaterally between the U.S. government and recipient countries, to a multilateral effort with international participation. To that end, the U.S. State Department was working with its European allies in the United Nations Development Program (UNDP). Overall, the Food for Peace and the WFP were engaged in similar projects, such as flood control and land reclamation, and both received U.S. aid grain under Title II Section 202 of PL 480.[37]

When the Rural Development Division (RDD) of USOM, which managed PL 480 programs in South Korea, disagreed with the World Food Program over the latter's river projects, the incident highlighted the difference in their priorities. The planners in World Food Program anticipated that flood control projects would produce crucial benefits for agricultural irrigation in comparison to the size of investment.[38] They argued that river projects made excellent use of surplus grain since the works were labor-intensive and thus would provide jobs to many unemployed people.[39] However, the Rural Development Division argued that dam projects were not suitable for self-help programs because they required large capital investment, scientific expertise, and machinery. The disagreement was over the use of grain. World Food Program in Korea sold aid grain to the market and purchased advanced machineries and skilled labor with the local currency raised through the sales. On the other hand, the Rural Development Division focused more on using PL 480 grain only to feed workers and their families.

Pursuing the dual goals of poor relief and development in the self-help community program was also at odds with South Korean government-led development programs. Park Chung Hee's regime aspired to build more key infrastructural facilities and heavy industries in its second Five-Year Plan (1967–1971). Highway construction was one of those monumental projects. In early 1967, the South Korean Ministry of National Construction inquired if the World Food Program could provide PL 480 grain for assistance in its six-year-long highway project.[40]

To this proposal, USOM's Seoul office assessed that the Highway Project was inappropriate for the self-help program. The consolidation of embankment was especially important for the project, and this required intricate technical design and sophisticated machines. The self-help program could not provide for those since it no longer sold grain to generate local currency. Instead, USOM suggested that the Ministry turn to provincial governments for technical assistance and machineries.[41]

In addition, USOM also pointed out that for the PL 480 self-help program in 1967, workers had to come from the list of relief recipients registered with the South Korean Ministry of Health and Social Affairs. However, the consolidation of base materials for the highway could not be performed by unskilled laborers who were from the relief list. The highway project also needed qualified field engineers and inspectors to supervise the laborers. Nor was it acceptable when the South Korean Ministry of Reconstruction proposed to use conscripted labor instead of hiring those who needed relief.[42] Thus, the Rural Development Division reminded the Ministry of Reconstruction that Food for Peace grain was reserved for village self-help and simple labor-intensive projects.

Perhaps, apart from the intentions behind the self-help programs, there was also an element of hesitation in the U.S. attitude towards Park Chung Hee's military regime, stemming from the earlier years of the junta. The U.S. government was not interested in assisting "PARK and COL. KIM Chung-pil, former head of the Central Intelligence Agency and once the number two man in Korea… in building "monuments" to the military regime through construction of big plants such as steal mills or oil refineries."[43] Highway project was definitely adding to the list of monuments.

The Origins of Self-Help (Jajo)

The idea of village community had a long history in Korea from the time of the Joseon Dynasty. The best known writing on village community was produced by Yi Yulgok, a sixteenth-century neo-Confucian literati. He followed Chinese neo-Confucian scholar Chu Hsi's (Song Dynasty Confucian scholar) example of the Lü-Family Compact in (1076), and proposed self-sufficient village and mutual aid system be established by Village Compact (Hyangyak).[44] The concept of self-sufficient village community provided an ideal of village life.

As for the term "self-help" (jajo), it was introduced to Korea from Japan in the 1900s. Japanese educator Nakamura Masanao (1832–1891) invented the term in the 1870s when he translated Samuel Smiles's *Self-Help (1859)*.[45] Nakamura found that there was no equivalent word for self-help in Japanese, and thus combined two Chinese characters "self" and "help" to create the term jijo in Japanese (jajo in Korean).[46] In the original book, Smiles gave a model for personal success in which individuals overcome hardship through extraordinary effort, and finally succeed. In Japan, intellectuals combined Smiles's notion of self-help for individuals with the theory of Social Darwinism among nations, and concluded that to be a strong nation, Japan needed individuals with the spirit of self-help. Thus, in the age of European colonialism in Asia, fostering people with the spirit of self-help became an urgent matter for the survival of the nation.[47] During that time, the opening line of Smiles's book "Heaven helps those who help themselves" became a well-known and oft-quoted adage.

Further, this self-help model of national strengthening found a venue for application through rural community development in colonial Korea in the 1930s. In the 1930s, both Korean agrarianists and the Japanese colonial state, albeit with different nationalist and colonialist goals in mind, began promoting the practice of self-help in rural communities. In 1932, Governor-General of the colonial state, Kazushige Ugaki, initiated the Rural Revitalization Campaign (nongchon jinheung undong, 1932–1940). In emphasizing the spirit of self-help, the campaign drew largely from the Economic Rehabilitation Campaign (keizai kōsei undō) in Japan that was being carried out around the same time.[48] Some projects in the Rural Revitalization Campaign, such as selecting "model villages" and advising them on increasing agricultural productivity, were similar to the Food for Peace's self-help programs carried out in the 1960s.[49]

However, with regard to poor relief, the Rural Revitalization Campaign of the 1930s presented a profoundly different position from that of the self-help programs in the 1960s. Historian Choi Hee-jung persuasively argues that rural self-help in the 1930s was instituted to discredit the need for poor relief and the concept of social welfare.[50] According to Choi, the colonial state inculcated the moral position that rural people should not rely on the government for material and policy assistance; they were expected to mend the problems by themselves. In other words, the rhetoric of self-help put the blame on the peasants and gave the message that their laziness and ignorance caused the hardship.[51] Choi Hee-jung argues that the notion of overcoming unfavorable conditions through individual persistence and diligence can be traced back to the discourse accompanying Smiles's "self-help."[52]

However, the rural problems in Korea had structural causes. It had the system of land tenancy that severely disadvantaged peasants and the falling prices of agricultural commodities aggravated the financial hardship of the peasants. The colonial division of agricultural economy prioritized the market in the Japanese metropole and adversely affected the rural economy in Korea, and the worldwide depression precipitated by the New York Stock Exchange crash of 1929 also had impacts. Rather than "relief," the Rural Revitalization Campaign focused on "reforming the spirit." However, when the rural communities faced the set of structural problems beyond their control, donning of colored clothing (a ban on white clothing), literacy campaign and night classes, self-production of animal manure instead of using chemical fertilizers, rice campaigns, and saving money were not likely to help them.[53]

During the Korean War (1950–1953), the U.S. military and foreign volunteer agencies in Korea combined the aspects of relief and self-help community development in their refugee and resettlement programs.[54] The larger "self-help" programs run by U.S. voluntary agencies received Food for Peace aid grain from the State Department. Under the provision for voluntary agency programs (Title III), Cooperative for American Remittance Everywhere (CARE) ran self-help programs in 153 refugee and "assimilation" (of people from North Korea) projects and 8 fishing village projects in 1959; they could be found in places such as Kisan, Sok Bong ri, Kimpo, Paju and Hwangsan.[55] The National Catholic Welfare Council (NCWC), another prominent voluntary agency, received funding for 175 "assimilation" projects for refugees in 1961. Food for Peace grain also paid for self-help community programs run by Catholic Relief Services (CRS), Church World Services (CWS), and Lutheran World Relief (LWR).[56]

The National Construction Services (NCS, Gukto Gaebal Saeop) in 1961 and 1962 preceded rural self-help community programs of the late 1960s in employing unemployed people in public work projects and paying them in PL 480 grain. After closing down the National Construction Services, which was funded as a short-term emergency aid, the Food for Peace national committee and the South Korean state continued the program under the new name "Work-Relief" (Geullo-Guho) in 1963. Work-Relief Program derived funding from the same source as the earlier National

Construction Service—Title II Section 202 of the Food for Peace Act—, and paid the workers partially in PL 480 grain. As explained earlier, this shift in focus from humanitarian relief to construction programs makes sense within the context of evolving anti-communist strategies associated with U.S. aid food. Self-help programs were an extension of earlier forms of U.S food aid, such as milk-gruel feeding stations and school lunch programs.

However, the South Korean government took the credit for the Work-Relief initiative in the media. The Work-Relief Program was promoted below in *Gyeonghyang Sinmun*:

> Work-relief programs prevent the harmful effects of free relief such as the reliance on the State, laziness, and unemployment. At the same time, the program also promotes sound motivation to work and the spirit of self-help (jajo). In addition to providing livelihood, they provide for comprehensive local development. With relief on one side and construction on the other side, this kills two birds with one stone.[57]

In introducing the Work-Relief Program to the public readership, Ha Sang-rak, Professor of Social Works at Seoul National University, chose not to bring attention to the fact that the U.S. Agency for International Development (AID) had been funding food-for-work aid programs in other countries as well as in South Korea. Instead, in acknowledging many precedents for "providing relief to the poor by giving them work," he chose an example not related to receiving foreign aid.[58] He used the example of the U.S. Federal Emergency Relief Administration (FERA, 1933–1935) and Work Project Administration (WPA, from May 1935) under Roosevelt as a precedent for the South Koreas Work-Relief Program. In a *Dong-a Ilbo* column, "A Path to Overcome Poverty: Work-Relief," Ha explains the ways that FERA and WPA provided jobs for the unemployed Americans during the decade of the Great Depression in the 1930s:

> The (U.S.) programs included the construction and repair of public facilities such as roads, bridges, sewers, schools, hospitals, sport stadiums, airfields. The programs also implemented projects reclaiming unused land and developing drinking water, and providing jobs to unemployed professionals like artists, teachers and nurses so that they could contribute to their local communities.[59]

While not acknowledging the direct and immediate support from the PL 480 funding, Ha credits the 1930s programs in the United States as a precedent. In the same article, he underlines the effectiveness of Work-Relief in creating self-sufficiency, citing the proverb, "give a man a fish and you feed him for a day; teach a man to fish and you feed him for a lifetime."

The ways in which the South Korean state used the Work-Relief Program to mobilize workers and consolidate the foundation for military dictatorship may not have been what the Food for Peace Congress in Washington had in mind in 1963. However, they did share the anti-communist goal. Work-Relief Programs made some contribution to legitimizing Park Chung Hee's hold on power after the coup, and Park was elected as President of the Republic of Korea in December 1963.

Munam-ri: A Model Fishing Village of the Provincial Development Program, 1967–1968

In 1966, the Provincial Government of Gangwon put forward the five villages of Jumunjin, Gisamun-ri, Oe-ongchi, Ingu-ri, and Munam-ri as candidates for creating a model fishing village project. The funding came from the Provincial Comprehensive Development Program of the U.S. Food for Peace Act, which was often called Self-Help Program. On March 6, 1967, L.E. Wakefield, Fishery Advisor in the Rural Development Division of USOM Korea notified the South Korean Office of Fishery Affairs that his committee, composed of two American Korean Foundation officials and four USOM officials, had selected Munam-ri as the site for the model fishing village. As a result, the village would receive Food for Peace grain for two years.[60]

The Munam-ri proposal was prepared at the county level. Goseong County introduced Munam-ri as a village adjacent to the East Sea, which was a habitat for squid and edible seaweed (miyeok). Munam-ri was a coastal village located 13 km north of Sokcho City, and in 1966 was home to 761 residents in 136 households. Most villagers identified themselves as fishermen.[61] Munam-ri was first registered as a village in 1919 under the Japanese colonial state. When Korea was divided in 1945, the village fell within the Soviet-occupied zone. However, after the Korean War (1950–1953), the South Korean state incorporated the area of Goseong County, which included Munam-ri, in Government Action Law for Reclaimed District in 1954.[62] After the war, a large number of refugees from the north settled in the Goseong area.[63]

The Pilot Fishing Village Program of Munam-ri aimed to build a village to sustain a fisherman's livelihood. Thus, projects included building port facilities for breakwater, anchoring yard, and fishing quay; developing marine product cultivation on the coast for seaweed, octopus traps, ear shell pearl cultures, and artificial fish habitat; and constructing public facilities such as a kindergarten, public hall, salty fish storage tank, public bath house, waiting room for fishermen, and a wholesale and retail store. Villagers also built new houses, improved latrines, a public well, and an electric power installation that connected all 136 households to radio broadcast. Finally, there was a project to establish a Fishing Cooperative.[64]

The pilot fishing village project was jointly operated by USOM Korea and the provincial government of Gangwon in cooperation with the South Korean Office of Fishery Affairs. USOM signed contracts with individual county heads (gunsu) and made efforts to maintain communication with field operations. The direct communication between USOM and the field programs provided advantages over other channels of U.S. food aid distribution through the South Korean government and U.S. voluntary agencies in Korea. In the 1950s, Syngman Rhee's government had obtained notoriety for distributing aid grain along the lines of political favoritism.[65] In addition, voluntary agencies with religious affiliations at times disregarded the principle of providing aid independent of religious affiliation, and prioritized their religious constituencies. These channels of aid distribution served the U.S. foreign policy agenda in Korea such as supporting the South Korean regime, which was a bulwark against Communist North, and promoting the image of humanitarian aid. However, by the mid-1960s, USOM was beginning to focus more on forming direct connection with local projects through the Provincial Development Program, bringing it closer to Food for Peace's strategy of "bypassing the governments" and reaching the people directly via food aid.

In 1967 and 1968, Food for Peace grain bore approximately half of the total funding for Munam-ri project, providing over 700 tons of grain as wages in kind.[66] The American Korean Foundation, another donor agency, was particularly interested in the housing project and provided half the funding for it, with the other being self-funded by each household.[67] CARE provided brick-making machines with which villagers could mold bricks out of mud and use them to build houses. The Central Federation of Fishing Cooperative (CFFC) had pledged to bring in bank loans to construct cuttlefish drying plant and seaweed multiplication, but it ended up only giving 10 percent of the promised amount. The rest of the funding came from the Central Government of South Korea and Provincial Government of Gangwon.[68]

As befitting the strategies of the self-help program, projects were intended to be completed by unskilled labor with minimum capital investment and technological expertise. The construction of wharves and breakwater at the port did not require many raw materials beyond roughly cut stones. Thus, the Provincial Development Program for South Chungcheong Province found it sufficient to allocate just 3 percent of the budget to purchase raw materials for the construction of breakwater and wharves in 1965; the other 97 percent of the budget was PL 480 grain as wages in kind.[69]

Likewise, the planners chose marine product cultivation projects that required only unskilled labor and dirt work for construction. Projects that needed technological expertise, use of machines and purchase of raw materials were avoided to the extent possible.[70] Marine product cultivation was an integral part of the self-help program to provide jobs for the villagers and thus sustain their livelihood after the completion of the construction programs. The planners often opted for oyster, cockle, short-necked clams, and agar-agar because cultivation fields for those species could be built with very little capital investment, and in the case of the Munam-ri project, seaweed (miyeok) farming was added to the list. These projects did not require skilled labor; the workers quarried and cut the stones, transported them to the construction site using hand-pulled carts, and, once the site was made operational, they spread marine products on stones for cultivation.

In fact, the oyster and clam farming industry had been providing a viable source of income for impoverished coastal people from long before because they could be conducted without capital investment and skilled labor. During the Japanese colonial era, Haechang Bay in Goheung in South Jeolla Province was a well-known site for oyster farming. When in 1927 Japanese entrepreneur Tomita Gisaku proposed a plan to reclaim the bay to set up a clam farm, it alarmed the locals who depended on oyster farming for their livelihood. Thus, 750 locals formed a cooperative to keep the coastal area for oyster farming.[71] Yeongheung in Hamgyeog Province was another well-known site for oyster farming; there and in other oyster farming villages in the 1930s, there was rising concern about Japanese companies taking over the oyster farming industry.[72] With knowledge of this history, the Provincial Comprehensive Development Program funded building cultivation fields for these particular products and supported the villagers in what they had already been doing; this fit the vision of self-help.

The Munam-ri project was a good reflection of what was taking place in self-help programs elsewhere where PL 480 grain was the major contribution for projects. For a 1965 Title II flat tidal area development program, the South Korean Ministry of Agriculture and Forestry calculated that PL 480 grain provided 80.7 percent of the funding for oyster and agar-agar culture fields. The central government and provincial governments contributed the rest of the funding, each approximately 10 percent.[73] In 1966, PL 480 grain made up 90.6 percent of the total expenditure for the forty eight oysters, short-necked clams, hard clam shellfish, and breakwater projects in South

Chungcheong Province.[74] The 1966 provincial projects employed 26,991 persons and paid for a total of 448,050 "man days" (the number of workers multiplied by the number of days they worked). In South Jeolla Province, PL 480 grain covered 75 percent of the total cost of the Provincial Development Program.

In line with its primary vision of self-help, Food for Peace's Provincial Program turned down projects that required cash input to purchase machines and materials, unless the village could procure extra funding from other sources. For example, in 1965, to the inquiry made by the Provincial Government of South Chungcheong, the Ministry of Agriculture and Forestry responded positively for oyster and short-necked clam (bajirak) projects but advised the province that the hard clam (baekhap) project might not qualify for the program. The Ministry found hard clam farming impractical because the bamboo fences it required would take 36 percent of the total expenditure. Since the cost of bamboo was a problem, the number of hard clam farming projects had to be reduced from six to four in South Chungcheong Province.[75]

The Effect of Self-Help Programs on Wheat Flour Consumption

Wheat flour constituted the majority of the U.S. donation for self-help programs in Korea.[76] Wheat flour from self-help programs affected the diet of relief recipients and their families. In 1967, only the workers from the families designated as the "general needy" in government rosters were eligible to participate in the programs. In 1968, 8.2 percent of the total population in South Korea was registered as the "general needy."[77] Food shortage was a chronic condition in South Korea until the end of the 1960s. Newspapers such as *Dong-a Daily* and *Gyeonghyang* frequently published stories about "farm families that exhausted their grain stock (jeollyang nong-ga)" and "underfed children (gyeolsik adong)" as social problems.[78] The Provincial Comprehensive Development Program's self-help projects helped alleviate the problem of food shortage in rural areas. Local participants in the program received food as wages in grain. As a result, U.S. wheat flour from the self-help programs affected specific sections of the population: it changed the diet of the rural poor and thus wheat flour formed a particular association with the rural poor.[79]

For self-help programs in Korea, the U.S. government distributed 75,000 tons of U.S. surplus wheat in 1964; 110,000 tons in 1965; 130,000 tons in 1966; and 100,000 tons in 1967.[80] Although the workers also received barley in their wage package, they particularly singled out the memory of eating wheat flour. This was perhaps because while barley had been a familiar part of Korean diet, wheat flour was a foreign food staple that changed the everyday food practices of their Korean recipients.[81] In any case, in 1966, the South Korean government contributed to the program for the first time with the provision of 20,000 tons of polished barley and in the following year, 25,000 tons of barley.[82] Since for the self-help programs, U.S. Food for Peace was to provided half the funding, and the South Korean government to take up the rest, the South Korean government paid the remaining percentage in local Korean currency for the 1967 program.[83]

The U.S. surplus wheat flour received through PL 480 Title II (self-help programs) and Title III (voluntary agency) programs took up approximately 1.8 percent of total grain consumption in Korea in 1967.[84] 1.8 percent may not seem to be a significant amount compared to the total grain consumption. However, when you consider that "the general needy" on the government list took up 8–9 percent of the total population and that it was they who consumed the wheat flour from self-help programs, that 1.8 percent becomes quite substantial for the diet of these people.

It is possible to estimate the number of people who were affected by the grain received from self-help programs from the following. In 1964, the agricultural section of the Food for Peace's provincial program mobilized 42,937 farm families and reclaimed 8,823 hectares of land. Including fishery and forestry projects, the whole Food for Peace Program fed approximately 397,564 people with PL 480 grain in 1964. In 1965, the program worked with 41,028 farm families. It reclaimed 28,858 hectares of new land and improved 21,142 hectares of less productive land.[85] In 1966, the Provincial Comprehensive Development Program had 12,676 project sites in upland development; 885 small reservoir projects; 3,669 project sites for reforestation and soil erosion; and 524 flood control projects.[86]

In 1967, local governments issued work permits to the families registered as the "general needy (yoguhoja)." To qualify for a work permit, the family had to earn an income of less than 3,000 won per month and had an ablebodied member who were unemployed or only partially employed. Food was rationed based on the number of days the participant worked. Workers could receive 3.6 kilograms (8 pounds) of grain for their daily labor. The amount of grain distribution was calculated based on the grain required to feed a family of five.[87] The planners argued that this would ensure that all grain be directly consumed by the family, and the family would not have extra grain to sell in the market. According to the program guide, a worker was to work 20 days a month, which would yield 72 kilograms of grain for his family. However, in reality, work was not consistently available, and most participants worked much less than 20 days a month.

As reflected in *Dong-a Daily*, some local villagers voiced that receiving grain from self-help programs was their last resort and the only solution to the predicament of hunger. In 1965, the villagers of Seongsan Burak in South Gyeongsang Province informed Dong-a reporter Go Su-gyun that most of the villagers would starve had it not been for the self-help (jajo) program.[88] Go Su-gyun reported that in March when grain was running low, only 10 families of the 116 families in the village had grain to eat. The rest of the villagers depended on the self-help program to obtain food. The self-help program site was in Dongjeon-ri was 20 *ri* (7.9 km) away from their village, so the villagers had to get up at dawn and walk 20 *ri* to get to the site. Self-help grain provided indispensable help to the hungry, but it was not enough to solve the problem of food shortage. The villagers were only given work for 10 days a month, instead of the 20 days a month as laid out by the program. With the grain they received for 10 days of labor, they could only feed their families for 7 days. The situation was as dismal in the neighboring village Dongchon where the villagers also depended on self-help grain. Despite the desperate situation, local government officials claimed that no household in Jindong myeon was experiencing grain shortage.[89]

While self-help programs proved to be indispensable for the survival of the rural poor, the programs did not run smoothly everywhere. Often, the projects were not carried out as planned, and participants blamed the South Korean government for the mismanagement and non-payment of wages in kind. As an example, or the 1965 program, the Food for Peace ("Pyeonghwa reul wuihan singryang") Committee had granted 1,096 project sites, but only 647 sites had commenced work by September.[90] In Bucheon, Gyeonggi Province, in 1965, 184 tons of grain was not paid to the workers. In 1968, Gim Baek-yong, a 29-year-old farmer, wrote to *Gyeonghyang Sinmun* that he had not been paid for a year of work-relief labor, and he asked the government to make the delayed payment.[91]

Wheat flour was becoming increasingly familiar in Korean diet through the commercial market and various aid programs in the 1950s and 1960s. However, in the predominantly rice-eating culture, feeding on wheat flour was still considered a sign of hardship that the poor had to endure. In 1968, a local government official named Mun Hong-gyu, who worked in the Bureau of Internal Affairs of Naju-gun, sent a letter to *Jibang Haengjeong*, the official gazette for local governments and shared his opinion on work-relief programs.[92] Mun pitied that self-help participants received wheat flour, and pleaded with the government to give workers rice instead of wheat flour.

This good hearted local official apparently did not understand that half of the funding for the program came from U.S. wheat flour and that the hallmark of the program was using U.S. surplus agricultural commodities to help relieve hunger and promote development in U.S. friendly nations such as South Korea.

The rest of Mun's letter published in the official gazette was also filled with misunderstandings about the intention of the self-help program. While the program sought to combine relief and self-help development by employing relief recipients and paying them in grain, Mun obliviously argued that the South Korean state should not base payment on the number of days the participants worked, but rather on their families' grain needs. In addition, he pointed out that while the government ordered one male member of the needy family to participate in the program, often women go to self-help work. He explained that it was because men could earn better wages in the market: the market price of 3.6 kilograms of wheat flour, which was the daily wage in the program, was 100 won, but a day laborer could earn 200 won. Mun missed the point of the program here as well since the whole point of work relief was providing work and wages to those who were unemployed. Despite all the problems, however, Mun remained hopeful about the benefits of the program. He claimed the self-help program was the only hope for Naju-gun, where he worked as a local official, and he also believed that the program may alleviate the problem of rural exodus to urban areas ("inong hyangdo").[93]

Overall, neither the recipients of the self-help aid nor the editors of *Jibang Haengjeong* to which Mun sent his letter seemed to put much meaning to the origin of wheat flour, which was the U.S. government. They did not comment on the U.S. intention behind the program which was to use community development as its global anti-communist tool. Still, they acknowledged that the program helped feed desperately poor families in rural areas. However, as a result, through the self-help program, wheat flour drew yet another association with poverty and hardship as the food for the poor in the 1960s.[94]

Conclusion

Food for Peace self-help programs were not designed to be a permanent commitment; the very goal of self-help anticipates the eventual superfluousness of further aid. In fact, the initiative for self-help programs began as short-term emergency relief under Title II, Section 202 of the Food for Peace Act (PL 480). From 1966, the Rural Development Division of USOM and U.S. voluntary agencies began phasing down their community development programs in South Korea. The remaining PL 480 funding was handed over to the South Korean government. This seemed to be an appropriate conclusion for a self-help initiative, not only for the U.S. donors but also for the South Korean government that was engaged in competition with North Korea regarding national self-reliance.[95]

In other words, the South Korean government inherited USOM's Food for Peace programs at the end of the 1960s. Thus, it was no coincidence that in 1970, Park Chung Hee's regime launched a set of rural programs that were very similar to USOM's earlier Provincial Comprehensive Development Program. The two looked alike in their self-help method and developmental intentions in peripheral regions of the country. The regime named the 1970s programs as the New Village Movement (Saemaeul Undong, 1971–1979). The New Village Movement largely shared the vision of a modernized village with earlier USOM's programs: New Village projects included building irrigation, water supply, and sewage pipes; roads to make villages accessible by car; dykes and public wells; electricity installations; telephone lines; and methane gas facilities.[96] One difference noted by the planners of New Village Movement planners was that USOM programs paid wages in food, and according to them, this was not a good practice since food made people dependent on aid. Instead, the New Village Movement funded the projects by distributing raw materials such as cement and slate roof tiles.

The elements of continuity in the transition from the 1960s USOM to the 1970s South Korean rural self-help programs have important implications on how we understand the 1950s and the 1960s in the narratives of South Korean development and of Cold War politics in the region. U.S. PL 480 food aid, distributed through various channels of distribution in the 1950s and the 1960s, interacted with and transformed the South Korean society much more than previously acknowledged. On the other hand, neither the state propaganda devised in the 1970s nor the revisionist historiographies seriously engaged with the legacies of U.S. food aid programs.

The term "aid economy" (wonjo gyeongje) is used to describe the 1950s and 1960s when the South Korean economy largely depended on U.S aid. Especially for the 1950s, "aid economy" is often invoked to decry the incompetence of South Koreans, who were floundering in poverty and in corruption of the authoritarian regime.[97] Describing the era in a lump as "aid economy" tends to work towards undermining the foundational work that was being done in the 1950s and the 1960s such as the self-help community development programs. In addition, this dismissing of post-1945 decades also hinders us from properly evaluating the legacies of development and industrialization during the colonial period (1910–1945).

According to the Park Chung Hee myth, the story of New Village Movement is a crucial piece in the narrative of successful South Korean modernization.[98] Carrying out dashingly successful large-scale industrialization in parallel, Park Chung Hee's regime publicized the New Village Movement as an embodiment of indigenously Korean characteristics, emphasizing the voluntary zeal of the people and its national origin. The fact that New Village Movement was largely based on self-help aid programs operated by foreign voluntary agencies and U.S. Food for Peace in the 1960s was not mentioned. The reason for this covering is obvious for a formerly colonial nation, now in the 1970s under U.S. patronage: the regime wanted to insist on the nation's independence.

Instead, in the Park Chung Hee myth, the memory of U.S. food aid acquired a different significance. The history of "aid economy" was celebrated as the memory that is overcome. While much of the Park Chung Hee myth has been dismantled in revisionist historiographies, the narrative of nationalistic pride in overcoming dependency and in achieving economic prosperity still remains immensely popular and enduring.[99] However, writing off the 1950s and the bulk of the 1960s as the time of misery and stagnation, with the country merely waiting for the 1970s, underestimates how much groundwork had been laid down in the 1950s and the 1960s and how much of it South Koreans inherited and appropriated.[100]

Notes

1. Letter of Appeal from fire-field farmers to Joel Bernstein, Director of USOM/K, November 17, 1966 (3190–3); Food For Peace I (FFP I), Container #16; Mission to Korea/Executive Office, P583; Agency for International Development, Record Group 286 (RG 286); National Archives at College Park, College Park, MD.

2. In another letter of appeal, 45 families, representing 238 people from Cheongsong-gun in North Gyeongsang, wrote a similar letter to the Director of US Operations in Korea, Joel Bernstein, Director of USOM/Korea. Undated letter from fire-field farmers (Hwa nongmin) (3194–3196); #16; P583; RG 286.

3. It began as a surplus food program in 1954. However, there were further changes made to the Food for Peace program in 1966. President Johnson in his February 10, 1966 message on his newly envisaged Food-For-Freedom approach laid out a number of changes. One was that PL 480 aid grain was no longer "surplus" but "reserve acreage be returned to production as needed," and another change was that grain was to be used for family planning programs in foreign countries. *The New Food Aid Program* (pamphlet), by U.S. Department of Agriculture, 1966.

4. Chung, "Foreign Things no Longer Foreign." Also see section, Food Aid as Anti-Communist Tool, in this paper.

5. In this paper, I do not mean modernization theory when I refer to modernization. In the peripheries of an under-developed country, community development was not dissociated from modernization such as building roads to the market, putting up electricity poles, and organizing fishing and agricultural cooperatives, which helped to link the villages to the larger capitalist economy. In that sense, village community development and modernization theory put forward two different models of development and modernization. I agree with Immerwahr when he points out that the discussion of modernization was too focused on modernization theory. Through his studies of community development in India and in the Philippines, he presents community development as a rival model to modernization theory and that the two models competed over the same pull of resources and in the same policy arena. See Immerwahr, *Thinking Small*.

6. U, "Joseon eui 'cheollima undong' gwa hanguk eui 'saemaeul undong' bigyo yeongu siron- jungguk eui 'daeyakjin undong' eul gyeotdeuryeo."

7. CARE's self-help program, January 1965 (4389 and 4397); #4; P589; RG 286. [1966 CARE's self-help program in Korea] April 20, 1967 (3762); Voluntary Agencies- Title III, #17; P583; RG 286.

8. "Report of Audit: Public Law 480 Title III Food Commodities Program of the Seventh-Day Adventists Welfare Service, INC." For the period from April 1, 1964 to December 31, 1966 (3766); #17; P583; RG 286.

9. The Etawah model (1946–1954) was the program of "decentralized development" which was funded by U.S. capital and supported by Nehru in India. The U.S. government intended to use the program to placate the rural discontent that might turn communist. See Immerwahr, *Thinking Small*, 66–99.

10. See Kim, "The Discursive Foundations of the South Korean Developmental State: *Sasanggye* and the Reception of Modernization Theory."

11. For U.S. foreign aid as the humanitarian aid, see Chung, chapters 3 and 4.

12. Presidential Speech, "War on Hunger," August 29, 1966 (3287–3288); Food for Peace, #16; P583; RG 286.

13. See Chung.

14. Perkins, *Geopolitics and the Green Revolution*; Connelly, *Fatal Misconception*; Cullather, *The Hungry World*; Immerwahr, *Thinking Small*.

15. See Chung, Chapter 1.

16. Ibid. Chapters 3 and 4.

17. Ibid. Chapter 4.

18. For North Korean reconstruction in the post-Korean War period, see Armstrong, "'Fraternal Socialism': The International Reconstruction of North Korea, 1953–1962."

19. Henry C. Alexander, "Look at what the Communists are doing- Berlin-Korea Train Off," May 21, 1954 (C. 2586); #16; 1276; Record Group 469 (RG 469); National Archives at College Park, College Park, MD.

20. Henry C. Alexander, "Look at what the Communists are doing- Berlin-Korea Train Off," May 21, 1954 (C. 2586); #16; 1276; Record Group 469 (RG 469); National Archives at College Park, College Park, MD.

21. Chung, Chapter 4.

22. 86th (U.S.) Congress, 1st Session (S. 1711- Humphrey Bill); amendment to Public Law 480. Food for Peace Act of 1959, April 16, 1959. International. FY.59, 265/329, Container #1; Food For Peace Files, 1960–1966/USAID/Material Resources, P153; RG 286.

23. ICA/Washington, ICATO CIRC 37, "Cooperatives," June 21, 1961 (3969); #1; Central Subject Files, 1961–1962: USAID Mission to Korea/Executive Office, P.582; RG 286. George McGovern, Special Assistant Director, Food For Peace, Memorandum for the President, *14th Semiannual report on activities of the Food for Peace Program carried on under Public Law 480, 83rd Congress, as amended*, period January 1 through June 30, 1961, 87th Congress, 1st Session, House Document No. 223.

24. For community development in the Philippines, see Immerwahr, *Thinking Small*, Chapter 4.

25. For National Reconstruction Program of 1961, see Chung, *Foreign Things No Longer Foreign*, Chapter 5.

26. For American influence in leading to the April Revolution, see Brazinsky, *Nation Building in South Korea*. For examples of political and economic corruption in Rhee's regime, see Chung, *Foreign Things No Longer Foreign*, Chapter 5.

27. Priority cablegram from Moyer, Seoul (Far East Program), to Sheppard, ICA, January 3, 1961 (1671); Agricultural Surplus, #139; U.S. Foreign Assistance Agencies, Headquarter Office of Far Eastern Operations; Record Group 469; National Archives at College Park, College Park, MD.

28. Ibid.

29. Priority cablegram from Moyer, Seoul (Far East Program), to Sheppard, ICA, January 3, 1961 (1671); Agricultural Surplus, #139; U.S. Foreign Assistance Agencies, Headquarter Office of Far Eastern Operations; Record Group 469; National Archives at College Park, College Park, MD.

30. *JCRR Newsreel*, February 3, 1962 (2174); #13; ICA Mission to Korea- Unclassified Subject Files, 1954–1961, P319; RG 469.

31. *National Conference on Food for Peace Booklet*, September 30, 1963 (3-4/329), #1; P153; RG 286.

32. Food for Peace National Conference Booklet, American Food for Peace Council, September 30, 1963, published by U.S. Department of State (4/329); #1; P153; RG 286.

33. Ibid.

34. 89th Congress, 2nd Session, House of Representatives, Report No. 1558, "THE FOOD FOR FREEDOM ACT OF 1966," May 27, 1966, p. 48.

35. David E. Bell, Administrator, Agency for International Development, "Some comments on the role of Food for Peace in the total U.S. foreign assistance effort," *Food for Peace National Conference Booklet*, September 30, 1963 (4/329), #1; P153;

RG 286. There were also concurrent community development projects in India that were funded by US Department of State in the 1950s. See Immerwahr, *Thinking Small*.

36. From AID/Washington to AID/TO Circular, "World Food Program," March 25, 1963 (2991); #12; P583; RG 286.

37. From AID/Washington to AID/TO Circular, sent on September 8, 1966 (3946); #22; P 583; RG 286.

38. World Food Program (WFP) (2984–3001); #12; and (3940, 3945, 3946); #22; P583; RG 286.

39. From FODAG/Rome to AID/Washington, Seoul, Subject: WPF/Korea 349- Flood Control, February 10, 1967 (3940); International Organization, #22; P583; RG 286.

40. From Brown, Seoul, to AID/W, "WFP Proposal- Highway Improvement Projects," May 10, 1967 (3323–3326, also noted as 136–139/241); Food For Peace II, #16; Central Subject Files: 1963–1979, Mission to Korea/Executive Office, P583; RG 286.

41. Ibid.

42. Ibid.

43. Philip C. Habib, Counselor of Embassy for Political Affairs, Submission of UPI Washington Report on the U.S. Attitude Towards the ROKG, to Department of State, May 21, 1963 (3058 of 3055–3058); #12; World Food Program, P583; RG 286.

44. See Palais, *Confucian Statecraft and Korean Institutions*, pp. 729–731.

45. Samuel Adams, *Self-Help*. John Murray, 1859.

46. Choi, "1930 nyeon dae 'jaryeok gaengsaeng' ron eui yeonweon gwa singminji jibae ideologi hwa," pp. 145–146.

47. Choi Hee-jung, "1910 nyeondae choe nam-seon eui jajo ron beonyeok gwa 'cheongnyeon' eui jajo," pp. 237–242. In the intellectual discourse, when a nation was conceived as the sum of each individual, individual ability for self-help would determine the overall strength of the nation. See Araki, "[Jajo] (Self-Help) eseo [gyoyang] (Culture) euro," p.160.

48. For the Japanese context of the rural problem, see Young, *Japan's Total Empire*, Chapter 7.

49. Shin and Do Hyun Han, "Colonial Corporatism: The Rural Revitalization Campaign, 1932–1940," pp. 83–84.

50. Choi Hee-jung, "Hanguk geundae wa jajo jeongsin- namhan eui saemaeul jeongsin gwa bukhan jaryeok gaengsaeng ron eui yeonweon," p. 202.

51. Gi-wook Shin and Do Hyun Han, "Colonial Corporatism" (1999).

52. Choi Hee-jung, "Hanguk geundae wa jajo jeongsin- namhan eui saemaeul jeongsin gwa bukhan jaryeok gaengsaeng ron eui yeonweon. Also see "Nongmin eui nagwon jeongmae [6]," *Dong-a Ilbo*, February 2, 1930.

53. *Dong-a Ilbo*, December 17, 1932; March 25, 1933; and February 20, 1934.

54. John E. Mills, "Evaluation Report: Resettlement and Assimilation projects," Community Development Division, OEC, June 30, 1959 (2150–2153); #3; P319; RG 469.

55. (1565–1566); #170; Headquarters: Office of the Far Eastern Operations; RG 469. (2155–62); MHSA, #7; P319; RG 469. From CINCREP Seoul "Request for additional surplus commodities, PL 480, Title III," June 17, 1959 (1564); #130; Headquarters of Office of Far Eastern Operations; RG 469. In 1960, CARE requested 1,480,000 lbs of flour and 1,980,000 lbs of cornmeal to some 99,000 persons residing in refugee assimilation projects and villages (79,000 refugees); 18,505 Taegu school lunch recipients; 20,000 in fishing villages) (1936); Relief, #170; Headquarters: Office of Far Eastern Operations, Subject Files, 1950–1961; U.S. Foreign Assistance Agencies, RG 469.

56. The number of recipients for refugee feeding programs proposed for 1961 were CARE 90,000; Catholic Relief Services (CRS), 100,000; Church World Services (CWS), 15,000; Lutheran World Relief (LWR), 5,000; National Catholic Welfare Council (NCWC)'s War Relief Services (WRC), 9,617 (total 219,617 recipients), March 22, 1960 (1937); #170; Office of the Far Eastern Operations; RG 469. From Seoul, Subject: Volage (voluntary agency) FY '62 PL 480 Title III, to ICA/Washington, July 11, 1961 (1902); #170; Headquarters, Office of the Far Eastern Operations; RG 469. The total number of assimilation recipients from voluntary agencies was 483,324 for 1961, September 15, 1961.

57. *Gyeonghyang sinmun*, September 14, 1963.

58. Ha, "Path to Overcome Poverty: Work-Relief (Bingon eul neomeo seoneun gil: Geullo Guho)."

59. Ibid.

60. From L.E. Wakefield, Fishery Advisor in the Rural Development Division, USOM/Seoul, to the South Korean Office of Fisheries Affairs, "Model Fishing Village," March 6, 1967 (4546); #2; Records Relating to Fisheries, 1964–9, USAID: Mission to Korea/Rural Development, P589; RG 286.

61. "Status of Pilot Village Candidate" (4473); #2; P589; RG 286.

62. Subok jigu imsi haengjeong jochi beop, July 27, 1954.

63. Munam-ri proposal, 1966 (4488); #2; P589; RG 286.

64. "Total Investment of Pilot Fishing Village Project- Munam Ri" (4475–6); #2; P589; RG 286.

65. Chung, Chapter 5.

66. Munam-ri (4501–4512); #2; P589; RG 286. The figure varies between 701 and 1,000 metric tons. (4475–6, 4531); #2; P589; RG 286.

67. For information on American Korean Foundation, see Chung, *Foreign Things*, Chapter 4.

68. The central government only sent 16.8 million weon out of 67.3 million weon that was initially promised. On CFFC (4506, 4462, 4520); #2; P589; RG 286.

69. Munam-ri file (4443), #4; P589; RG 286.

70. For example, drainage system needed input other than "food." From Seoul to AID/Washington, "WFP Proposal- Highway Improvement," May 10, 1967 (3324); #16; P 583; RG 286.

71. "Jopaeryu yangsik euro yeonsan baek'isip manweon," *Dong-a Daily Newspaper*, June 27, 1927.

72. The journalist interpreted the crowding-out of the locals by Japanese firms as a class struggle between labor and capital. "Ilbon Susan Heungeopsa Seollip- Yeongheung gul eojang jeomryeong," *Dong-a*, April 3, 1931.

73. "1965 nyeon-do Title 2 e daehan susan jeungsik sa-eop." Nonglim Bu, Susan Guk, P.5 (4363); #4; P589; RG 286.

74. "1966 Self-help fisheries project plan and status by species," Chungchung Namdo (4326); #4; P589; RG 286.

75. "Paejoryu jeungsik sa-eop gisul geomto euiroe" from Tcha Kyun Hi, South Korean Minister of Agriculture and Forestry, to the South Korean Minister of Health and Social Affairs on April 21, 1965; also see (4333); Munam-ri, #4; P589; RG 286.

76. From 1959 to 1966, U.S. Title II (including school lunch program and others) Food for Peace commodities to Korea, and of this, wheat took 76.6 percent of the total cost for the US government. Title II total CCC cost $119,054.9; wheat varieties $91,246,800. wheat= 76.6 percent of the CCC dollar cost. *Summary of U.S. Economic Aid to Korea, FY 1954-FY 1966 as of 30 June 1966*, United States Operations Mission to Korea (3916); #22; Central Subject Files, Mission to Korea, P583; RG 286.

77. Jeong, "Jajo-geullo Sa-eop," pp. 56–59.

78. The percentage of income that families spend on food was high for an average household, not just the "general needy" household. On average, food took up 64.4 percent of the total family expenditure in 1959; 59.2 percent in 1962; 58.6 percent in 1966; and 55.7 percent in 1969 on average. Bogeon Sahoe Bu, *Bogeon Siljeok gwa Jeonmang [Bogeon Sahoe Haengjeong Baekseo]* (Bogeon Sahoe Bu, 1971), p. 77.

79. Self-help programs were one of many distribution channels of U.S. surplus wheat flour. South Korean private companies bought and sold U.S. surplus wheat flour in the commercial market (Title I, PL 480) and U.S. voluntary agencies also distributed surplus wheat flour to their program constituencies (Title III, PL 480).

80. 1966 was the first year that South Korea contributed grains with the 20,000 tons of barley. Before 1966, all Provincial Program grain was American donation. 3266–3275, #16; P583; RG 286; In the 1967 program, U.S. Food for Peace provided 48.8 percent of the funding. The rest was Korean. (4310–13, 4320); #4; P589; RG 286.

81. See Chung, Chapters 1 and 5.

82. Before 1966, South Korean government only provided cash contribution. (3267–9); #16; P583; RG 286.

83. The South Korean state paid its 51.2 percent with 25,000 tons of barley and the rest in local Korean currency. (4320); #4; P589; RG 286.

84. In 1967, total grain consumption in South Korea was approximately 10.4 million metric tons, and of this, wheat (commercial+ aid programs) took up 849,000 metric tons, comprising 8.2 percent of total grain consumption. From Seoul to

AID/W, "War on Hunger- Supplemental Data," September28, 1966 (3263–3276); #16; P583; RG 286.

85. Report from Paul H. Russell, AD/P-FFP to L. Wakefield, RDD, 1966. "Provincial Comprehensive Development Program (Title II Section 202)" (4315); #4; P589; RG 286.

86. Newman, Seoul, to AID/W TOAID A 442, "On WFP flood control project," October 11, 1966 (3253–4); #16; P583; RG 286.

87. From Paul H. Russell, AD/P-FFP, to L. Wakefield, RDD, "CY 1967 Provincial Comprehensive Development Program (Title II-Section 202)" (4319); #4; P589; RG 286.

88. Go Su-gyun, "Seongsan Burak, Jindong myeon, Changweon-gun, Gyeongsang Namdo," *Dong-A Daily Newspaper*, March 16, 1965.

89. Ibid.

90. *Gyeonghyang*, September 22, 1965.

91. *Gyeonghyang*, August 10, 1968.

92. Mun, "Jajo Geullo Sa-eop gwa Guho," pp. 162–165.

93. Ibid.

94. For the various meanings of wheat flour in the 1920s and 1930s, see Chung, Chapter 1.

95. Between 1966 and 1971, U.S. AID (Agency for International Development) phased down Title II and Title III community development programs, and the South Korean government took over the programs. From Seoul to AID/W, "War on Hunger- Supplemental data," September 28, 1966 (3267); #16; P583; RG 286. The phase-down of Title III Voluntary agency community development programs with increasing responsibility of the ROKG (1967–1971), December 21, 1966 (3204); #16; P583; RG 286. Title III phase-down (3745); #17; P583; RG 286.

96. *Gyeonghyang Sinmun*, October 2, 1970.

97. For reference to wonjo-gyeongje (periodization varies), see March 8, 1995, *Maeil Gyeongje*; May 18, 1981, *Gyeonghyang Sinmun* among others.

98. *Gyeonghyang*, October 2, 1970; Naemubu, *Yeonggwang eui baljachui: maeul danwi saemaeul undong chujinsa*; Park, *Saemaul*.

99. For research on New Village Movement, see Bak, Seop, and Yi, Haeng, "Geun hyeondae hanguk eui gukka wa nongmin: saemaeul undong eui jeongchi sahoe jeok jogeon"; Kim, "Maeul eui geundae hwa gyeongheom gwa saemaeul undong-yicheon a*ri maeul eui sarye reul jungsim euro"; Kim, "Nongchon jeongi gonggeup sa-eop gwa saemaeul undong"; Lee, "1960 nyeon-dae maeul gaebal gwa nongchon saemaeul undong eui chogi jeongae gwajeong"; Choi, "Hanguk geundae hwa wa jajo jeongsiin- namhan eui saemaeul jeongsin gwa pukhan jaryeok gaengsaeng ron eui yeonweon"; Heo, Eun, "Dong asia naengjeon eui yeonswae wa bak jeong-hi jeongbu eui 'daegong saemaeul' geonseol."

100. On the other hand, there is significant research done on the American influence in South Korean nation-building, see Brazinsky, *Nation Building in South Korea*.

Bibliography

Archival Sources
National Archives and Records Administration, College Park, MD
Record Group 286
Record Group 469

Other Sources
Araki, Masazumi. "[Jajo] (Self-Help) eseo [gyoyang] (Culture) euro," *Ilbon Munhwa Yeongu*, No. 4 (April 2001).
Armstrong, Charles. "'Fraternal Socialism': The International Reconstruction of North Korea, 1953–1962," *Cold War History*, Vol. 5, No. 2 (May 2005).
Bak, Seop, and Yi, Haeng. "Geun hyeondae hanguk eui gukka wa nongmin: saemaeul undong eui jeongchi sahoe jeok jogeon," *Hanguk Jeongchi Hakhoe Bo*, Vol. 31, No. 3 (November 1997).
Brazinsky, Gregg. *Nation Building in South Korea: Koreans, Americans, and the Making of a Democracy* (University of North Carolina Press, 2007).
Choi, Hee-jung. "1930 nyeon dae 'jaryeok gaengsaeng' ron eui yeonweon gwa singminji jibae ideologi hwa," *Hanguk Geunhyeondae Sa Yeongu*, Vol. 63 (2012).
———, "1910 nyeondae choe nam-seon eui jajo ron beonyeok gwa 'cheongnyeon' eui jajo," *Hanguk Sasang Sahak*, Vol. 39 (2011).
Chung, Dajeong. "Foreign Things no Longer Foreign" (PhD Dissertation, Columbia University, 2015).
Connelly, Matthew J. *Fatal Misconception: The Struggle to Control World Population* (Cambridge: Belknap Press of Harvard University Press, 2008).
Cullather, Nick. *The Hungry World: America's Cold War Battle against Poverty in Asia* (Cambridge: Harvard University Press, 2010).
Ha Sang-rak. "Path to Overcome Poverty: Work-Relief (Bingon eul neomeo seoneun gil: Geullo Guho)," *Dong-a Daily Newspaper*, July 13, 1963.
Heo, Eun. "Dong asia naengjeon eui yeonswae wa bak jeong-hi jeongbu eui 'daegong saemaeul' geonseol," *Yeoksa Bipyeong*, No. 11 (May 2015).
Immerwahr, Daniel. *Thinking Small: The United States and the Lure of Community Development* (Cambridge: Harvard University Press, 2015).
Jeong Heui-seop. "Jajo-geullo Sa-eop," *Jibang Haengjeong*, Vol. 17, No. 171 (1968).
Kim, Michael. "The Discursive Foundations of the South Korean Developmental State: *Sasanggye* and the Reception of Modernization Theory," *Korea Observer*, Vol. 38, No. 3 (Autumn 2007).
Kim, Yeong-mi. "Maeul eui geundae hwa gyeongheom gwa saemaeul undong-yicheon a*ri maeul eui sarye reul jungsim euro," *Jeongsin Munhwa Yeongu*, Vol. 110 (2008).
Kim, Yeon Hee. "Nongchon jeongi gonggeup sa-eop gwa saemaeul undong," *Yeoksa Bipyeong*, No. 97 (Fall 2011).

Lee, Hwan-Byung. "1960 nyeon-dae maeul gaebal gwa nongchon saemaeul undong eui chogi jeongae gwajeong," *Yeoksa Yeon-gu*, No. 23 (December 2012).

Mun, Hong-kyu. "Jajo Geullo Sa-eop gwa Guho," *Jibang Haengjeong*, Vol. 17, Issue 174.

Naemubu. *Yeonggwang eui baljachui: maeul danwi saemaeul undong chujinsa* (Seoul: Maeul Mungo Bonbu, 1978).

Palais, James B. *Confucian Statecraft and Korean Institutions: Yu Hyŏngwŏn and the Late Chosŏn Dynasty* (Seattle: University of Washington Press, 1996).

Park Chung Hee. *Saemaul: Korea's New Community Movement* (Seoul: Korea Textbook Co., 1979).

Perkins, John. *Geopolitics and the Green Revolution: Wheat, Genes and the Cold War* (New York: Oxford University Press, 1997).

Shin, Gi-wook, and Do Hyun Han. "Colonial Corporatism: The Rural Revitalization Campaign, 1932–1940," in *Colonial Modernity in Korea*, edited by Gi-Wook Shin and Michael Robinson (Cambridge: Harvard University Press, 1999).

U, Sang-yeol. "Joseon eui 'cheollima undong' gwa hanguk eui 'saemaeul undong' bigyo yeongu siron- jungguk eui 'daeyakjin undong' eul gyeotdeuryeo," *Tongil Inmunhak Nonchong*, No. 55 (May 2013).

Young, Louis. *Japan's Total Empire: Manchuria and the Culture of Wartime Imperialism* (Berkeley: University of California Press, 1998).

CHAPTER THREE

"The Carter Zeal" versus "The Carter Chill"

U.S. Policy Towards the Korean Peninsula in the Carter Era

Khue Dieu Do

During his 1976 presidential campaign, Jimmy Carter promised to withdraw all American troops stationed in the Republic of Korea (ROK), resulting in the so-called "Carter Chill"[1] with regard to a close U.S. ally in the Asian-Pacific region. At the same time, his "zeal" for approaching North Korea surprised many. Due to its critical strategic implications for South Korea at that time, Carter's troop withdrawal plan has received much attention among scholars.[2] However, there has been relatively little interest paid to the other side of the story, that is, the U.S.'s attempts at engagement with the Democratic People's Republic of Korea (DPRK) during the Carter era.[3] The period of the late 1970s was a crucial one for understanding contemporary Northeast Asian geopolitics: it was during this time that concepts such as "tripartite talks" and "four-party negotiations" with respect to resolving the Korean issue and engaging North Korea were first officially endorsed by the related governments.

Utilizing primarily archival research, particularly recently declassified materials in U.S. archives, this chapter explores the Carter administration's policies towards the two Koreas, with the "China factor" as the backdrop for the U.S.'s broader strategy. It particularly focuses on U.S. policy towards the DPRK and views American engagement with North Korea as part of a larger policy regarding the Korean peninsula and Sino-American relations. Initially, Carter's plan was to launch "détente at a smaller scale," or to approach "minor" Communist regimes, including Vietnam, North Korea, and Cuba.

With respect to North Korea, Carter suggested contact with Pyongyang and called for the resumption of inter-Korean dialogues or the establishment of trilateral talks between North Korea, the U.S., and South Korea. Washington also put great pressure on Seoul by announcing the eventual withdrawal of American troops and issuing a critique of human rights violations by the Park Chung Hee government. However, changes in international politics surrounding the normalization of Sino-American relations resulted in the Carter administration's failure in both North and South Korea. Carter's parallel plan for the two Koreas will be analyzed within the context of global relations in the late 1970s in East Asia, an element missing from previous studies.

Carter's Korea Plan

On January 16, 1975, two weeks after leaving the governorship of Georgia and a month after declaring his candidacy for president, Jimmy Carter stated that he favored pulling U.S. troops out of South Korea. Reiterating this desire during a campaign speech in June 1976, Carter further announced his extreme dissatisfaction with South Korea's human rights record. From that point on, a unilateral withdrawal of U.S. ground forces stationed in Korea became one of Carter's major foreign policy initiatives in East Asia. To this end, the improvement of North-South Korean relations and a less antagonistic environment around the peninsula would be vital. It is also important to emphasize that one of Carter's stated goals during his presidential campaign was the establishment of normal relations between the U.S. and fourteen nations, including the Communist regimes of North Korea, Cuba, and Vietnam, which had no official ties with Washington. Soon after taking office, Carter instructed his Secretary of State Cyrus Vance to draw up a list of nations with which Washington did not enjoy diplomatic relations and to give comments on the "prospects" and "advisability" of normalization.[4] He then enthusiastically announced U.S. wish to seek reconciliation with all states in the first address before the United Nations (UN) General Assembly.[5]

In his memoirs, the president argues that automatic recognition of all established governments, which most European nations already adhered to, "would give us a toehold in the unfriendly country and an opportunity to ease tensions, increase American influence, and promote peace."[6] Moreover, this stance revealed Carter's wish to view Third World countries as independent states, rather than superpower proxies, torn between the two camps and potentially targets for the expansion of Soviet hegemony abroad. Such an approach in Carter's words would be conformable with "a new world-wide mosaic of global, regional and bilateral relations,"[7] a "global community" of interdependent and cooperating nations.[8]

The DPRK was quick to seize this opportunity of possible policy change in Washington. From the end of 1976 to mid–1977, North Korea toned down its usually shrill anti-American rhetoric and refrained from attacking Carter personally. In November 1976, Kim Il Sung sent a personal letter through Pakistani Prime Minister Bhutto to the U.S. president-elect at Plains, Georgia, asking for direct contact. In his 1977 New Year address, Kim proposed a peace treaty with the U.S., making sure to differentiate between the old and new administrations in Washington. In denouncing the "aggressive machinations" of the "U.S. imperialists" against North Korea, Kim specifically referred twice to the "Ford administration of the United States."[9] It was likely that President Carter's troop withdrawal plans resulted in a "cautious optimism" in Pyongyang that followed the 1975 fall of Saigon, but quickly turned sour during the Axe Murder incident of August 1976.

Meanwhile, South Korea found ways to cope with the president-elect's plan. During a 1977 New Year's press conference, President Park stated that he would not oppose the withdrawal of American troops stationed in Korea after the conclusion of a South-North Mutual Non-Aggression Pact. However, Seoul was not happy with Carter's attempt to engage Pyongyang. Ambassador Richard Sneider was questioned by the ROK Ministry of Foreign Affairs (MOFA) about the list of fourteen nations with which the U.S. government did not have diplomatic relations; the Koreans inquired as to whether the list included North Korea.[10] Clearly concerned, President Park paid close attention to the negotiating process between the U.S. and the Socialist Republic of Vietnam (SRV). He was afraid that the talks would lead to a U.S. recognition of the SRV and pave the way for Vietnam's entry into the UN, which would in turn swing two votes against the ROK on the Korean question.[11] Vance recognized that although U.S. normalization with Vietnam would not directly affect South Korea, it would trigger worries about a possible U.S. move to improve relations with North Korea.[12] Therefore, the Carter administration kept the Park government closely informed of the negotiating process with Vietnam throughout 1977 and 1978.[13]

At the same time, Carter's plan for Korea faced opposition in Washington, especially from the Congress. Before leaving office, Gerald Ford warned that sudden changes in Korea policy would be harmful and negatively affect U.S. relations with Japan, the People's Republic of China (PRC), and the Union of Soviet Socialist Republics (USSR). Carter's White House staff was also suspicious of North Korean intentions. Nonetheless, the National Security Council (NSC) fully recognized the importance of Carter's Korea plan for the North Koreans. NSC staffer Mike Armacost concluded, "The U.S. is the key to North Korea's strategy."[14] Armacost therefore suggested to the U.S. to try and take the upper hand in dealing with the North. In February 1977, he advised National Security Adviser Zbigniew Brzezinski not to receive a letter from North Korean Foreign Minister Heo Dam, which had been carried by a friend of Jerry Cohen, a Marxist; this was another attempt by Pyongyang at direct communication with the Carter administration.[15] Brzezinski advised President Carter not to pay attention to the reports of a North Korean proposal for talks with South Korea due to its "limited significance," concluding that "the North was playing an old record."[16]

Jimmy Carter came into office with high hopes for an improvement of U.S. relationships with the international community in general and Third World nations in particular. His expectations for the Korean peninsula were even higher due to its geopolitical importance and uniqueness. He had in mind a parallel plan for the two Koreas: ground force withdrawal in the South and diplomatic contact with the North. While many view his attempts to establish contact with North Korea as merely a way to facilitate his troop withdrawal plan in South Korea, I argue that it was Carter's regionalist vision of world affairs both prior to and during the early stage of his presidency that led him to approach Pyongyang.

During Carter's first year in office, Kim Il Sung tried to approach him privately for direct talks that would exclude South Korea,[17] but the U.S. was unwilling to accept these terms that would mean cutting out its ally. At the same time, President Park Chung Hee's strong opposition to troop withdrawal forced Carter to hold back information regarding his initiatives with the North and consent to his NSC advisors of not accepting Pyongyang's offer for contact. The best Carter could do was instruct his staff to provide a thorough study of Pyongyang and its relationships with other Communist states. As discussed in the next section, the U.S. proceeded cautiously on North Korea in the first six months of the Carter presidency before officially embarking on a diplomatic initiative.

Observing Pyongyang

Washington carefully considered Pyongyang's reactions to the troop withdrawal plan, an issue the NSC thought "as important as it is conjectural."[18] Various courses of action from the North had been drafted a week before the Policy Review Committee (PRC) meeting on Presidential Review Memorandum/PRM-13 of troop withdrawal was scheduled. The Central Intelligence Agency (CIA) had also investigated the possibly reactions by Pyongyang's major allies. It was concluded that both Moscow and Beijing saw the U.S. as generally on the defensive internationally, and more specifically as unwilling to become engaged in a future land war in Asia.[19]

The CIA also saw "important differences" in the ways the Chinese and the Soviets viewed, respectively, an American reduction of forces in South Korea. Whereas the troop withdrawal would not significantly complicate U.S.-Soviet relations or lead Moscow to conclude that the U.S. was less of a global adversary, it could, felt the CIA, raise some troublesome implications for Beijing. This is because the U.S. saw Chinese support for U.S. military presence in South Korea not only as a deterrent to rash action by Kim Il Sung, but also as a strategic counterweight to the threat of "Soviet military encirclement of China."[20] If we look at the situation in Indochina, it is clear that the predictions of the CIA proved to be accurate. Chinese fear of a Soviet encirclement resulted in its leaders' decision to support the Pol Pot regime (the Khmer Rouge) in Cambodia beginning in December 1978 and—with the underground support of President Carter himself—to launch a war against Vietnam, a country which Vice Premier Deng Xiao Ping called "a Cuba of Asia," in February 1979. As long as the U.S. maintained the ability to project military force as a Pacific power, thus blocking the expansion of Soviet influence in the region, China would be pleased.

On May 5, 1977, Jimmy Carter issued Presidential Directive/NSC-12, ordering a substantial troop withdrawal from Korea, including the removal of one brigade by the end of 1978 and the complete removal of all ground forces by 1981–1982.[21] The South Korean government showed disappointment, but, viewing Carter's determination to implement his plan, accepted the U.S. ground force withdrawal. In a consultation meeting between President Park and Under Secretary of State for Political Affairs Phillip Habib on May 25, Park harshly questioned Habib about U.S. plans in the event of a North Korean attack, and whether the U.S. was prepared to provide air and naval support.[22] Moreover, Park did respond to a query from Habib's as to whether the U.S. could be helpful in facilitating a North-South Korean dialogue, particularly as the U.S. entered into serious discussions with Beijing about normalization. Park's refusal to consider dialogue with the North, assisted by the U.S. and China, shows his hardline attitude towards the two powers' attempted interference in the Korean peninsula.

North Korean leaders joined Park in condemning another interference effort by outsiders. In July, U.S. Secretary of State Cyrus Vance reprised Henry Kissinger's old notion of "cross-recognition"—the USSR and the PRC would recognize the ROK and the U.S. and Japan recognize the DPRK—and concurrent recognition of both Koreas within the United Nations. Vance's actions triggered vocal disapproval from Pyongyang regarding the U.S.'s policy of "brutal interference in Korea's internal affairs and endorsement of Korean division."[23] North Korean centralized press, radio, and television actively campaigned against these American ideas. In an interview with *Yomiuri Shimbun*, Kim Il Sung stated that while North Korea was taking a "wait and see" attitude toward President Carter, it was nonetheless disturbed by what it perceived as a discrepancy between Carter's campaign pledges and his action since taking office.[24] It is true that the U.S. continued to refuse to be drawn into direct discussion of the Korean problem with Pyongyang without the participation of ROK representatives. Furthermore, the withdrawal plan was gradual in nature, not affecting air and naval units, and would be accompanied by an increase in assistance to the ROK. Thus, the North actually feared that the South was getting politically and militarily stronger, regardless of the American troop presence, and that the removal of troops did not necessarily give the North an advantage over the South.

However, Vance's scheduled visit to China at the end of August was widely publicized. Pyongyang considered the possibility that Vance's Beijing visit would enable unofficial contact between the U.S. and the DPRK "in view of clarifying the main problems between the two."[25] As a result, during and after the July 14 incident—the incursion of a U.S. military helicopter into the North's airspace—Pyongyang reacted in a surprisingly "calm and highly balanced manner."[26] The press also objectively presented the facts, without any rhetoric against the U.S. This "understanding" reaction by the North Korean authorities was attributed first to the fact that the U.S. assumed responsibility for the incident, and second to the North's desire to create favorable conditions for initiating dialogue with Washington.

On July 27, 1977, the Carter administration decided to take one step forward, constructing a diplomatic strategy to accompany the troop withdrawals. Carter agreed to his staff's idea that talks between South and North Korea with or without PRC participation was "the missing dimension" in the troop withdrawal policy.[27] A scenario was enabled for the first time: tripartite talks (North Korea-U.S.-South Korea) or talks that would involve the major powers in the region, including Japan. The U.S. would move forward with the troop withdrawal plan in parallel with dialogue with both Koreas. This decision was made for several reasons. The first was the American evaluation of the great significance the Chinese attached to the presence of U.S. forces in Korea and thus, the problems that would follow the reduction of these forces. The second was a positive signal from Pyongyang. Taking into account the rapid progress of Sino-American normalization of relations and the current tilt of Pyongyang towards Beijing, the U.S. had important reasons to move forward with the North. As a result, despite Seoul's opposition to the idea, Washington quickly launched the very first initiative: wooing Seoul into talking with Pyongyang.

Reviving Inter-Korean Dialogue

The idea of North-South Korean dialogue was first introduced by the South Korean government in 1971 as one of Seoul's reactions to the Nixon Doctrine, which resulted in the gradual U.S. withdrawal from the Asian geopolitical sphere and the Vietnam quagmire. Following the North-South Korean joint statement on July 4, 1972 were short-lived efforts from both sides for true dialogue and cooperation. This process of dialogue was actually used by President Park to strengthen his political power. However, once it was revived by the Carter administration, Park strongly opposed the idea for which he had been the primary proponent.

South Korea's negative reaction was based on two main reasons. First, it opposed the idea of leaving China out and recalled Washington's most recent proposal, which had called for four-party talks that included the Chinese. Seoul, following developments related to the Sino-American détente, was trying to develop a relationship with China and excluding the Chinese might diminish Seoul's prospects for achieving this objective. Second, and more importantly, there was anxiety on the South Korean side of a repetition of the Paris peace talks in which trilateral discussions between the U.S., North Vietnam, and South Vietnam served essentially as a "cover" for bilateral discussions between Washington and Hanoi. In a conversation with Brzezinski in May 1978, right after his China visit—during which the intention for trilateral talks was directly discussed—Park showed his explicit disdain for the idea. In his words, "in such circumstances, the ROK would look simply like a bridesmaid with the United States and North Korea serving as the bride and the groom."[28]

Seoul's fear of a possible Washington-Pyongyang "wheel and deal" was not unfounded. Right after the decision was made in July 1977, the East Asia Inter-Departmental Group (EA-IG), chaired by the State Department, started to prepare a study of diplomatic initiatives on Korea designed to encourage an early resumption of North-South talks with or without U.S. involvement. Brzezinski instructed the EA-IG that such diplomatic initiatives should not exclude an analysis of ways to implement the troop withdrawal plan to promote inter-Korean dialogue.[29] Essentially, the Carter administration was using the troop withdrawal issue as a "bargaining chip" to obtain political concessions from North Korea. Armacost, while wary about the rationality of such an idea, supported his boss, saying, "I am not sure there is anything to look at here given the way we have defined our policy publicly. But since there is no precise terminal date for the third withdrawal stage, there is at least a small opening for this."[30]

As the Sino-Soviet split intensified while the Carter administration was opening diplomatic channels with Beijing, the North Koreans became skeptical of China's real intentions with regard to Korea in later 1977. At this moment rumor has it that the PRC was interested in retaining American troops in South Korea spread out, which undeniably affected North Korean leaders. As a result, the DPRK decided against contacting Cyrus Vance during his visit to Beijing. In a discussion with Romanian Ambassador to North Korea Dumitru Popa, Heo Dam noted that "there are currently no favorable conditions for an American-North Korean dialogue."[31] Asked by Popa of the rumors of China's duplicitous policy on Korea, Heo Dam replied that "North Korean officials are not fully aware of their Chinese counterparts' intentions." Heo also added, however, that "in official talks, the PRC declares to support the DPRK in terms of Korean unification."[32]

North Korea did in fact receive Chinese support during the Vance visit. Foreign Minister Huang Hua criticized Carter's half-hearted troop withdrawal policy and the warlike actions of the Park Chung Hee government. Vice Premier Deng advised the Secretary of State that the Korean issue belonged in the same category as the question of "two Chinas, two Germanys, two Vietnams, and the two Koreas."[33] Citing Vietnam as a typical example, Deng said that the struggle for reunification was inevitable and the issue of division would be solved eventually, whether it took one hundred or one thousand years.[34]

The latter half of 1977 also witnessed visits by various Communist leaders to Pyongyang, which reflected North Korea's vision of world affairs. On August 24–28 Josip Broz Tito, President of the League of Communists of Yugoslavia and of the Socialist Federal Republic of Yugoslavia, visited the DPRK and conferred with Kim Il Sung. During his visit to the U.S. in March 1978, Tito proposed to President Carter the idea of Yugoslavians as mediators for tripartite talks on Korea, with the Park government as a full participant but without the presence of President Park Chung Hee himself. Carter immediately rejected this proposal,[35] as did Brzezinski when Romanian president Nicolae Ceausescu suggested a similar framework for trilateral talks.[36] Surprisingly, Tito's proposal received widespread media attention everywhere except in Pyongyang, where it was greeted with stony silence,[37] obviously due to the North Korean desire for direct talks with the U.S.

On December 10, 1977, Erich Honecker, General Secretary of the Central Committee of the Socialist Unity Party of Germany and Chairman of the Council of State of the German Democratic Republic (GDR), arrived in Pyongyang. In contrast with Honecker's visit to Hanoi, the Pyongyang visit was not a great success, largely due to ideological differences between the GDR and DPRK over the question of divided states.[38] Similarly divided as North Korea, however, East Germany did not pursue unification, as a unified Germany was perceived a threat to peace in the USSR's view. Honecker, acting at the behest of the Soviets, lectured Kim on the applicability of a two Germanies solution for Korea. In reply, Kim took pains to persuade him that North Korea was not a blind follower of either Chinese or Soviet leadership.[39]

Meanwhile, according to the observation of some Australian diplomats in Beijing, after retaining Chinese backing in the latter half of 1977, North Korea was able to reestablish a close relationship with the Soviets.[40] The Kremlin also responded positively: in January 1978, Dinmukhamed Akhmedovich Kunayev, a member of the Soviet Politburo, headed a Soviet delegation to Pyongyang. During his visit, Kunayev delivered the Order of Lenin to Kim Il Sung and agreed to expand cultural and trade relations with the North.[41] In May the Soviet government sent an invitation to Kim Il Sung to visit the USSR and Kim accepted.

To check the rise of Soviet influence in North Korea, Beijing quickly planned a visit to Pyongyang by Chairman Hua Guofeng. No Chairman of the Communist Party of China had gone abroad in twenty years; accordingly, the visit marked a milestone in China's efforts to strengthen foreign relations with neighboring countries. Hua's Pyongyang visit in May turned out to be highly successful, as the two sides reached "a full identity of views on the issues discussed," including direct contact between the DPRK and the U.S.[42] Moreover, the Chinese expressed a notably moderate position toward both the U.S. and South Korea. This was evidenced by both the absence of military personnel within the delegation of Hua and the rejection of North Korea's request for military aid.

Washington observed these developments within the Communist bloc with great interest. The CIA, while maintaining its initial evaluation that both the Chinese and Soviets held little enthusiasm for Kim Il Sung's reunification efforts, now predicted that Kim would abandon his efforts to preserve a balance in ties with Moscow and Beijing, and might even consider aligning with one or the other.[43] The CIA acknowledged Pyongyang's great concern over the possibility of a Korean settlement imposed by the major powers, which was best reflected in its intense attacks on various proposals for "two Koreas" or "cross-recognition." An important CIA report prior to Brzezinski's visit to China in May 1978 concluded that his trip would promote even greater anxiety in Pyongyang.[44] Sensing that China was trying to regain total influence over North Korea, and that the concern of Great Power politics on the side of the North was rising, Washington decided to play the "China card." The plan for trilateral talks, therefore, was one of the key issues raised during Brzezinski's talks with top Chinese leaders.

Bringing in the Chinese

Amidst the confusion caused by the "Koreagate" investigation, the Carter administration announced the delay of the First Command Brigade withdrawal in April 1978. In May, Brzezinski made a path-opening visit to China, a breakthrough in the process of U.S.-Chinese normalization that echoed his predecessor Kissinger's 1971 Beijing visit. In their official talks, Brzezinski affirmed to the Chinese the "depth, durability and firmness" of the American commitment to the security and well-being of the ROK.[45] Several times he emphasized U.S. readiness to organize tripartite talks if both of the Koreas were amenable. In turn, he received firm assurance from Foreign Minister Huang Hua and Chairman Hua Guofeng that North Korea had no intention of moving southward and attacking the ROK. China supported North Korea's desire to obtain independent and peaceful unification free from foreign interference, and Hua told Brzezinski that a unified Korea would "make it difficult for Soviet revisionists" to interfere in the affairs of Korea.[46]

What is noteworthy is Brzezinski's understanding of the Chinese position on North Korea. At the Blue House following his China visit, the National Security Advisor lectured President Park Chung Hee, who confessed that he could not decipher the real thoughts of the Chinese. Brzezinski saw China's concern about North Korea as very similar to that of Vietnam, in that its political influence would deteriorate if the Chinese did not provide strong support for Kim, at least officially. The National Security Advisor concluded, "the Chinese face an uncertain situation in Korea, a Soviet controlled Mongolia and expanding Soviet influence in Vietnam."[47] This assessment and reference to Vietnam was crucial in that it impacted Brzezinski's understanding of both Chinese and North Korean actions. To avoid another pro-Soviet satellite in North Korea, the only thing China could do was support the North. Therefore, for Brzezinski, Chinese support for North Korea was almost formalistic. Overall, he found the Chinese assessment of the international scene to be "realistic, undogmatic" and aware that "to a large extent they share broad strategic objectives with the U.S."[48] His NSC staff agreed completely, and evaluated the China visit thus: "The real differences between us at this point are less than the rhetoric suggests. But we harm the Chinese cause by saying this. Hence, in our public statements, it is best to ignore the genuine commonality of our views."[49]

It appears that it was not just Communist thought, but also the calculations of Washington—Seoul close ally—that were difficult for President Park to apprehend. After complicating matters for Park by speaking about the "real" Chinese and North Korean intentions, Brzezinski returned to his ultimate goal: wooing South Korea to talk with the North. According to Brzezinski, in this complex situation, trilateral talks would help Park to "leave it to the North to demonstrate their own intransigence or modify its position" and "make it less necessary to understand what the Chinese really have in mind."[50] In other words, engaging in talks with North Korea would solve all the problems and, above all, ease Park's mind.

CIA reports in the latter half of 1978 show a great deal of confidence in Pyongyang's increased dependence on Beijing amidst North Korea's intensified fears.[51] Strengthening this belief were reports on North Korean military activities in Cambodia assisting the Pol Pot army against the Vietnamese, with or without Chinese encouragement.[52] Added to this was the rumor of Vice Premier Deng's visit to Pyongyang prior to his departure for the U.S.[53]

Above all, the international events in late 1978 strongly contributed to U.S. confidence in "Chinese flexibility." In November, the Soviet Union concluded the Treaty of Friendship and Cooperation with Vietnam, heightening a sense of crisis among the Chinese. Deng broke the deadlock by making concessions to the U.S. on Taiwan, a sticking point that prevented the immediate conclusion of the Washington-Beijing normalization negotiations. As a result, a week before Deng's historic visit to Washington, the CIA, on Brzezinski's order, provided an overly positive report of the situation. Citing "Chinese flexibility" since the start of Sino-U.S. normalization, and contact with Taiwan as an example, the CIA expected the same flexibility of Beijing regarding the Korean issue. They even expected the Chinese to request "parallel actions" in Washington in the form of flexibility on establishing contact with Pyongyang.[54] Following the positive Four-Point Proposal[55] by North Korea announced on January 23, 1979, the Carter cabinet was instantly deceived by the vision of "the beginning of a Chinese-inspired effort to preempt the Korea issue."[56] The "China card" was apparently bearing fruit and the U.S. was preparing for a historical breakthrough in terms of the two Koreas.

One of the main topics for Carter in discussions with Deng during the latter's visit was Korea. The agenda was clear, though difficult to achieve. It included urging the Chinese to restrain any potential North Korean effort to take the South militarily, influence the North to talk to the South, and engage directly with the South.[57] While confirming no military attack from the North, Deng refused to put pressure on North Korea and thus avoided working with South Korea. The reason, as pointed out by Deng during a discussion with Senator Sam Nunn prior to his U.S. visit, was China's historic "relationship of trust"[58] with the North Koreans. Deng explained that China had never interfered in the internal affairs or decision-making process of the North as the Soviet Union had, and which had resulted in North Korea's break from the Soviets. The U.S suggestion of an "exchange of trade relations"—the U.S. would open trade relations with North Korea if China would do so with South Korea—and that China should cooperate with the U.S. in establishing offices to mediate between the two Koreas received a sharp rejection from Deng. Carter was also unable to convince Deng to change the North Korean position of including "different parties and peoples organizations" in any North-South Korean dialogue. This was the main cause for unproductive inter-Korean contact in early 1979. Until May, the Carter administration still optimistically held hopes of the Chinese influencing Kim Il Sung to come to terms with three-way talks. Chinese Ambassador Chai Zemin subtly refuted Brzezinski's pressing imploration, saying that he believed the National Security Advisor was "good at finding solutions to all kinds of problem."[59] In reality, this was not at all the case.

Ironically, it was South Korean President Park who realized that the Americans were being overly optimistic in relying on the Chinese. Park frankly told Senator Nunn that East Asian security was being placed in danger as a result of U.S.-PRC normalization and he felt that many U.S. statements were "too optimistic."[60] In a letter to Carter regarding Deng's visit, Park voiced his concern with the U.S.'s mistake in "overestimating the role of China and of underestimating the impact of diplomatic and military maneuvers of the Soviet Union."[61] Nevertheless, Park perhaps never understood that it was the overly confident U.S. assessments of both the Chinese and the North Korean positions that resulted in the final suspension of U.S. troop withdrawal, the very objective he wished to achieve in dealing with the "Carter Chill." A group of NSC and State Department staff and senators succeeded in persuading Carter to make the tough decision on the same day as the North Korean Four-Point Proposal announcement. In a favorable situation that included a Sino-American consensus, concessions from Pyongyang, and improved U.S.-South Korean alliance, the U.S. should have grasped the opportunity of potential dialogue with North Korea. Sam Nunn, indifferent to president Park's concerns, stated bluntly to Carter, "let our withdrawals become contingent upon progress in reducing tensions on the peninsula."[62] The troop withdrawal plan, which was once considered a bargaining chip for inter-Korean dialogue in 1977, was now dependent on the results of the upcoming trilateral talks in 1979. Even though he disagreed with his staff, Carter could not help but announce the freeze on troop withdrawals on February 9, 1979.

In early 1979, while Sino-American normalization of relations resulted in the U.S. sacrificing its diplomatic efforts with Vietnam, it was assumed that Carter's idealistic plan in Korea would be successful, given the close-knit relationship between Beijing and Pyongyang and Chinese "flexibility." However, as history has shown, despite President Park's concession to participate in tripartite talks, on the other side of the table the Communists proved to be intransigent.

Trilateral Talks: Carter's Final Shot

After three rounds of talks in February and March 1979, North-South relations were suspended because each side failed to attend a subsequent meeting called by the other. Ultimately, inter-Korean talks achieved limited success because they could not address the security problem in the absence of the Americans. Frustrated, different attempts were planned in Carter's White House. The president himself, out of the desire to bring the two Koreas into one place, wanted to make his upcoming visit to Seoul an occasion for a three-way meeting, or at least a chance for a joint U.S.-ROK proposal for tripartite summit talks. Consequently, Ambassador William Gleysteen "exploded with surprise and anger" when he received a phone call from the State Department informing him of Carter's wish to invite President Kim Il Sung to Seoul to join him and President Park.[63]

For Brzezinski and his NSC staff, continuing with the "China card" solution seemed like the best option for the stalemate. Therefore, a four-way meeting was proposed that would involve the Chinese during a future presidential visit to Beijing.[64] Confident that the Chinese would be willing to exercise leverage to produce a flexible North Korean posture during any trilateral talks, China experts within the NSC even suggested using Taipei as a bargaining chip to woo China to open economic negotiations with South Korea. Contact between Beijing and Seoul would be one result of the trilateral talks and, in exchange, the U.S. would put pressure on Taipei to establish economic relations with Beijing.[65]

To the surprise of American counterparts as well as his staff in the Blue House, President Park agreed to the three-way talks proposal. Initially, Park hoped this tripartite meeting would not be a repetition of that between Egypt and Israel where President Carter was essentially an intermediary, and he stated that he would consider the proposal if the U.S. was "on our side."[66] Whereas the South Korean MOFA still had doubts about the real intentions behind the U.S. proposal, Park simply questioned Cyrus Vance if President Carter felt confident enough in the ROK-U.S. security relationship to embark on such a proposal.[67] After receiving a nod from the U.S. government regarding the possibility of linking the proposal with security issues and the confirmation that there would be no tradeoff on human rights, Park ordered his administration to accept tripartite talks. On June 19, the ROK government announced as one of the conditions for positively considering the proposal that:

> if President Carter could directly and privately guarantee to President Park that no additional troop withdrawal will take place and make an announcement around July 15 (but make it clear that the trilateral meeting is not a condition to be exchanged for the postponement of troop withdrawal).[68]

President Park finally achieved all of his objectives and in mid-July, the final decision on U.S. ground force withdrawals was made, leaving further withdrawals of combat units suspended; the resumption of further withdrawals would be reviewed by 1981 and depend on evidence of reduced tensions on the peninsula. Brzezinski believed that this option would be the most successful, since it could achieve both domestic and international goals. In his words,

> making the resumption of further withdrawals contingent upon North Korea's willingness to join actively in an effort to reduce tensions on the peninsula will enable us to place future withdrawals in a broader diplomatic context, strengthen our hand in promoting a resumption of serious North-South dialogue, and enable us to explain the policy persuasively to the Congress and to the American public.[69]

USFK troop withdrawal—the only possible incentive for a more flexible North Korean response—disappeared, and one could easily predict the DPRK's rejection of the proposal. Park's apparent concession of tripartite talks, therefore, can be seen as a successful strategic move.

North Korea rapidly rejected the tripartite talks proposal revealed in the Carter-Park joint communiqué of July 1. Before the official rejection was announced, the State Department naively expected that, following several counter-proposals, the North Koreans would eventually agree to tripartite talks "on the grounds that from the wider political angle they cannot afford not to."[70] This erroneous prediction from the Carter administration was probably based on its expectations of immanent high-level meetings with the Chinese. Surprisingly, even when Pyongyang continued to voice strong criticism of the proposal, and Chinese Foreign Minister Hung Hua adhered faithfully to the North Korean line during meetings with the Assistant Secretary of State for East Asian and Pacific Affairs Richard Holbrooke, hopes were still high in both Seoul and Washington that this was not a final rejection.[71] The two governments, therefore, moved to the second approach of UN Secretary General good offices. When North Korea officially rejected UN Secretary General Kurt Waldheim's offers to help initiate talks between the two Koreas, expectations were shifted to Vice President Walter Mondale's visit to Beijing to change Deng Xiao Ping's mind. Mondale, in fact, did a poor job of discussing the Korean issue with the Chinese.[72]

Political crisis in South Korea following a series of events (the Park assassination, the military coup by Chun Doo Hwan, the Kwangju uprising) and similar turmoil in Washington during the Iran hostage crisis further doomed the three-way talks initiative. The year 1980 also witnessed Pyongyang's tilt towards Moscow. At the Sixth Party Congress in October 1980, North Korea officially designated Kim Jong Il as his father's successor.[73] Chinese newspapers indirectly criticized this hierarchical succession. The wind hauled again in the relationships among the Communists comrades, and so did the political situation in Washington: Carter did not win reelection and Ronald Reagan would soon assume the office of the presidency.

Conclusion

Jimmy Carter entered the White House with a pacifist vision of world affairs, seeing it as "global community" in which the U.S. played the key role as a pioneer in peace-building initiatives and cooperative actions. He viewed countries within their regional and national contexts, rather than as merely satellites of the two superpowers. However, as the Carter administration's foreign policy became more and more influenced by the NSC, which was headed by a globalist National Security Advisor, Carter's objectives gradually changed. The Sino-American diplomatic normalization, a big success of the Carter presidency, turned out to be an obstacle for Carter's initiatives, not only in Korea but also in Vietnam and Cuba. This was due to not only the complex Washington-Beijing-Moscow relationship but also the American strategy of using the "China card." By placing relations with China as the top priority and being too confident in Chinese flexibility and in the amount of Chinese influence on North Korea, Carter's policies for Korea ended up bearing no fruit.

For South Korea, Carter's parallel policy raised great concern for the Park administration. Already troubled by the plan for phased American troop withdrawal, Park became even more fearful of Carter's efforts to engage North Korea and U.S.-ROK relations dipped to a new low point during the first two years of the Carter presidency. Therefore, even though the plan for trilateral talks was consolidated as soon as 1977, it took Carter's staff two years to slow down the troop withdrawals, reassuring Park and improving this alliance; this had been the vital factor for the implementation of three-way talks. However, one thing remained strong during the Carter presidency: the U.S.-ROK alliance. The Carter administration never sacrificed its alliance with the South to agree on bilateral talks or a secret deal with the North. The Cold War framework was still a significant undercurrent during one of the most idealistic eras of U.S. foreign policy.

In terms of North Korea, it was a surprise to both Washington and Seoul that the tripartite talks proposal received such a strong rejection from Pyongyang. Unlike the Vietnam case, in which the U.S. government could directly negotiate for diplomatic normalization to achieve certain goals, the U.S. was unable to break the Cold War alliance framework to make direct contact with the North. The Carter administration also misread the North Koreans somewhat in that it had hoped for more flexibility from Pyongyang following Sino-American normalization. The DPRK turned out to be more inflexible, and at the same time attached less importance to its "comradeship" with the Chinese than expected. As is shown in this chapter, Chinese influence over North Korea had limits and Beijing frankly announced its unwillingness to affect Pyongyang's decisions despite a closer Sino-American relationship.

Notes

1. I have borrowed the term "Carter Chill" from Don Oberdorfer's *The Two Koreas: A Contemporary History*.

2. These include studies by Taehwan Ok (1990, 1998); Ho–hwon Jeon (2008); Jin–hwan Kim (2010); Kwan–haeng Cho (2011, 2015, 2016); Hun Yu (2012); Jung–sik Um (2012, 2013).

3. Some comparative studies of foreign policy systems and unification policies of South and North Korea, such as that of Hakjoon Kim (1987), Sung Chul Yang (1981), and Byung Chul Koh (1984) covered the Carter administration period. However, as these studies were published in the 1980s and based roughly on periodical research, many assessments are found outdated, especially those on the calcula-

tions of the actors involved. Recent studies by Jung–sik Um (2013), Seuk Ryule Hong (2016), and Wan Bom Lee (2017) which were based on advanced archival research are highly updated and valuable.

4. Handwritten memorandum from Jimmy Carter to Cyrus Vance, January 28, 1977, Name File, "Vance, Cyrus (Secretary of State)" Carter Presidential Library (CPL).

5. United Nations—Address Before the General Assembly, March 17, 1977. The American Presidency Project, http://www.presidency.ucsb.edu/ws/?pid=7183

6. Carter, *Keeping Faith*, 195.

7. Address at Commencement Exercises at the University of Notre Dame, May 22, 1977, The American Presidency Project, http://www.presidency.ucsb.edu/ws/index.php?pid=7552

8. United Nations—Address Before the General Assembly. October 4, 1977, The American Presidency Project, http://www.presidency.ucsb.edu/ws/index.php?pid=6744

9. Koh, *The Foreign Policy Systems of North and South Korea*, 169.

10. Telegram from the U.S. Embassy in Seoul to the Secretary of State, "MOFA Inquiries About List of 14 Nations with which U.S. Desires to Normalize Relations," February 18, 1977. The National Archives Access to Archival Databases (AAD).

11. Telegram from Ambassador Sneider to Secretary of State Vance, "U.S.–Vietnamese Relations," February 10, 1977. Declassified Document Reference System (DDRS).

12. Cable from Secretary of State Vance to the Embassies, "East Asian Attitudes toward U.S. Normalization with Vietnam Not Releasable to Foreign Nationals," March 15, 1977, AAD.

13. For example, despite its "confidential basis," Assistant Secretary Richard Holbrooke briefed South Korean Foreign Minister Park Tong Jin in details of the state of dialogue between Vietnam and the USG. See Telegram from Seoul, "Tour D'Horizon with ROK Foreign Minister Park—International Issues," September 23, 1978, DDRS.

14. Memorandum for Zbigniew Brzezinski from Mike Armacost, "Contact and Communications with North Korea," February 28,1977. Records of the Office of the National Security Advisor Zbigniew Brzezinski's Country File (NSA6), Box 43, CPL.

15. Ibid.

16. Memorandum for Jimmy Carter from Zbigniew Brzezinski, "North Korean Proposal for Discussions of Reunification with South Korea," March 14, 1977. NSA6, Box 43. CPL.

17. Two approaches came via letters to Carter in May and October 1977 from President Bongo of Gabon and Yugoslav President Tito, respectively. Memo for Dr. Zbigniew Brzezinski, "HIRC Request for Our Responses to NK Approaches," March 30, 1978, DNSA.

18. Memorandum for Zbignew Brzezinski from Mike Armacost, "North Korea Reactions to U.S. Forces Reductions," April 12, 1977. NSA6, Box 43. CPL.

19. CIA and National Intelligence Reports on Ground Troop Withdrawals, April 28, 1977. CIA Records Search Tool (CREST), National Archives and Records Administration.

20. Central Intelligence Agency, "U.S. Ground Forces Withdrawal: Korean Stability and Foreign Relations," June 7, 1977. CREST.

21. Presidential Directive/NSC–12, "U.S. Policy in Korea," May 5, 1977. DNSA.

22. Telegram from the American Embassy in Seoul to the Secretary of State, "U.S. Ground Force Withdrawal: Consultations with President Park," May 25, 1977. NSA6, Box 43, CPL.

23. Telegram 066667 from the Romanian Embassy in Pyongyang to the Romanian Ministry of Foreign Affairs, July 7, 1977. Ostermann, Person, Kraus (2013), "The Carter Chill: US–ROK–DPRK Trilateral Relations, 1976–1979," 171.

24. Op cit in Note 8.

25. Telegram 0666678 from the Romanian Embassy in Pyongyang to the Romanian Ministry of Foreign Affairs, "US Helicopter Incident of July 14," July 19, 1977. "The Carter Chill," 190.

26. Ibid.

27. Memorandum for Mike Armacost from David Aaron, "Talks between North Korea and South Korea," July 26, 1977. NSA 6, Box 43, CPL.

28. Memorandum of Conversation between Zbigniew Brzezinski and Park Chung Hee, May 28, 1978. DNSA.

29. Memorandum from Zbigniew Brzezinski to Cyrus Vance, "Talks Between North Korea and South Korea," August 5, 1978. DDRS.

30. Memorandum from Mike Armacost to Robert Rich, "EA–IG Study of Additional Diplomatic Initiatives for Korea," August 17, 1977. DDRS.

31. Telegram 066691 from the Romanian Embassy in Pyongyang to the Romanian Ministry of Foreign Affairs, July 31, 1977. "The Carter Chill," 217.

32. Ibid.

33. Memorandum of Conversation with the U.S. Secretary and PRC Foreign Minister et all, August 23, 1977. *Foreign Relations of the United States, 1977–1980: Volume XIII: China*, 204 (hereafter FRUS).

34. Ibid.

35. Carter strongly confirmed this to Park in a personal letter. Letter from Jimmy Carter to Park Chung Hee, May 17, 1978. President's Personal Foreign Affairs Files, Box 2, CPL.

36. Memorandum of Conversation Between Takeo Fukuda and Zbigniew Brzezinski, May 23, 1978. DNSA.

37. Intelligence Memorandum, "Korea and the Major Powers," October 30, 1978. CREST.

38. Telegram from U.S. Embassy in Berlin to Secretary of State, "GDR Leaders Visit North Korea," December 19, 1977. The National Archives AAD.

39. Don Oberdorfer. 2011. *Two Koreas: A Contemporary History*. Basic Books, 99–100.

40. Letter from C.G. Woodard to Andrew Peacocks, "DPRK: The Year in Review," 3 January 1978. "The Carter Chill," 264.

41. Telegram to the Minister of Foreign Affairs from the Ambassador in the United Kingdom, March 31, 1978. Ibid., 291.

42. Memorandum from Zbigniew Brzezinski to the President, "Information Items," May 8, 1978. DDRS.

43. Central Intelligence Agency, National Foreign Assessment Center, "The Seoul–Pyongyang Dialogue on Reunification: Origins, Decline, and Prospects," May 10, 1978. DDRS.

44. Central Intelligence Agency National Foreign Assessment Center, "The Pyongyang–Beijing–Moscow Triangle," May 10, 1978. Remote Archives Capture (RAC), CPL.

45. Memorandum of Conversation Between Dr. Brzezinski and Foreign Minister Huang Hua, May 20, 1978. FRUS, 429.

46. Ibid., 456.

47. Conversation between Park Chung Hee and Zbigniew Brzezinski, May 25, 1978, DNSA.

48. Ibid.

49. Memorandum From Michel Oksenberg of the National Security Council Staff to the President's Assistant for National Security Affairs (Brzezinski), "Appraisal of the China Trip," May 25, 1978. FRUS, 465.

50. Op. cit. in Note 46.

51. Reports such as: Intelligence Appraisal, "Great Power Relations with the Two Koreas, September 22, 1978. DNSA; Intelligence Memorandum, "Korea and the Major Powers," October 30, 1978. CREST.

52. Memorandum from East Asia for Zbigniew Brzezinski, "Weekly Report," June 15, 1978. DDRS.

53. Memorandum for Dr. Brzezinski from The Situation Room, "Noon Notes," January 11, 1979. DDRS.

54. Intelligence Memorandum, "Chinese Leverage on North Korea," January 23, 1979. DNSA.

55. The Central Committee of the Democratic front of the Reunification of the Fatherland (DFRF) responded positively to President Park Chung Hee's proposal on January 19, offering a "Four Point Proposal" for accelerating the reunification process, including holding a grand national convention. The ROK delegation for the South-North Coordinating Committee (SNCC) finally met the DFRF on February 17, but talks came to nowhere after three rounds of meeting.

56. Memorandum from Cyrus Vance for the President, January 23, 1979. DDRS.

57. Memorandum from the President's Assistant for National Security Affairs (Brzezinski) to President Carter, January 25, 1979. FRUS, 718.

58. Telegram from the Liaison Office in China to the Department of State, January 11, 1979. FRUS, 762.

59. Memorandum of Conversation between Dr. Zbigniew Brzezinski and PRC Ambassador to the U.S., May 4, 1979. DDRS.

60. Telegram from Ambassador Gleysteen to Cyrus Vance, "Codel Nunn's Talk with President Park," January 13, 1979. The State Department E–Reading Room.

61. Letter from Park Chung Hee to Jimmy Carter, January 31, 1979. "The Carter Chill," 458.

62. Memorandum of Conversation between the President and Senators, State Department and NSC staff, January 23, 1979. DDRS.

63. Gleysteen, *Massive Entanglement, Marginal Influence*, 42.

64. Memorandum from Nick Platt for Zbigniew Brzezinski, "A Korea Trialogue in June," May 7, 1979. DDRS.

65. Memorandum from Michel Oksenberg and Nick Platt for Zbigniew Brzezinski, "Beijing, Taipei, and the Korean Issue," May 24, 1979. DDRS.

66. Telegram from the Embassy in Seoul to the Secretary of State, "Coordination of Initiative with President Park to Reduce Tensions on the Korean Peninsula," May 29, 1979. DDRS.

67. Cable from the Embassy in Seoul to the Secretary of State, "Coordination of Initiative with President Park to Reduce Tensions on the Korean Peninsula," June 8, 1979. DDRS.

68. Ministry of Foreign Affair, "ROK's Position Regarding the Trilateral Meeting (Draft Plan)," June 19, 1979. "The Carter Chill," 601.

69. Memorandum for Jimmy Carter from Zbigniew Brzezinski, "U.S. Ground Force Withdrawals from the Republic of Korea," July 12, 1979. Zbigniew Brzezinski Collection, Subject File, Box 20, CPL.

70. Telegram 1794 from Washington to the Foreign and Commonwealth Office, "Korea: North/South Talks," July 5, 1979. "The Carter Chill," 639.

71. Telegram from W. Morris, "Tripartite Talks Proposal," July 31, 1979. Ibid., 661.

72. Mondale did not show any of American position and ignored Deng's positions to quickly move to other issues. See Memorandum of Conversation Between the Vice President and the PRC Vice Premier Deng Xiaoping, August 28, 1979. FRUS, 959–960.

73. Kim, *North Korea Foreign Policy*, 42.

Bibliography

Archival Sources
The National Archives Access to Archival Databases (AAD)
Declassified Document Reference System (DDRS)
Carter Presidential Library (CPL)
Central Intelligence Agency Research Tool (CREST)
Digital National Security Archive (DNSA)

Other Sources
Armstrong, Charles. *Tyranny of the Weak: North Korea and the World, 1950–1992* (Columbia University Press, 2013).

Brazinsky, Gregg. "Korea's Great Divergence: North and South Korea between 1972 and 1987," in ed. Tsuyoshi Hasegawa, *The Cold War in East Asia 1945–1991* (Stanford University Press, 2011) 241–265.

Brzezinski, Zbigniew. *Power and Principle: Memoirs of the National Security Adviser, 1977–1981* (New York: Farrar, Straus, Giroux, 1983).

Carter, Jimmy E. *Keeping Faith: Memoirs of a President* (Collins, 1982).

Cho, Kwan-haeng. 2011. "Kateo haengjeongbu ui Ju Han Miji sanggun cheolsu gyeoljeong si Bukhan gunsaryeok pyeonggae gwahan yeongu—Gukbangbu mit gunbu ui pyeongga byeonhwa reul jungsim euro" (A Study on North Korea Military Evaluation During Carter Administration Decision Making towards the US Troops Withdrawal Policy—Focused on Evaluation Change of DoD and Military Authorities), *Gunsa* (81), 261–295.

———. 2015. "Kateo haengjeongbu ui Ju Han Migun cheolsu gyeoljeonge dae Han yeongu—Jeongchaek geomto wiwonhoe wa gukga anbohoe ui nonui reul jungsim euro" (The Study on Carter Administration's U.S. Troops Withdrawal Policy from the ROK), *Gunsa* (94), 281–322.

———. 2016. "Kateo haengjeongbu ui Ju Han Migun cheolsue dae Han miuiheoui ipjang byeonhwae gwanhan yeongu—Kateo haengjeongbu chulbeomihu 77nyeon 6wol misangwon ui bonhoe ui jeonhu reul jungsim euro" (The Study on the change of U. S. Congress' perspective for the Carter Administration's U. S. Troops withdrawal policy from the ROK), *Gunsa*, (100), 303–330.

Chung, Il Yung ed. *Korea and Russia: Toward the 21st Century* (The Sejong Institute, 1992).

Glad, Betty. *An Outsider in the White House: Jimmy Carter, His Advisors, and the Making of American Foreign Policy* (London: Cornell University, 2009).

Gleysteen, William. *Massive Entanglement, Marginal Influence: Carter and Korea in Crisis* (Brookings, 1999).

Hasegawa, Tsuyoshi. "A Strategic Quadrangle: The Superpowers and the Sino-Japanese Treaty of Peace and Friendship, 1977–1978, " in ed. Tsuyoshi Hasegawa, *The Cold War in East Asia 1945–1991* (Stanford University Press, 2011), 213–240.

Holdrige, John H. *Crossing the Divide: An Insider's Account of the Normalization of U.S.–China Relations* (Rowman & Littlefield, 1997).

Hust, Steven. *The Carter Administration and Vietnam* (Palgrave Macmillan, 1996).

Jeon, Ho-hwon. 2008. "Miguk ui dae Han gunwon jeongchaek (1976–1980) yeongu—Kateo haengjeongbu ui Teukjing jeokin jeongchaek naeyong eul jungsim euro" (A study on U.S. military assistance policy toward Korea), *Gunsa* (66), 225–255.

Hong, Seuk Ryule. 2016. "Kateo haengjeongbugi Miguk ui dae Hanbando jeongchaek gwa 3ja hoedam" (The U.S. Polict toward Korea and Tripartite Talks during the Carter Administration), *Hanguk gwa gukje jeongchi*, 32(2), 33–71.

Kaufman, Scott. *Plans Unraveled: The Foreign Policy of the Carter Administration* (Northern Illinois University Press, 2008).

Kim, Bong Joong. 2003. "Jeonhwangi ui Miguk oegyo wa Kateo Ingwon oegyo ui deungjang" (American Diplomacy in Transition and the Rise of Human Rights Policies of Jimmy Carter). *Miguksa yeongu*, 17, 213–237.

Kim, Hakjoon. *Unification Policies of South and North Korea, 1945–1991: A Comparative Study* (Seoul National University, 1987).

Kim, Hyong-Gon. 2003. "Jimi Kateo daetongnyeong ui Jidoryeoke gwanhan sogo" (A Study on the Leadership of President Jimmy Carter). *Chungang Saron*, 18, 177–216.

Kim, Jin-hwan. 2010. "Kateo wa Kimilsungman chaseonghaetdeon Ju Han Migun cheolsu" (Cater and Kim Il Sung's USFK Withdrawal), *Minjog21*, 98–103.

Kim, Yong Ho. *North Korea Foreign Policy: Security Dilemma and Succession* (Lexington Books, 2010).

Kim, Yong-Jick. "The Security, Political, and Human Rights Conundrum, 1974–1979," in ed. Byung-Kook Kim, Ezra F. Vogel, *The Park Chung Hee Era: The Transformation of South Korea* (Harvard, 2011) 457–482.

Koh, Byung Chul. *The Foreign Policy Systems of North and South Korea* (University of California Press, 1984).

Koh, Je-sik. 1986. "Wollam jeonjaeng ihu ui jeollyak (Kateo wa Podeu)" (Strategy after the Vietnam War (Carter and Ford). *Shinhak yeongu*, 27, 325–334.

Lee, Wan Bom. 2017. "Kateo ui Nam-Buk-Mi 3ja hoedam jeui, 1977–1979 nyeon," *Hanguk minjok undongsa yeongu*, 90, 417–526.

———. 2017. *Kateo sidae ui Nam-Bukhan: Dongmaeng ui wigi wa minjok ui galdeung*. Seongnam: Hangukhak Chungang yeonguwon chulpanbu.

Ma, Sang Yoon, Park Won Gon (2009) "Detangteugi ui Han-Mi galdeung—Nikseun, Kateo wa Bak Jeonghui" (ROK-US Conflicts during the Era of Detente: Nixon, Carter, and Park Chung Hee), *Yeoksa bipyeong*, 2, 113–139.

Mitchell, Nancy. *Jimmy Carter in Africa: Race and the Cold War* (Stanford, CA: Standford University Press, 2016).

Niksch, Larry. 1981. "US Troops Withdrawal from South Korea: Past, Shortcomings & Future Prospects," *Asian Survey*, 21(3).

Oberdorfer, Don. *Two Koreas: A Contemporary History* (Basic Books, 2001).

Ok, Taehwan. "President Carter's Korean Withdrawal Policy" (Ph.D. Diss., Loyola University of Chicago, 1990).

———. 1990. "Japanese Reactions on President Carter's Korean Withdrawal Policy," *Asian Perspective*, 14(2). 157–166.

———. 1998. "Hanbando munje reul wiyohan Mi haengjeongbu wa uihoe ui hyemneok gwa galdeung," *Tongil yeonguwon yeonguchongseo*, 1–113.

Ostermann, Christian F., Person, James, and Kraus, Charles. 2013. "The Carter Chill: US-ROK-DPRK Trilateral Relations, 1976–1979," Woodrow Wilson International Center for Scholars.

Park, Insook. 2008. "Kateo haejeongbu wa 'Bongswaegunsaui' ui seungri" (The Carter Administration and the 'Containment Militarism'), *Miguksa yeongu*, 27, 145–186.

Park, Won Gon. *Kateo haengjeongbu ui dae Han jeongchaek 1977–1980: Dodeog oegyo ui jeogyong gwa tahyeop* (Jimmy Carter administration's policy toward South Korea 1977–1980: (The) accommodation and concession of moral diplomacy) (Ph.D. diss., Seoul Daehakgyo, 2008).

———. 2009. "Kateo haejeongbu ui dae Han jeongchaek—10/26 ul jeonhuhan Dodeog oegyo ui jeogyong" (Carter Administration's Policy Toward South Korea: The Accommodation of Moral Diplomacy around the 10/26 incident), *Hanguk jeongchihak hoebo*, 43(2), 215–234.

———. 2010. "1979 nyeon 12.12 Kudeta wa Kateo Mi haejeongbu daeeung: Dodeog oegyo ui tahyeop" (The US Carter Administration and Korea in the 12/12 Incident: Concession of Moral Diplomacy), *Gukje jeongchi nonchong*, 50(4), 81–102.

———. 2011. "5.18 Gwangju minjuhwa hangjaeng gwa Miguk ui daeung" (5.18 The Kwangju Uprising and the US Response), *Hanguk jeongchihak hoebo*, 45(5), 125–145.

Skidmore, David. *Reversing Course: Carter's Foreign Policy, Domestic Politics, and the Failure of Reform* (Vanderbilt University Press, 1996).

Smith, Gaddis. *Morality, Reasons & Power: American Diplomacy in the Carter Years* (Hill and Wang, 1987).

Sneh, Itai Nartzizenfield. *How the Future Almost Arrived: How Jimmy Carter Failed to Change U.S. Foreign Policy* (New York: Peter Lang, 2008).

Um, Jung-sik. Kateo haengjeongbu sigi dae Han mugijeon jeongchaek ui byeonyong: baekgom misail ui gaebal gwa F-5E/F gongdongsaengsan ui habui" (Adaptation of arms transfer restraint policy toward South Korea during the Carter administration) (Ph.D. diss., Seoul Daehakgyo, 2012).

———. 2012 "Miguk mugijeon jeongchaek ui Hanguk jeokyong: Kateo haejeongbu sigi Ju Han mijisanggun cheolsue ttareun jangbi ijeon (1977–1978)" (US Arms Transfer Policies' Application of Korea—Equipment Transfer based on Carter's Withdrawal Plan of US Forces in Korea, 1977–1978), *Gunsa*, (82), 275–303.

———. 2013 "1979 nyeon Kateo daetongnyeong ui 3ja hoedam chujin gwa Bak Jeonghui jeongbu ui insik" (President Carter's North-South-US Tripartite Talks in 1979 and the Perception of Park Chung Hee Administration), *Hanguk jeongchihak hoebo*, 47(1), 243–259.

Vance, Cyrus R. *Hard Choices: Critical Years in America's Foreign Policy* (New York: Simon and Schuster, 1983).

Yang, Sung Chul. *Korea and Two Regimes: Kim Il Sung and Park Chung Hee* (Schenkman Publishing, 1981).

Yu, Hun. Kateo haengjeongbu ui segye joellyak gwa Ju Han Migun jeongchaek (Carter administration's global strategy and US troop withdrawal policy from Korea) (Ph.D. diss., Seoul Daehakgyo, 2012).

CHAPTER FOUR

Armed with Notebooks and Pencils

North and South Korean Students at the Tehran Foreign School, 1983

Benjamin R. Young

During the Cold War era, the North and South Korean governments established missions, trade offices, and embassies throughout the Global South as part of their diplomatic offensives to be the true, legitimate Korean government. This diplomatic competition between the two Koreas also extended to the sons and daughters of the North and South Korean diplomats and officials as they often went to the same schools together in remote capital cities in Africa, Latin America, the Middle East, and southern Asia. These inter-Korean student interactions in the Global South became spaces of intense competition between Seoul and Pyongyang. This paper specifically focuses on the Tehran Foreign School in 1980s Iran and argues that it was a microcosm of the global inter-Korean conflict as it was one of the few spaces in which citizens from the two Koreas interacted and competed on a daily basis.

The microhistory framework, which "scrutinizes isolated topics [in order] to come to grips with the larger universe of historical circumstances and transformations," suits the reality of the inter-Korean conflict as interactions between citizens from the two Koreas were kept to a bare minimum by the governments in Seoul and Pyongyang.[1] Studying the history of inter-Korean relations from *the margins* refers to both physical location and scale.[2] In terms of physical location, rare moments of interaction between North and South Korean citizens primarily occurred outside the Korean peninsula.[3] This was due to the fact that the loyalty of most overseas North or South Koreans to their respective government was typically unwavering during the Cold War era so interactions with citizens from the opposing Korea were technically prohibited but nonetheless tolerated by Seoul and Pyongyang. Also, strict restrictions on interactions between North and South Koreans could rarely be enforced in remote Third World countries and occurred primarily due to the limited amount of resources available to diplomats and workers abroad. For example, there were few educational options available for foreign students living in 1980s Iran, which was in the middle of a brutal war with neighboring Iraq. Nonetheless, the children of North and South Koreans living in Tehran had to attend school somewhere so most, if not all, Korean students attended the Tehran Foreign School. Thus, this school becomes a valuable and unique vantage point from which to assess inter-Korean relations during the Cold War era.

This paper borrows its methodology from the school of Italian microhistory, with its focus on "idiosyncratic figures and phenomena rather than ordinary people and consistent patterns."[4] The North and South Korean students at the Tehran Foreign School, while exceptional in their location and their parents' status, also reflect the attitudes of their respective governments. However, as Francesca Trivellato explains, practitioners of Italian microhistory have struggled to connect microhistory with global history.[5] Nonetheless, the Italian microhistory approach "can provide a device (or at least a prod) to balance abstraction and detail, to pause on apparent inconsistencies and detect parallelisms that a hasty emphasis on structural breaks would dismiss unjustly."[6] This paper hopes to connect the lived experiences of North and South Korean students at the Tehran Foreign School with the larger geopolitical realities of the inter-Korean conflict. These student experiences, although limited in scope, expose the contradictions within the North and South Korean political systems. More specifically, in combatting North Korean communism abroad during the 1980s, the South Korean government adopted many of the same tactics and surveillance techniques used by the North Korean government and thus became strikingly similar to the authoritarian menace it tried to destroy. On the other hand, the North Korean students' displays of wealth at the Tehran Foreign School was strikingly at odds with the DPRK's anti-capitalist discourse and highlights the bourgeoisie culture of the North Korean elite.

The Tehran Foreign School was one of the few places in the Cold War world where the fears and anxieties of the two Koreas were played out on a daily basis. North and South Korean students uneasily passed each other in the school hallways, played near each other on the playground, and sometimes even took classes together. A folder consisting of South Korean students' reports from this school, found in the microfilm of the ROK's Diplomatic Archives, illustrates the degree to which inter-Korean politics influenced the daily lives of these students. Similar to the way in which Carlo Ginzburg read records from inquisition trials "against the grain" to illuminate the worldview of a sixteenth century miller, I also hope to use these students' reports to reveal the behaviors of the children of the North Korean elite who rarely defect or leave written or oral records accessible to the outside observer. This "reading against the grain" of South Korean documents to gain a better understanding of the culture of the North Korean elite is rather unorthodoxly borrowed from Ginzburg's highly influential study, *The Cheese and the Worms*.

Overview of North and South Korean Relations with Iran

In 1962, the ROK established diplomatic relations with Iran. More than ten years later, the DPRK established diplomatic relations with Iran in 1973.[7] Thus, Iran became one of the few countries in the world to hold diplomatic relations with both Koreas at the same time. However, Iran, under the Pahlavi Dynasty, retained closer ties with South Korea while Iraq, under the leadership of Saddam Hussein, had close ties with North Korea. The North Korean ambassador to Iran, Ri Yong-ho, told his Romanian colleagues in 1978, "In its relations with Iran, the DPRK is confronted with South Korean competition. Every time North Korea discusses a problem with Iran, the South Korean embassy was fully informed in the next few days by the Iranians."[8]

From May 20–24, 1978, the vice president of North Korea, Gang Ryang-uk, visited Iran and met with the Shah. However, no joint communiqués or trade agreements were signed. The Romanian embassy in Tehran commented, "North Korea's trade with Iran is almost equal to zero; North Korea's presence in Iran is not felt in any way."[9] On the other hand, Iran was South Korea's largest export market in the Middle East by 1975. In addition, a trade deal was signed in 1975 between Seoul and Tehran, which increased the total volume of bilateral trade from $79 million in 1974 to $158 million in 1975. Between 1975 and 1977, trade more than doubled between Iran and South Korea and reached $350 million in 1977.[10] In addition, large numbers of South Korean workers came to work in Iran. According to a 1978 Romanian embassy in Tehran report, "5000 South Korean qualified workers and technicians were hired in Iran and they work in various economic facilities: building harbors, drivers on trucks, etc."[11] Before the Islamic Revolution, the ROK, compared to the DPRK, had a much stronger presence in Iran.

However, all of that changed in 1979 as the Islamic Revolution changed the nature of Iran's foreign policy. Revolutionary Iran, with its fervent anti-Americanism, naturally gravitated towards the anti-imperialist North Koreans. This relationship was solidified during the early part of the Iran-Iraq War when North Korea supplied $800 million worth of weapons to Iran from 1980 to 1982 and sent three hundred military technicians to Iran in 1984.[12] The Iran-DPRK military trade angered Saddam Hussein who quickly broke off diplomatic relations with the DPRK in October 1980. The North Koreans even lobbied for the location of the 1983 Non-Aligned Movement Summit to be moved from Baghdad to Pyongyang. North Korean diplomats and publication spread rumors that Baghdad was a dangerous place and that a summit there would endanger the safety of foreign heads of state.[13]

The North Koreans continued to strengthen its military relations with Revolutionary Iran during the 1980s. Al-Seyassa, a Kuwaiti newspaper, reported that DPRK weapon supplies to Iran amounted to $400 million in 1983.[14] An Iraqi military commander noted, "We know the countries that help Iran and support it with arms, such as North Korea. Not only this, but we have captured a number of North Koreans and Libyans, who have fought, side by side, with Iranians."[15] The Iraqi ambassador in Sri Lanka confirmed to his South Korean colleagues that Iraqi troops had arrested a few North Koreans alongside Iranian soldiers during the war in early 1984.[16] The Iraqi government later discovered that several experts from the DPRK helped the Iranians produce mustard gas and a nerve agent, called *Tabun*.[17] In return for providing weapons and military assistance, Pyongyang received large amounts of crude oil from Tehran. Economic and political cooperation agreements signed in 1984 between Iran and the DPRK stated that the North Koreans would receive 1 million tons of oil, which was valued at $2 million U.S. dollars, in exchange for providing $50 million U.S. dollars worth of steel and $150 million dollars worth of weapons to Iran.[18] North Korea's ample supply of wartime materials fueled the Iranian war machine and the Ayatollah Khomeini was all too willing to participate in barter trade with the foreign oil-dependent North Koreans.

Rumors spread in 1984 that China used North Korea as a medium to sell weapons and military equipment to Iran. *The Washington Post* reported on April 2, 1984 that Tehran agreed to pay Beijing $1.3 billion in spring of 1983 for fighter jets, tanks, artillery, and light arms over a three-year period. Anonymous sources in Beijing also told *The Washington Post* that Iran agreed to let the Chinese inspect Soviet-made weapons captured from the Iraqis during the war. According to an Arab analyst quoted in *The Washington Post* article, "North Korea can do nothing without getting the green light from

China."[19] This Cold War-era mindset that small nations could do nothing without approval from their superpower patrons neglects the agency of Pyongyang in navigating the complexities of regional military conflicts.

While Iran engaged in close military cooperation with the North Koreans, South Korea was essentially kicked to the corner. An Iranian-South Korean joint venture between the National Iranian Oil Company and the Korean Ssangyong Cement Industrial Company was cancelled in 1980. The Iran-Iraq War also had larger consequences for South Korean export trade to the Middle East. In the period between 1972–1977, the Middle East accounted for 12 percent of South Korea's total export trade. By 1986, it decreased to less than half and the region made up only 5.2 percent of South Korea's export trade. Nonetheless, around 2,000 South Korean workers remained in Iran and worked on industrial projects, such as the Tabriz power plant, the Shiraz petrochemical plant, and the Bafg-Bandar railway.[20]

The Iran-Iraq War changed the nature of Iran's relations with the two Koreas. Tehran's shift from Seoul to Pyongyang was based on North Korea's ample supply of weapons and willingness to sell them to the Ayatollah Khomeini. Nonetheless, South Korean workers remained in the Islamic Republic and continued to design and build Iranian infrastructure. The situation of wartime Iran led to the creation of a divisive Korean community at the Tehran Foreign School, which became one of the few spaces in the Cold War world where North and South Koreans interacted on an everyday basis. Thus, the North and South Korean students at the Tehran Foreign School uniquely became part of a war within a war.

North and South Korean Students at the Tehran Foreign School

On April 5, 1983, the children of North Koreans living in Tehran transferred from the Pakistani School to the Tehran Foreign School due to "the poor quality" of instruction at the Pakistani school. However, only one of the North Korean students, a ninth grader, was placed in the same class as South Korean students. Nonetheless, the sudden appearance of seven North Korean students at the Tehran Foreign School put the ROK embassy in Tehran on high alert. They worried that the administrators and teachers at the Tehran Foreign School might not understand the nuances of inter-Korean relations so clashes would break out between the North and South Korean students.[21]

The embassy quickly summoned the parents of the eleven South Korean students and formed a special committee for rapid communication between the two parties. The embassy and the parents also agreed to meet once a month to discuss the North Korean situation at the school. The students and their parents were also invited to a luncheon on April 29, 1983 at the ROK diplomatic residence. The embassy saw the parents as vital conduits of information on the North Korean students at the Tehran Foreign School and also for uplifting the national pride of their children.[22] The embassy also established "protective measures" for the students, such as holding a monthly meeting in which the students would watch a propaganda film on the ROK and learn what to do when encountering a North Korean student.[23] These monthly anti-communist "training" sessions for the students were designed to "instill a sense of superiority over the North Korean puppet regime."[24] In one of these sessions, the ROK embassy explained the "miserable living conditions" in North Korea and compared the economic power between the two countries. They also watched South Korean news and a film about the Korean War.[25]

The South Korean students also had to follow strict rules regarding contact with the North Korean students. The first rule stated, "When our students encounter North Korean students, they should be very proud and behave naturally and they should try to outperform the North Korean students in all activities including academic areas."[26] The code of conduct also stated that students "should look closely at the actions of the North Korean students and report them to the embassy through the Vice Principal of the Korean school as often as possible."[27] The code also told students "to avoid direct confrontation with the North Korean students at all costs and when there is a possibility a problem could occur, tell the teachers and seek help." Korean cultural traditions regarding age and hierarchy also played a role in the code of conduct. For example, the code stated that "older students should protect younger students from provocative acts and the younger students should follow the older students' orders." They were told to go and come from school in groups of two to three students. The South Korean students were also told to not have needless conversations with the North Korean students and to never visit their homes. In addition, the rules prohibited the exchange of gifts between South and North Korean students. The last rule said, "If a North Korean student criticizes South Korea or says false propaganda, refute the message in a calm and logical way. Do not get into a physical confrontation."[28] The South Korean students at the Tehran Foreign School became pseudo-fighters on the frontline of the propaganda war with the North Koreans.

The majority of students, around 80 percent, at the Tehran Foreign School came from Taiwan.[29] This pleased ROK embassy officials as they thought having students from an allied Asian anti-communist nation at the same school would reduce the possibility of communist indoctrination by the North Korean students. However, soon after the North Korean students arrived at the Tehran Foreign School, South Korean students reported that the Taiwanese students were "slowly forming a close relationship with the North Korean students."[30] Thus, the ROK embassy urged its students to quickly befriend the Taiwanese students. The parents of the South Korean students even got involved as the parent representatives of the Tehran Foreign School's students requested cooperation from the Taiwanese students' parents in regard to the inter-Korean conflict at the school. The embassy also hoped to strengthen South Korean students' relations with other foreign students by holding parties, film showings, and distributing propaganda materials.[31]

The ROK embassy in Tehran depicted the Tehran Foreign School as not only an educational institution but also as a battlefield of ideas. The embassy stated, "There is a psychological war going on between the South Korea and North Korean students."[32] Students reported back to the embassy their analysis of North Korean students' movements. For example, South Korean students reported, "In and out of school, the North Korean students always have a communalistic behavior."[33] Since students from the two Koreas were prohibited from interacting with one another, the South Korean students reported that the North Koreans formed friendships with other foreign students in order to learn about the personal information of the South Korean students.[34] The details recorded within these students' reports illustrate the degree to which the ROK government, as a whole, feared North Korean influence.

The South Korean student closely monitored the clothing, material purchases, and transportation of the North Korean students at the Tehran Foreign School, which they later relayed to the ROK embassy. For example, the South Korean students reported that all North Korean female students wore Islamic outfits and that the seventh grade North Korean student routinely wore perfume. The South Koreans also noted that the ninth grade North Korean student did not wear a Kim Il Sung pin, which was typically required for all North Korean citizens.[35] The North Koreans also took a Mercedes Benz going to and from school or would sometimes walk together to school. On the other hand, all the other students, including the South Koreans, at the Tehran Foreign School rode on a school bus. The South Korean students suspected that one North Korean student was responsible for distributing money to all the other North Korean students for school supplies and lunches.[36]

In addition to being closely monitored by the South Koreans, the North Korean students were also being closely monitored by their own government. South Korean students noticed that North Koreans usually possessed notebooks "in which they recorded something" and that an eight grade North Korean student who wore a suit and put grease in his hair looked much older than the rest. The South Korean students' report stated, "Visibly, he looks twenty years old. In behavior, you can see many differences so it is assumed that he is the student responsible for monitoring the others."[37] The observation, recording, and reporting conducted within the walls of the Tehran Foreign School was indicative of the general lack of trust between the two Korean governments. Each side tried to gain an advantage over the other so the frontlines of the Korean conflict, whether it was the DMZ or an international school in Iran, became highly contested spaces of legitimacy and superiority.

The South Korean government tried to protect all their students at the Tehran Foreign School from North Korean influence. However, they were especially concerned with the safety of their female students. This can be traced to traditional Korean cultural stereotypes surrounding female fragility and their supposed need for male protection.[38] The South Korean students reported, "North Korean male students come near our country's female students" and that "North Korean male students followed South Korean female students."[39] This focus on North Korean aggression also reflects South Korean fears of unprovoked actions from the DPRK, whether it be at the Tehran Foreign School or the DMZ. The memory of the North Korean invasion in June 1950 still lingered in the background of inter-Korean relations and influenced South Koreans' perceptions of North Koreans.[40]

The South Korean students also noticed that the North Korean students repeatedly showed off their new purchases. For example, it was reported that a North Korean female student flaunted her new blouse and skirt in front of her South Korean classmates. Meanwhile, an eighth grade North Korean student was driving a white Mercedes Benz near the school and when he spotted South Korean students, he pressed on the gasoline. South Korean students "cleared their throats" when they saw a first grade North Korean student riding in the passenger's seat of the Mercedes Benz.[41] The South Korean students' reports portrayed the North Korean students as being reckless and materialistic. This countered propaganda from the DPRK that depicted North Koreans as being selfless, highly disciplined believers of socialism. The fact that North Koreans could not represent the virtue of their political system abroad strengthened the ROK's claims for legitimacy and exposed the materialistic culture of the North Korean elite.

South Korean performance in the classroom was the area that primarily concerned the ROK embassy in terms of competitiveness vis-à-vis the North Korean students. According to South Korean students' reports, the North

Korean students at the Tehran Foreign School were more interested in the belongings of the South Korean students than performing well in the classroom. On May 12, 1983 at a meeting held between the parents of the South Korean students and the ROK diplomatic personnel in Tehran, the parents relayed the message to the ROK embassy that "North Korean students have become more active but they skip school and do not behave well in classes."[42] They also reported that a seventh grade North Korean female student was continuously absent and that a ninth grade North Korean female student was often sent to the principal's office for not bringing her books to class and "problematic classroom behavior."[43]

Besides not behaving well in classes, the North Koreans were also suspected of stealing from the South Koreans. For example, on April 24, 1983, a South Korean student noticed that his homework went missing. Other students, within the vicinity of where the incident happened, reported that North Korean students took it. A week later, a South Korean student accidentally left English language books related to South Korea, titled, "Facts about Korea," "Korea," and "My Country," in the locker room. When he went back to retrieve them, they were gone. The student speculated that a North Korean student took the books. The ROK embassy urged South Korean students to not take materials distributed by the embassy to school since the North Koreans might steal them.[44] This bandit-like character of the North Korean students stands at odds with the DPRK propaganda's official portrayal of North Koreans as being extremely moral and virtuous.[45] However, it is also important to acknowledge that South Korean students often had their own self-interests at play. By reporting on the nefarious activities of their North Korean classmates, the South Koreans could carry out their patriotic duties and make their parents proud. Thus, the South Korean students may have falsely blamed their North Korean classmates due to pressure from elders.

The South Korean embassy in Tehran encouraged its students to behave well in school in order to improve their reputation vis-à-vis the North Korean students. The South Korean students reported that the North Koreans had violent outbursts at times. For example, a Taiwanese student splashed a little bit of water on a North Korean student's clothes so the North Korean student hit him in the stomach with a ball. Two North Korean students had also previously shoved a Taiwanese student.[46] In many ways, the South Korean students' reports of the North Koreans at the Tehran Foreign School mirrored the ROK government's views of the North Korean government as a whole. Whether it was at an international school in Iran or at the negotiating table in Panmunjom, the South Koreans saw the North Koreans as inherently violent, untrustworthy, and duplicitous.

The South Korean students' reports included vivid descriptions of the North Korean students' physical abilities and behaviors. For example, they noticed that there were two cases when two North Korean students, a middle schooler and a first grader, went underneath a barbed wire fence to retrieve a ball from a swimming pool.[47] In physical education class, the South Korean students observed that the eighth grade North Korean student "adjusted well" to playing a game of dodgeball and that the North Korean elementary school students excelled at running. The report states, "In terms of behavioral characteristics, the North Koreans are very agile and organized. They are also very brutal."[48] South Korean students' were told by the ROK embassy to observe the North Korean students' physical characteristics and odd behaviors. For example, a South Korean student noticed that the eighth grade North Korean student cut his hand and then bit his hand to drain the blood.[49] They also noted that North Korean students performed military drills during the school year and vacation periods.[50] This suggests the ROK government feared these sons and daughters of the North Korean elite could potentially grow up to be spies or a member of the DPRK military's Special Forces. No detail was too small to go unnoticed in the inter-Korean conflict.

Similar to the way in which the two Korean governments refused to acknowledge the other, North and South Korean students at the Tehran Foreign School mostly ignored each other. For example, the North Korean students ate their lunch in an isolated place outside of the school cafeteria.[51] In many ways, the relations between South and North Korean students at the Tehran Foreign School echoed the relations of their respective governments. South Korean students observed, "The North Korean students are avoiding any conversation with South Korean students, especially during class time. When the teacher lets South Korean students translate, as the North Korean students are not good at English, they would never answer."[52] On another occasion, a North Korean first grade student tried to pick up a piece of candy that was dropped on the ground but he suddenly made eye contact with a South Korean student so he dropped the candy. The North Korean students' decision to ignore the South Koreans even when they offered help or made eye contact suggests that they were directed to do so by their government. South Korean students overheard a conversation between North Korean students in which they said, "Isn't it impossible to not talk to the South Korean students?"[53] Despite the fact that only 120 miles separated the two capital cities, the governments in Seoul and Pyongyang refused to talk to each other or acknowledge the existence of the other. This decision to ignore the other Korean government had reverberations beyond the peninsula, as shown in the lack of communication between North and South Korean students at the Tehran Foreign School.

However, according to the South Korean students' reports, the North Koreans had increasingly displayed friendlier behavior towards the South Koreans in May 1983. The ROK embassy warned its students to "be suspicious of the North Korean students' unusually gentle attitudes." While encounters between students from the two Koreas were kept to a minimum, the few instances of interaction were typically short-lived and full of tension. In the middle of a class, a South Korean student, who was sitting beside a North Korean student, dropped a pen. The North Korean picked up the pen and returned it to the South Korean student. He then showed off his pencil case to the South Korean student. On another occasion, the North Korean students returned a ball to South Korean students playing a game of volleyball. The North Korean students told the South Koreans, "If you run after the ball in the mud, it is dangerous." The ROK embassy concluded, "It seems like the North Korean students have been closely observing South Korean students and have concluded that they are not dangerous."[54] The Taiwanese students at the Tehran Foreign School even mocked the awkward tensions between the North and South Korean students.[55] These fleeting moments of interaction between students from the two Koreas are indicative of the general apprehension that existed between these two countries. Each side thought the other was deceitful and manipulative.

The South Korean students at the Tehran Foreign School were not only representatives of the Republic of Korea's educational system but also important intelligence gatherers for the South Korean government as they recorded the behaviors and actions of their North Korean classmates, which they later reported back to the ROK embassy in Iran. Thus, the South Korean students at the Tehran Foreign School were forced to become part of the broader inter-Korean competition and essentially soldiers on the frontline of the global Korean conflict. Instead of bayonets and rifles, these South Korean soldiers were armed with notebooks and pencils.

While the ROK Foreign Ministry's files on the Tehran Foreign School are rather limited in number and confined to a narrow time period, they nonetheless provide a unique window into the inter-Korean conflict from the ground level. As Richard Hoffman said, microhistory is "is much like the poet William Blake's injunction to see a world in a grain of sand."[56] Similarly, historians can see the inter-Korean conflict encapsulated in the Tehran Foreign School.

The history of the Tehran Foreign School is shrouded in mystery. However, it appears that the school was closed in the mid–1980s and most of the foreign students living in Tehran started going to the new Tehran International School in 1985. Holly Dagres, an Iranian-American who attended the Tehran International School from 1999–2006, said that South Korean students also attended this school at the same time but that were no North Korean students present. Dagres noted, "The [South] Korean girls were often cliquish, as in they kept to themselves and mostly spoke in Korean. Occasionally, there'd be a lone [South] Korean girl in a class and she'd make friends with Iranians and other foreigners." According to Dagres, most of the South Korean students were the children of businessmen or diplomats.[57] The brief period of a North and South Korean student presence in Tehran seems to be limited to the 1980s.

Conclusion

The students at the Tehran Foreign School did not arrive out of thin air. They were the products of broader diplomatic relations between Iran and the two Koreas in the 1980s. A May 1989 visit to the DPRK by Iranian president Seyed Ali Khamenei strengthened the revolutionary friendship of the two nations. Over 100,000 North Koreans lined the streets of Pyongyang to welcome Khamenei on May 14, 1989. At a mass rally in Pyongyang, Khamenei said, "We think that the root cause of the instability and disputes existing in the world is the interference of the dominationist forces in others' internal affairs." Khamenei continued, "We believe that foreign armed forces, particularly the military bases of the United States, must be withdrawn from the Persian Gulf and the Korean peninsula and the security in these regions must be guaranteed only by the local nations." Kim Il Sung held a luncheon for Khamenei on May 17, 1989 in which the North Korean leader proclaimed, "The Iranian people are an industrious and courageous people with a long celebrated cultural tradition. Some time ago, the Iranian people celebrated the 10th anniversary of the victorious Islamic revolution which opened up a new epoch in their life." Kim added, "Under the leadership of their outstanding leader His Eminence Ayatollah Imam Khomeini, the Iranian people overthrew despotic monarchism and won victory in the Islamic Revolution."[58] Less than a month after President Khamenei's visit to the DPRK, the Ayatollah suddenly passed away. Perhaps acknowledging his own mortality and declining health, Kim Il Sung visited the Iranian embassy in Pyongyang on June 6, 1989 to pay his condolences to his fallen revolutionary comrade.[59]

Despite the passing of the Ayatollah, North Korea and Iran continued to have strong relations with each other in the post-Cold War era. The most important area of collaboration between Tehran and Pyongyang revolved around ballistic missile development. When Iran test launched a cruise missile from a submarine in May 2017, U.S. intelligence quickly discovered that the submarine was the same type of North Korean submarine that torpedoed the South Korean *Cheonan* navy vessel in 2010. In addition, North Korean and Iranian missiles have been nearly identical. Jeffrey Lewis, a missile proliferation expert at the Middlebury Institute of International Studies at Monterey, also explained, "The very first missiles we saw in Iran were simply copies of North Korean missiles. Over the years, we've seen photographs of North Korean and Iranian officials in each other's countries, and we've seen all kinds of common hardware."[60] While close military ties between Iran and the DPRK increasingly worry U.S. officials, it is important for the U.S. government to understand that the relationship is historically rooted in the Iran-Iraq War of the 1980s and it will take more than sanctions to untangle the two regimes.

Meanwhile, South Korea continued its economic dealings with Iran in the post-Cold War era. South Korean companies began investing in Iran's energy sector during the 2000s. In addition, South Korea's Minister of Foreign Affairs Han Seung Soo visited Iran in August 2001. The two countries also agreed to an investment deal in 2005 in which the two would build a liquefied natural gas project. Despite these economic dealings, political differences hindered any development of close economic ties between the two nations.[61] The two would remain pragmatic economic partners but ideology and militarism remained most important to the Islamist regime in Tehran. Thus, Pyongyang was the more imperative ally for Revolutionary Iran in the post-Cold War era.

Notes

1. Ronald Hoffman quoted in Woodward, "Historians to Debate Value of New Historical Approach."

2. Iggers, *Historiography of the 20th Century*, 143.

3. These inter-Korean interactions during the Cold War era were often violent and deadly. For example, the 1983 North Korean bombing in Rangoon, Burma nearly killed the South Korean president Chun-doo Hwan and the 1987 North Korean bombing of Korean Air flight 585 killed all 115 people on board. However, in 1991, athletes from the two Koreas competed together at the World Table Tennis Championships in Japan and at the World Youth Football Championships in Portugal.

4. Trivellato, "Is There a Future for Italian Microhistory in the Age of Global History?" 3.

5. For two of the most well-known and distinguished works of Italian microhistory, see Ginzburg, *The Cheese and the Worms* and Levi, *Inheriting Power*.

6. Trivellato, "Is There a Future for Italian Microhistory in the Age of Global History?" 20–21.

7. Chung-in Moon, "Between Ideology and Interest: North Korea in the Middle East," in Jae-Kyu Park, B.C Koh, Tae-hwan Kwak, eds., *The Foreign Relations of North Korea: New Perspectives* (Boulder, CO: Westview Press, 1987), 379–410.

8. "TELEGRAM 075.205 from the Romanian Embassy in Tehran to the Romanian Ministry of Foreign Affairs," April 6, 1978, Wilson Center History and Public Policy Program Digital Archive, AMAE, Folder 784/1978, Issue 220: Features of political-diplomatic relations between the Democratic People's Republic of Korea and some countries in Europe, Asia, Africa, America (Cyprus, Spain, USA, Bangladesh, Philippines, India, Indonesia, Japan, Pakistan, Sri Lanka, Central African Republic, Egypt, Gabon, Iraq, Iran, Libya, Nigeria, Mozambique, Syria) January 7, 1978—September 23, 1978. Obtained and translated for NKIDP by Eliza Gheorghe. < http://digitalarchive.wilsoncenter.org/document/116499 > (Accessed April 10, 2017).

9. "TELEGRAM 075.345 from the Romanian Embassy in Tehran to the Romanian Ministry of Foreign Affairs," May 24, 1978, Wilson Center History and Public Policy Program Digital Archive, AMAE, Folder 784/1978, Issue 220: Obtained and translated for NKIDP by Eliza Gheorghe. < http://digitalarchive.wilsoncenter.org/document/116429 > (Accessed April 10, 2017).

10. Azad, "Iran and the two Koreas: A Peculiar Pattern of Foreign Policy," 171.

11. "TELEGRAM 075.345 from the Romanian Embassy in Tehran to the Romanian Ministry of Foreign Affairs," May 24, 1978, Wilson Center History and Public Policy Program Digital Archive, AMAE, Folder 784/1978, Issue 220: Obtained and translated for NKIDP by Eliza Gheorghe. < http://digitalarchive.wilsoncenter.org/document/116429 > (Accessed April 10, 2017).

12. Moon, "Between Ideology and Interest: North Korea in the Middle East," 402.

13. The summit was eventually held in New Delhi, India. "Hungarian Embassy in the DPRK, Report, 11 March 1982. Subject: North Korean activities in the Non-Aligned Movement," March 11, 1982, History and Public Policy Program Digital Archive, MOL, XIX-J-1-j Korea, 1982, 80. doboz, 10, 002796/1982. Obtained and translated for NKIDP by Balazs Szalontai. < http://digitalarchive.wilsoncenter.org/document/116016 > (Accessed April 10, 2017).

14. Al Seyassa, March 17, 1984 found in "Pukhanŭi taeiran kunsa chiwŏn, 1984," March 18, 1984, ROK Diplomatic Archives (Microfilm Roll number) 2014-036/(File number) 16/(Document number) 28.

15. Sawt Al-Shaab Daily News, March 29, 1984 found in "Pukhanŭi taeiran kunsa chiwŏn, 1984," March 30, 1984, ROK Diplomatic Archives 2014-036/16/41–43.

16. "Pukhanŭi taeiran kunsa chiwŏn, 1984," March 2, 1984, ROK Diplomatic Archives 2014–036/16/9.

17. "Letter of General Military Intelligence Directorate about Iranian Use of Chemical Weapons on Iraqi Troops," April 14, 1987, History and Public Policy Program Digital Archive, Conflict Records Research Center, National Defense University, SH-GMID-D-001-125 < http://digitalarchive.wilsoncenter.org/document/111667 > (Accessed April 10, 2017).

18. "Pukhanŭi taeiran kunsa chiwŏn, 1984," June 30, 1984, ROK Diplomatic Archives 2014–036/16/5–6.
19. Weisskopf, "China Secretly Selling Arms to Iran."
20. Azad, "Iran and the two Koreas," 173–175.
21. "Pukhan haksaeng t'eheran oegugin hakkyo iphage ttarŭn taech'aek hyŏbŭi, 1983," April 1983, ROK Diplomatic Archives 2013–0120/17/1–9.
22. "Pukhan haksaeng t'eheran oegugin hakkyo iphage ttarŭn taech'aek hyŏbŭi, 1983," April 14, 1983, ROK Diplomatic Archives 2013–0120/17/15.
23. "Pukhan haksaeng t'eheran oegugin hakkyo iphage ttarŭn taech'aek hyŏbŭi, 1983," April 19, 1983, ROK Diplomatic Archives 2013–0120/17/5.
24. "Pukhan haksaeng t'eheran oegugin hakkyo iphage ttarŭn taech'aek hyŏbŭi, 1983," April 14, 1983, ROK Diplomatic Archives 2013–0120/17/9.
25. "Pukhan haksaeng t'eheran oegugin hakkyo iphage ttarŭn taech'aek hyŏbŭi, 1983," April 22, 1983, ROK Diplomatic Archives 2013–0120/17/19.
26. Pukhan haksaeng t'eheran oegugin hakkyo iphage ttarŭn taech'aek hyŏbŭi, 1983," April 14, 1983, ROK Diplomatic Archives 2013–0120/17/9.
27. Details are hard to gather from the ROK Foreign Ministry documents about this Korean school but it seems that many of the South Korean students also attended a late night Korean school (*hagwon*) in Tehran. This Korean school had a partnership with the Tehran Foreign School.
28. "Pukhan haksaeng t'eheran oegugin hakkyo iphage ttarŭn taech'aek hyŏbŭi, 1983," April 14, 1983, ROK Diplomatic Archives 2013–0120/17/15.
29. On slide 4, the report refers specifically to Taiwanese-based Chinese students as forming the majority at the school. However, in the rest of the documents, the Taiwanese students are referred to as Chinese students. Pukhan haksaeng t'eheran oegugin hakkyo iphage ttarŭn taech'aek hyŏbŭi, 1983," April 17, 1983, ROK Diplomatic Archives 2013–0120/17/4.
30. "Pukhan haksaeng t'eheran oegugin hakkyo iphage ttarŭn taech'aek hyŏbŭi, 1983," April 14, 1983, ROK Diplomatic Archives 2013–0120/17/8.
31. "Pukhan haksaeng t'eheran oegugin hakkyo iphage ttarŭn taech'aek hyŏbŭi, 1983," April 1983, ROK Diplomatic Archives 2013–0120/17/1–10.
32. "Pukhan haksaeng t'eheran oegugin hakkyo iphage ttarŭn taech'aek hyŏbŭi, 1983," April 14, 1983, ROK Diplomatic Archives 2013–0120/17/8.
33. "Pukhan haksaeng t'eheran oegugin hakkyo iphage ttarŭn taech'aek hyŏbŭi, 1983," April 14, 1983, ROK Diplomatic Archives 2013–0120/17/8.
34. "Pukhan haksaeng t'eheran oegugin hakkyo iphage ttarŭn taech'aek hyŏbŭi, 1983," May 12, 1983, ROK Diplomatic Archives 2013–0120/17/30.
35. The Kim Il Sung pins were introduced in the 1970s. See Lankov, *North of the DMZ*, 7.
36. "Pukhan haksaeng t'eheran oegugin hakkyo iphage ttarŭn taech'aek hyŏbŭi, 1983," April 25, 1983, ROK Diplomatic Archives 2013–0120/17/17.
37. "Pukhan haksaeng t'eheran oegugin hakkyo iphage ttarŭn taech'aek hyŏbŭi, 1983," April 14, 1983, ROK Diplomatic Archives 2013–0120/17/8.

38. Park, "Patriarchy in Korean Society: Substance and Appearance of Power," 48–73.
39. "Pukhan haksaeng t'eheran oegugin hakkyo iphage ttarŭn taech'aek hyŏbŭi, 1983," April 25, 1983, ROK Diplomatic Archives 2013–0120/17/17.
40. Kim, *The Unending Korean War*.
41. "Pukhan haksaeng t'eheran oegugin hakkyo iphage ttarŭn taech'aek hyŏbŭi, 1983," May 12, 1983, ROK Diplomatic Archives 2013–0120/17/28–29.
42. "Pukhan haksaeng t'eheran oegugin hakkyo iphage ttarŭn taech'aek hyŏbŭi, 1983," May 12, 1983, ROK Diplomatic Archives 2013–0120/17/24.
43. "Pukhan haksaeng t'eheran oegugin hakkyo iphage ttarŭn taech'aek hyŏbŭi, 1983," May 12, 1983, ROK Diplomatic Archives 2013–0120/17/28.
44. "Pukhan haksaeng t'eheran oegugin hakkyo iphage ttarŭn taech'aek hyŏbŭi, 1983," May 12, 1983, ROK Diplomatic Archives 2013–0120/17/25, 28.
45. Myers, *The Cleanest Race*, 35.
46. "Pukhan haksaeng t'eheran oegugin hakkyo iphage ttarŭn taech'aek hyŏbŭi, 1983," May 12, 1983, ROK Diplomatic Archives 2013–0120/17/28–29.
47. "Pukhan haksaeng t'eheran oegugin hakkyo iphage ttarŭn taech'aek hyŏbŭi, 1983," April 25, 1983, ROK Diplomatic Archives 2013–0120/17/18
48. "Pukhan haksaeng t'eheran oegugin hakkyo iphage ttarŭn taech'aek hyŏbŭi, 1983," May 12, 1983, ROK Diplomatic Archives 2013–0120/17/24, 29.
49. "Pukhan haksaeng t'eheran oegugin hakkyo iphage ttarŭn taech'aek hyŏbŭi, 1983," May 12, 1983, ROK Diplomatic Archives 2013–0120/17/29.
50. "Pukhan haksaeng t'eheran oegugin hakkyo iphage ttarŭn taech'aek hyŏbŭi, 1983," May 12, 1983, ROK Diplomatic Archives 2013–0120/17/9.
51. "Pukhan haksaeng t'eheran oegugin hakkyo iphage ttarŭn taech'aek hyŏbŭi, 1983," April 25, 1983, ROK Diplomatic Archives 2013–0120/17/17.
52. "Pukhan haksaeng t'eheran oegugin hakkyo iphage ttarŭn taech'aek hyŏbŭi, 1983," April 25, 1983, ROK Diplomatic Archives 2013–0120/17/18.
53. "Pukhan haksaeng t'eheran oegugin hakkyo iphage ttarŭn taech'aek hyŏbŭi, 1983," April 25, 1983, ROK Diplomatic Archives 2013–0120/17/18.
54. "Pukhan haksaeng t'eheran oegugin hakkyo iphage ttarŭn taech'aek hyŏbŭi, 1983," May 12, 1983, ROK Diplomatic Archives 2013–0120/17/29.
55. "Pukhan haksaeng t'eheran oegugin hakkyo iphage ttarŭn taech'aek hyŏbŭi, 1983," April 25, 1983, ROK Diplomatic Archives 2013–0120/17/18.
56. Hoffman quoted in Woodward, "Historians to Debate Value of New Historical Approach."
57. Personal communication with Holly Dagres, March 15, 2017. She noted that the Tehran International School was gender segregated. It does not appear that its predecessor, the Tehran Foreign School, was gender segregated.
58. "Iranian President Visits DPRK," May 20, 1989, *The Pyongyang Times*.
59. "President Kim Il Sung Visits Iranian Embassy, Gives Condolences," June 10, 1989, *The Pyongyang Times*.
60. Tomlinson and Griffin, "Pentagon eyes Iran-North Korea military connection."
61. Hunter, *Iran's Foreign Policy in the Post-Soviet Era*, 139–140.

Bibliography

Archival Sources
ROK Diplomatic Archives
Wilson Center History and Public Policy Program Digital Archive

Other Sources
Azad, Shirzad. "Iran and the two Koreas: A Peculiar Pattern of Foreign Policy," *The Journal of East Asian Affairs* 26 (Fall/Winter 2012).
Ginzburg, Carlo. *The Cheese and the Worms: The Cosmos of a Sixteenth-century Miller*, Translated by John Tedeschi and Anne Tedeschi (Baltimore, MD: Johns Hopkins University Press, 1980).
Hunter, Shireen. *Iran's Foreign Policy in the Post-Soviet Era: Resisting the New International Order* (Santa Barbara, CA: ABC-CLIO,LLC).
Iggers, George G. *Historiography of the 20th Century: From Scientific Objectivity to the Postmodern Challenge* (Middletown, CT: Wesleyan University, 1997).
Kim, Dong-Choon. *The Unending Korean War: A Social History*, trans. by Sung-Ok Kim (Larkspur, CA: University of Hawaii Press, 2009).
Lankov, Andrei. *North of the DMZ: Essays on Daily Life in North Korea* (Jefferson, North Carolina: McFarland & Company, Inc., 2007).
Levi, Giovanni. *Inheriting Power: The Story of an Exorcist*, Translated by Lydia G. Cochrane (Chicago: University of Chicago Press, 1988).
Moon, Chung-in. "Between Ideology and Interest: North Korea in the Middle East," in Jae-Kyu Park, B.C. Koh, Tae-hwan Kwak, eds., *The Foreign Relations of North Korea: New Perspectives* (Boulder, CO: Westview Press, 1987).
Myers, B.R. *The Cleanest Race: How North Koreans See Themselves and Why It Matters* (Brooklyn: Melville House, 2011).
Park, Boo Jin. "Patriarchy in Korean Society: Substance and Appearance of Power," *Korea Journal* 41, no. 4 (Winter 2001).
Tomlinson, Lucas, and Jennifer Griffin. "Pentagon eyes Iran-North Korea military connection," May 5, 2017, *Fox News Politics*. < http://www.foxnews.com/politics/2017/05/05/pentagon-eyes-iran-north-korea-military-connection.html > (Accessed January 5, 2017).
Trivellato, Francesca. "Is There a Future for Italian Microhistory in the Age of Global History?," *California Italian Studies* 2, no. 1 (2011), < http://escholarship.org/uc/item/0z94n9hq > (Accessed April 3, 2017).
Weisskopf, Michael. "China Secretly Selling Arms to Iran," *The Washington Post Foreign Service*, 2 April, 1984.
Woodward, Walt. "Historians to Debate Value of New Historical Approach," (October 22, 1999), *UConn Advance*, < http://advance.uconn.edu/1999/991011/10119912.htm > (Accessed April 3, 2017).

CHAPTER FIVE

North Korea's Changing Policy Toward the United Nations

Jie Dong

On September 17, 1991, the United Nation's 46th General Assembly admitted North Korea and South Korea, under the names the Democratic People's Republic of Korea (DPRK) and the Republic of Korea (ROK), as the 160th and 161th members of the United Nations. The simultaneous joining of North and South Korea as two separate members was a significant event for both sides of the Korean peninsula and has had an important ripple effect on Northeast Asia and the rest of the world. To enable this event, North Korea abruptly reversed its previous long-held policy that the two Koreas should join the UN with one joint seat. As late as April 1991, North Korea reiterated its position in the *Rodong Sinmun*, the official newspaper of the Central Committee of the Workers' Party of Korea, that the two Koreas should join the UN as one country. Nonetheless, less than two months later, on May 27th, the DPRK foreign ministry surprised the world by officially announcing that it would seek separate UN membership along with the ROK. It is crucial to investigate why North Korea changed its stand on UN membership so abruptly, abandoning a decades-old policy.

Existing research has focused on the background and accounts of the events leading up to this historical moment, but not on the reasons behind North Korea's abrupt policy change.[1] South Korean scholars have explored a few factors that enabled the two Koreas to join the UN with separate seats. However, these studies have not provided a detailed discussion of this issue. South Korean scholar Kim Hong Nack stated, "The single most important reason for Pyongyang's policy reversal appears to have been China."[2] Still, analysis is lacking regarding how China influenced North Korea on this issue, and more importantly, why China was able to achieve this, since North Korea had held a one Korea policy since the foundation of the DPRK, insisting that separate UN membership would "legitimize the two Koreas" and "perpetuate the division of the two Koreas."[3] This chapter will investigate this issue further by providing a historical account of the reasons for and mechanisms of China's influence. It will also discuss the effect of this influence on the relationship between China and North Korea in the following years. Due to the limited space, this analysis cannot address in detail why China changed its position and stopped opposing South Korea's bid for UN membership, a topic that requires a separate chapter.

The Two Koreas' Policies Towards UN Membership: A Historical Review

The issue of United Nations membership for the two Koreas dates back to 1949, shortly after the division of the Korean peninsula into two political entities in 1948. Both North Korea and South Korea applied to be admitted to the UN as a way of establishing legitimacy for their respective governments. On January 19, 1949, South Korea presented its application for UN membership as the sole legal government in Korea. Consequently, on February 10, North Korea sent a cable to the Security Council, requesting unilateral admission into the UN and opposing South Korea's application on the ground that the latter was an "illegal" government under the occupation of foreign forces.[4] On February 15, the UN Security Council discussed whether to include the membership applications from both Koreas in the official agenda. The U.S. and Soviet Union fought bitterly over this, resulting in South Korea's application being vetoed by the latter, and North Korea's application not even being placed on the official agenda. On December 22, 1951, South Korea filed an application for UN membership for the second time, again presenting itself as the sole legal government of Korea. North Korea also submitted another application on January 2, 1952. Since this was during the Korean War, neither application made it into the official agenda.

Besides these official applications, during the second half of the 1950s, the question of Korea's admission had been intermittently discussed in both the Security Council and the General Assembly.[5] Invariably the result was the same: the U.S. and Soviet Union each used their veto power to block the other side's application. However, the Soviet Union changed its policy of the unilateral membership for North Korea to propose the parallel membership of the two Koreas on September 9, 1957, which was immediately rejected by

Washington. During the 1960s, neither sides of the Korean peninsula paid much attention to UN membership. Only South Korea filed for admission again, in April 1961, again unsuccessfully.

With Cold War frictions on the wane during the 1970s due to détente between the Great Powers, the two Korean governments signed the South and North Korea Joint Statement on July 4, 1972. The statement reached agreement on various principles and other issues concerning the reunification of the Korean peninsula. On June 23, 1973, South Korean president Park Chung-hee announced a special foreign policy declaration, claiming that South Korea would not oppose joining the UN "together" with North Korea if this was the wish of a majority of member states and if it would not stand in the way of eventual unification.[6] This was the first time South Korea officially proposed dual memberships, and it was regarded at the time as an important strategy for unification. North Korea, on the other hand, had an entirely different view; it regarded this proposal as an effort to "legitimize the two Koreas" and "perpetuate the division of the two Koreas."[7] North Korea proposed a confederated format for Korea's UN membership on the same day. Two days later, during an enlarged session of the political bureau of the Central Committee of the Workers' Party of Korea, Chairman Kim Il-sung provided more details about the five principles for unification. They included: (1) resolving the situation of the military confrontation between the South and the North to ease tensions, (2) establishing various joint cooperative enterprises and exchanges, (3) convening a large national conference composed of representatives from various political parties and social organizations, (4) forming "a confederate republic of Goryeo" named after the Goryeo Dynasty, and (5) joining the UN under the single name of the Goryeo Confederated Republic.[8]

On July 29, 1975, South Korea applied for UN membership once again; it had been 14 years since its last attempt. On August 6, South Korea's application did not obtain the necessary nine votes and failed to be placed on the agenda of the Security Council by a vote of seven against, six in favor, with two abstentions.[9] On September 21, South Korea made another effort by sending a letter to the UN secretary-general requesting a review of its case. This effort did not have enough support in the Security Council and failed by a vote of seven to seven, with one abstention.[10] South Korea did not attempt to join the UN again for several years.

During the 1980s, there was little movement to join the UN by either North or South Korea. Instead, the two sides fought with each other, each seeking international support for its cause. In general, South Korea was more active in seeking UN membership throughout this process, while North Korea took no affirmative initiative during this time. North Korea's only two official applications for UN membership entailed counteracting the South Korean applications. It has been pointed out by some South Korean scholars that North Korea was more interested in preventing South Korea's membership than in its own admission.[11]

There were two major reasons for North Korea's objection to South Korea's bids for UN membership. First, North Korea had long insisted on a "one Korea" policy and regarded South Korea's attempt to join the UN as an effort to legitimize the two-Korea model and perpetuate the division of Korea. The second reason, and possibly a more important one, was North Korea's general lack of trust towards the UN. From North Korea's viewpoint, it was the UN that had acted with hostility towards North Korea from the very beginning, and that had, in fact, caused the division of Korean peninsula. Moreover, it was the United Nations Command that North Koreans had fought against during the Korean War. While South Korea obtained observer status in the UN in 1948, North Korea did not become a UN observer until 1971. Thus, North Korea held a consistent policy on the UN membership issue that a separate seat solution was totally unacceptable, and that the only viable means was a joint seat under a federal republic flag.

Primary Reasons for North Korea's UN Policy Change

Multiple factors contributed to the abrupt change in North Korea's UN policy. The fall of communism in eastern Europe and the Soviet Union was a major blow for North Korea. North Korea's economy depended heavily on aid and trade with Soviet bloc countries, and its economy suffered significantly with the fall of the Soviet Union. The fall of the Berlin Wall, the demise of another communist regime, and German reunification was another shock for North Koreans. Finally, the establishment of diplomatic relations between South Korea and the Soviet Union and other Communist Bloc nations, which was done without notifying North Korea, also struck a blow to North Korea politically.[12]

The shift in global politics had an important impact on North Korea. As a response, North Korea made some adjustments in its unification policy, resumed the North-South talks, and made plans to establish dialogue between the two prime ministers. The first talks between North Korean Prime Minister Yon Hyong-muk and South Korean Prime Minister Kang Young-hoon took place in Seoul from September 4–7, 1990. These were the highest-level talks since the division of Korean Peninsula. North Korea proposed three major problems that needed to be resolved: joining the UN with a joint single-seat membership; stopping the South Korea-U.S. joint military exercise named "Team Spirit"; and releasing political prisoners that were jailed for visiting North Korea. The talks didn't achieve much agreement between the two sides. An analysis by China's Ministry of Foreign Affairs pointed out that the talk was more for the purposes of propaganda than a meaningful negotiation; North Korea intended to use the peace talks to improve its international image instead of expecting to reach any agreement with the South.[13] Nevertheless, it is important and interesting to note that North Korea listed the UN membership problem as one of the three major issues, which indicates that it was one of the most important issues for the government.

Shortly after the end of the North-South talks, the 45th UN General Assembly was held in 1990. At the assembly, 155 member states made addresses, and 118 referred to the Korean question. Of these, 71 expressed their support for South Korea's position, whereas only nine states endorsed the North Korean position that opposed two separate UN memberships. Not one member-state supported North Korea's single-seat membership proposal.[14] Thus, South Korea gained substantially greater support from the international community, leveraging its growing influence.[15]

Encouraged by this trend, South Korea further accelerated its efforts to join the UN in January 1991. On April 5, South Korea sent an official government memorandum on obtaining UN membership in 1991 to the UN Security Council. Meanwhile, the government also sent delegations to 37 countries to secure their support. In April, President Gorbachev announced that the Soviet Union would support South Korea's bid for UN membership during his visit to South Korea. All the pieces were falling into place for South Korea.

In response to the diplomatic success of South Korea, North Korea did not stay silent. On April 8, 1991, *Rodong Sinmun* published an editorial, reiterating that the two sides must use the joint-seat formula to join the UN.[16] Apparently, North Korea was not backing down from its position despite dramatic changes in the international situation. Instead, it was clinging more tightly to its agenda. North Korea was likely counting on China's veto of South Korea's proposal. *The People's Daily*, the official newspaper of the Chinese Communist Party, republished *Rodong Sinmun's* editorial the very next day, suggesting that North Korea's confidence in China was not unfounded.[17]

In past decades, the Soviet Union and China had played an important role in North Korea's fight to prevent South Korea from joining the UN. The Soviet Union exercised its veto power multiple times to oppose South Korea's application for UN membership during the 1950s and 1960s. The

PRC replaced the Soviet Union as North Korea's unofficial representative in the UN with the expulsion of Taipei and the assignment of China's seat at the UN and on Security Council to Beijing 1971.[18] Since the Soviet Union had already abruptly changed its policy and announced that it would support South Korea's bid for UN membership, China's attitude was crucial.

North Korea's abrupt position change occurred at the end of May 1991, two months after the *Rodong Sinmun* had issued a statement insisting on a dual admission formula. Chinese Prime Minister Li Peng's visit to North Korea at the invitation of North Korean Prime Minister Yon Hyong-muk in early May was critical. It was obvious that the issue of South Korea's proposal for UN membership was a major item on the agenda. This visit was very important to Pyongyang, and the authorities went out of their way to show hospitality to Premier Li. Upon his arrival on May 3, Pyongyang held a grand ceremony to welcome him with more than half a million people singing and dancing in the streets. Even Premier Li, who was accustomed to this kind of welcome, wrote in his diary that "this is an unprecedented experience for me."[19] *Rodong Sinmun* published an editorial that day entitled "Friendly Messenger from Our Brothers of China," praising Li's visit and China's friendship with North Korea.[20] It was apparent that North Korea was trying its best to thank China for its continuing support.

At the welcoming banquet that evening, Premier Li brought up the matter of South Korea's UN membership issue. Kim Yong-nam, North Korean Vice-Prime Minister and Minister of Foreign Affairs, told Li that, according to an Nippon Hōsō Kyōkai (NHK, Japan Broadcasting Corporation) report, Zhu Liang, the head of the International Liaison Department of the Central Committee of the Communist Party of China (CPC), said China supported North Korea's position on this issue. Premier Li responded that this report on Zhu Liang was not accurate, and that if North Korea couldn't reach an agreement with South Korea on joining the UN, it was possible that South Korea would seek membership on its own, which would put China in an awkward position. The next morning, Premier Li met with Kim Il-sung at Kumsusan Memorial Palace. Although Kim restated his position regarding a joint-seat UN membership solution, Premier Li repeated that China would be put in a difficult position if South Korea filed a unilateral UN application. Kim responded by saying that North Korea was looking at all possible solutions and reassured Premier Li that North Korea "would not embarrass our Chinese comrades."[21]

Premier Li Peng made it clear to Kim Il-sung that China would not veto or oppose South Korea's proposal for UN membership, thus reversing its support of North Korea's position. There were many reasons behind China's decision, including the international sanctions on China after the Tiananmen Square protests in 1989; the political pressures from the U.S. and EU to support South Korea's application; and the ongoing negotiations with South Korea to establish diplomatic relations.[22] Thus, China's attitude change forced North Korea to adjust its long-standing position on this issue.

Likely due to the withdrawal of China's support, North Korea declared officially on May 27 that it would send an official application letter to the UN general-secretary. In the statement, North Korea stated that "as the South Korean authorities insist on their separate UN membership," the government of DPRK "has no choice but to enter the United Nations at the present stage as a step to overcome these temporary difficulties created by the South Korean authorities."[23] The next day, the spokesman of China's Foreign Ministry supported North Korea's declaration by stating that it would help maintain peace and stability in the Korean peninsula.[24] On May 29, *Rodong Sinmun* restated that joining the UN was a measure to "overcome temporary difficulties" and prevent the UN from handling the Korean issues in a partial way.[25] On June 1, Kim Il-sung told Japanese reporters that although North Korea had decided to join the UN, it had not altered its "one Korea" policy, that both sides would eventually hold one UN membership jointly.[26]

Premier Li made an agreement with North Korea to continue discussing and comparing notes on the UN membership issue. From June 17 to 20, China's Foreign Minister Qian Qichen visited Pyongyang and met with North Korea Foreign Minister Kim Yong-nam and Kim Il-sung. Kim Yong-nam asked China to veto South Korea's application in the event that the U.S. vetoed North Korea's application. Qian Qichen explained to Kim the procedure of the UN's membership admission and promised that China would do everything in its power to see that the admission of both sides went smoothly. Kim Il-sung told Qian Qichen that the UN had to admit North Korea and South Korea simultaneously, and that it was crucial to prevent the U.S. from vetoing North Korea's application. Kim emphasized that North Korea would not put China in a difficult position and embarrass China on the UN membership issue, and asked China to return the favor. Qian Qichen repeatedly stressed that North Korea had nothing to be worried about.[27] It is obvious that although North Korea reluctantly accepted the simultaneous admission to the UN with South Korea, it still lacked trust towards the UN. Apparently, China was able to convince North Korea to move forward with its UN application largely because Beijing's influence on Pyongyang was still paramount during this period.

After Qian Qichen's visit, North Korea filed an official application to join the UN on July 9. South Korea submitted its application on August 5. On

September 17, North Korea and South Korea were simultaneously admitted to the UN.

How was North Korea Persuaded?

Although it is clear North Korea was "persuaded" by China to reverse its longstanding policy regarding UN membership, it is interesting to investigate how China influenced North Korea, and why China was able to do so. The last few years of the Cold War were difficult ones for both China and North Korea. China was facing its biggest challenges after its reforms and the process of opening up to the world. The Tiananmen Square protests of 1989, commonly known in China as the June 4 incident, shook the legitimacy of the Communist Party's rule. The subsequent sanctions and blockade from the Western world and the fall of the Eastern Bloc left China isolated. At the same time, North Korea was suffering an economic meltdown and consequently lost its advantage and initiative on the Korean reunification issue. These challenges would bring China and North Korea closer.

The Chinese government was widely denounced by the world after the Tiananmen Square protests. Isolated internationally, China was in desperate need of international support and North Korea stepped in. It sent a delegation led by Vice Chairman Lee Jong-ok to celebrate the 40th anniversary of the People's Republic of China on October 1, 1989. The North Korean delegation received a warm welcome by Chinese leaders, including Deng Xiaoping and the newly appointed General Secretary of the Communist Party of China, Jiang Zemin.[28] Soon after, China sent a Foreign Ministry delegation to North Korea to celebrate the 40th anniversary of the establishment of diplomatic relations between the two allies. North Korean Prime Minister Yon Hyong-muk praised China's handling of the Tiananmen Square protests and stated that the relationship between North Korea and China was a "special relationship unlike any other," indestructible by any means.[29]

From November 5 to 7, North Korean leader Kim Il-sung paid an unofficial visit to China. He was the first foreign leader to visit China after the Tiananmen Square protests. Kim had two agendas: to discuss the unsettling situation in Eastern Europe with Chinese leader Deng Xiaoping and meet with new generation of Chinese leaders. Regarding the international situation, Deng gave Kim three suggestions: observe calmly, secure our position, and cope with affairs patiently. Deng admitted that the situation in the Soviet Union was very uncertain, but that the most important thing for China and North Korea was to reinforce socialist ideology and uphold the leadership of the Communist Party. Deng introduced Jiang Zemin to Kim and told

Kim the new leadership team of China—including Jiang, Li Peng, and Yang Shangkun—would handle affairs from then on.[30]

Kim's visit to China was an important gesture of support. China expressed its gratitude by holding an unusual welcoming ceremony at the railway station led by Deng Xiaoping himself, with the participation of four members of the standing committee of the political bureau. Deng and Jiang even boarded the train to welcome Kim Il-sung, which moved Kim. During Kim's visit, he met with almost all members of the political bureau who were in Beijing. Traditionally, China's media did not report on unofficial visits of leaders to China, but this time was different. Media outlets from both China and North Korea conducted joint reporting on this visit, and People's Daily published a headline news on Kim's visit on November 13.[31] Evidently, Kim's visit strengthened the relationship between North Korea and China.

China quickly returned the favor. In March 1990, General Secretary Jiang Zemin visited North Korea, his first international visit after his appointment to the position. Kim Il-sung, who was already 78 years old, welcomed Jiang at the airport. Hundreds of thousands of North Koreans stretched 12 km on Pyongyang's streets to greet Jiang. Jiang met many important North Korean leaders during his visit.[32]

With the worsening of the situation in Eastern Europe and the Soviet Union, North Korea needed China's support on reunification and Soviet-DPRK relations more than ever. In September 1990, while China was preparing for the 1990 Asian Games in Beijing, North Korea requested an urgent visit by Kim Il-sung to China. After negotiations, the meeting place was set in Shenyang. This urgent trip was triggered by the bad news brought by the Soviet Foreign Minister during his visit to Pyongyang earlier that month that the Soviet Union would soon establish a diplomatic relationship with South Korea. North Korea needed reassurance that China would not do the same. During the meeting, Jiang Zemin clearly stated that China would not establish diplomatic ties with South Korea, but that a trade office with South Korea was under consideration. Jiang pointed out that it was a necessary step for China to maintain and strengthen its special position in the Korean peninsula, and that consequently it was better for the stability and eventual reunification of the two Koreas, given the fact that trade between China and South Korea was more than three billion dollars per year and growing.[33]

China had been trying to achieve an understanding from North Korea on the trade office with South Korea issue for a while. In November 1988, China's Foreign Minister Qian Qichen discussed the issue with North Korean Foreign Minister Kim Young-nam during Kim's visit to China. Qian informed Kim that China was considering setting up trade offices with South

Korea. Due to North Korea's strong opposition, China did not move forward.[34] However, in April 1989, Deng Xiaoping asked then general secretary Zhao Ziyang to forward a message to Kim Il-sung during Zhao's visit to North Korea about the trade office issue. Deng said that China had already lost many opportunities to establish a strong economic relationship with South Korea because of North Korea's opposition, and that it was time for China to move forward on this issue, although China would continue its political support of North Korea.[35] North Korea remained stubbornly opposed. Kim Il-sung again expressed his opposition during his visit to China in November 1989. Kim said, "I am not against China doing business and trade with South Korea, but please do not set up a trade office with them. If China set up a trade office in South Korea, then all socialist countries would all have trade offices in South Korea, it would put North Korea in an isolated and difficult position."[36] Jiang Zemin agreed to postpone a decision on this issue after hearing Kim's plea. Finally, during his visit to China in September 1990, Kim backed down and told Chinese leaders that he understood their position. Kim said he would no longer oppose China setting up a trade office in South Korea, but it was essential that China would not establish a diplomatic relationship with South Korea. China agreed.[37] After obtaining North Korea's understanding, China and South Korea quickly reached agreement on the trade office issue and the offices were established in early 1991 in Beijing and Seoul.

Kim Il-sung's "major concessions" on the China-South Korea trade office issue constituted a typical "retreat in order to advance" political maneuver. Kim realized that China was determined to establish the trade office with South Korea and used this issue as a bargaining chip to obtain a promise to not establish a diplomatic relationship with the South. In the meantime, South Korea's "Northern Policy" of reaching out to traditional allies of North Korea was bearing fruit, and North Korea's response was a very passive one: stalling or attempting to slow the pace of South Korea's agenda.[38] When this strategy did not work—as evidenced by the fact that eastern European countries had established diplomatic relationships with South Korea and the Soviet Union was about to do the same—China was North Korea's last hope of avoiding complete international embarrassment. Therefore, North Korea was willing to give up almost anything to retain a small measure of pride. It was due to this situation that China managed to persuade North Korea in 1991 to reverse its position on UN membership; at this point, China was the only friend North Korea had left in the socialist bloc.

A related issue was that North Korea was depending on China more and more economically. With the fall of the Soviet Bloc, North Korea lost the bulk of its economic aid and its entire foreign trade system was left in chaos; trade with the Soviet Union had made up half of North Korea's entire foreign trade until 1989.[39] On September 20, 1991, Soviet Deputy Foreign Minister Kunadze made an appointment to meet the North Korean Ambassador in Moscow and criticized North Korea's failure to honor the two countries' trade agreement. At that time, North Korea owed almost three billion rubles to the Soviet Union. Kunadze informed the North Korean ambassador that it would be reevaluating economic and military relations with North Korea because of domestic pressure coming.[40]

During his visit to North Korea in May 1991, Li Peng noticed the difficult economic situation of North Korea, mentioning in his diary that the country was having trouble feeding its people. Kim Il-sung admitted that North Korea's economy was in trouble due to the cessation of trade with the Soviet Union and eastern Europe during his November 1991 visit to China. There was a shortage of oil and coal, and Kim estimated that it would continue for two more years. Kim wanted China to help North Korea develop hydroelectric power on the Yalu River. He did not want to change the trade relationship between North Korea and China from barter trade to direct trade. Li Peng agreed that the trade status would remain unchanged—part of it was barter and part of it was direct trade—but China wanted North Korea to improve its commitment to trade contracts.[41]

In fact, China had continuously supported North Korea with economic aid. From 1986 to 1990, China provided 150 million RMB economic and military aid to North Korea each year. After the expiration of the aid, China agreed to continue this 150 million per year support from 1991 to 1995.[42] Beyond this ongoing aid, China also tried its best to fulfill North Korea's other needs. For example, Kim Il-sung told Chinese leaders in his 1990 visit that since the Soviet Union had stopped providing aviation gasoline to North Korea, their pilots could not even perform regular training. Kim requested 150,000 tons of aviation gasoline from China and Deng Xiaoping personally instructed China's economic and trade department to fulfill the request, even though China also had an inadequate supply for itself.[43] From an economic standpoint, North Korea needed China more than ever.

Finally, China was helping North Korea to join the international community. Besides urging it to join the UN along with South Korea, China also tried to help North Korea establish a relationship with Japan and the U.S. In October 1990, Kim Il-sung informed China that North Korea was making progress with Japan and there would soon be a negotiation on establishing diplomatic relations.[44] Unfortunately, this negotiation didn't bear much fruit. In early April 1991, Premier Li Peng urged Japanese Foreign Minister

Taro Nakayama to establish a diplomatic relationship with North Korea. Li Peng pointed out that a normal relationship with North Korea from Japan would make the former feel less isolated and this was beneficial to the peace and stability of the Korean peninsula.[45] Kim Il-sung informed China during his November 1991 visit about the progress regarding the normalization of relations with Japan. Kim told Chinese leaders that although there had been a few rounds of talks, it was not easy to achieve a diplomatic relationship because Japan's autonomy was limited by its alliance with the United States.[46]

In November 1991, after both Koreas were admitted to the UN, Kim Il-sung visited China for the last time. General Secretary Jiang Zemin congratulated Kim on obtaining UN membership and stated his wish that the fourth round of South-North talks between the prime ministers would generate positive results. Jiang also stated that China supported North Korea's reunification formula under a Koryo federal republic.[47] Deng Xiaoping had already stopped meeting with foreign guests, but he made an exception for Kim. Deng told Kim that although the international communist movement was hitting a low point, there was still hope for global socialism as long as they held firm to their beliefs and continued developing their economies.[48] Before Kim's return, he told Jiang Zemin, "Other countries said that since North Korea has joined the UN, China would soon establish diplomatic relations with South Korea. I told my comrades, China would not do so. Last year I told Comrade Jiang Zemin, please, do not establish diplomatic relations with South Korea before the United States recognizes us."[49] Jiang reassured Kim by saying that China remembered all conversations with North Korea, and that it would only pursue a non-government trade relationship with South Korea. On the train back to North Korea, Secretary of the Central Committee of the Workers' Party of Korea Kim Yong-sun met alone with Zhu Liang, head of the International Liaison Department of the Central Committee of the CPC, to confirm that Jiang Zemin had honored his oral commitment and that North Korea did not need to worry. The purpose of Kim's trip to China had been the commitment of China to "only establish a non-government trade relationship with South Korea." Jiang's reassurance finally satisfied Kim.

North Korea was very happy with the results of this visit, claiming that it had achieved a new climax in its friendship with China. An editorial on Rodong Sinmun stated that the people of both China and North Korea "support each other's endeavor to reunify its own country," North Korea objected to the idea of "two Chinas" and supported the "one country, two systems" principle that Chinese leaders had articulated.[50]

Conclusion

In Sino-DPRK relations, China is much more powerful than North Korea. However, this unbalanced position did not lead to North Korea's political dependence on China. On the contrary, due to complicated geopolitical and ideological issues, China has sometimes been manipulated by North Korea—a phenomenon often described as tail wagging the dog. Since the deterioration of political and ideological relations between China and USSR and the eventual and inevitable Sino-USSR split, China was eager to earn North Korea's political support. As a direct result, China had to tolerate North Korea's unstable, pragmatic, and opportunistic policies. Therefore, North Korea was able to take a manipulative role in its relations to China.[51]

In this way, the case of North Korea being persuaded by China to join the UN simultaneously with South Korea was an exception. In spite of this, North Korea never abandoned its "one Korea" policy. North Korea's reversal of its joint-seat UN membership proposal was a reluctant move and the result of the realization that it could not prevent South Korea from joining the UN alone. North Korea hoped that China would not establish a diplomatic relationship with South Korea, or at least postpone it, in exchange for its concession to China on the UN membership issue. China played an important role in persuading North Korea to adopt this policy change. From China's standpoint, it was the first step towards cross recognition of both sides of Korean Peninsula. It effectively enabled China to establish diplomatic relations with South Korea while maintaining its own "one China" policy. From this viewpoint, North Korea's joining the UN simultaneously with South Korea was actually more important to China than to North Korea.

After the fall of the eastern bloc and before the establishment of diplomatic relations between China and South Korea, the Sino-DPRK relationship was unbalanced: North Korea needed China's support more than China needed North Korea's. To maintain the special relationship with China, and particularly to delay China's establishing formal relationship with South Korea as long as possible, North Korea was willing to show cooperation with China and make certain concessions. In other words, as long as China did not establish diplomatic relationship with South Korea, which was the bottom-line for North Korea, China was capable of influencing North Korea to a certain degree. Although this influence would not be a lasting one, China might have been able to use this influence to help North Korea normalize its relations with the United States, Japan, and South Korea, and eventually become a member of international community.

Notes

1. Pak, *Korea and the United Nations*; Jonsson, *South Korea in the United Nations*; Kim, "Bukhan ui UN gaib ijeon gwa ihu ui bigyoleur jungsimeulo," 91–103; Lee, "bukhan ui UN gaib gyeoljeong gwa tongil ui jeonmang," 240–249; Kim, "Bukhan ui UN gaib seoneon gaehyeok ui sijakingan—UN gaib gyeorjeong baegyeong gwa daenae byeonhwa jeonmang," 86–88; Caoliqin, "Beinan chaoxian jiaru lianheguo hou de chaoxian bandao tongyi wenti"; Lin Xiaoguang, "chaoxian beinan shuangfang jiaru lianheguo de jiannan lichen."

2. Jonsson, "South Korea in the United Nations," 58.

3. "Jin Richeng tong Bajisitan yisilan gongheguo jizhe de tanhua (Conversation between Kim Il Sung and the Pakistani journalist)," 27 May 1976, Pyongyang: Waiguowen chubanshe,1976.

4. UN Doc. S/1247;GAOR: Fourth Session, 1949,Suppl, No. 2 (A/945), 85–86.

5. South Korea's UN membership was discussed for: once in 1954, 3 times in 1955, twice in 1957, and once in 1958; North Korea's UN membership was discussed for: twice in 1957, once in 1958. Pak, *"Korea and the United Nations,"* 64–66.

6. *JoongAng Daily*, 24 June 1973.

7. "Jin Richeng tong Bajisitan yisilan gongheguo jizhe de tanhua (Conversation between Kim Il Sung and the Pakistani journalist)," 27 May 1976, Pyonyang: Waiguowen chubanshe, 1976.

8. Kim, "Guanyu zuguo tongyi wuda fangzhen," 213.

9. UN Doc. S/11828.

10. UN Doc. S/PV 1842, 20 September 1975, 4.

11. Chi Young Pak, *Korea and the United Nations*, 67.

12. In February 1989, Hungary became the first socialist country to break the taboo and established diplomatic relations with South Korea. Subsequently Poland (November 1989), Yugoslavia (December 1989), Czechoslovakia (March 1990), Bulgaria (March 1990), Romania (March 1990) established diplomatic relations with South Korea. Finally on September 30 1990, the Soviet Union also established diplomatic relations with South Korea.

13. "Chaoxian beinan zongli juxing shouci huitan (The first round of talks between North and South Korean prime minister)," 11 September 1990, People's Republic of China Foreign Ministry (PRCFM), *Xin Qingkusng (The New Situation)*.

14. Pak, *Korea and the United Nations*, 66.

15. Compared to North Korea, South Korea was in a historically strong position in all fields such as economy, international diplomacy and support, and even military power at that time. South Korea had the world's 12th largest trade and an economy 10 times larger than that of the North. The successful 1988 Summer Olympic Games in Seoul also boosted South Korea's confidence tremendously. The "Northern Policy" proposed by South Korean president Roh Tae-woo, which aimed to reach out to North Korea's traditional allies, also gave South Korea an advantage in international support.

16. *Rodong Sinmun*, 8 April 1991.
17. *Renmin Ribao (People's Daily)*, 9 April 1991.
18. Shen, "Miandui lishi jiyu: zhongmei guanxi hejie yu zhongchao guanxi (1971–1974) (Facing historical opportunities: Sino–US relations reconciliation and Sino–DPRK relations)," 10.
19. Li, *Heping Fazhan Hezuo: Lipeng waishi riji (LiPeng's Diary on Foreign Affairs)*, 338.
20. *Rodong Sinmun*, 3 May 1991.
21. Li, *Heping Fazhan Hezuo*, 338, 347.
22. Jonsson, *South Korea in the United Nations*, 57.
23. *Renmin Ribao*, 29 May 1991.
24. *Renmin Ribao*, 29 May 1991.
25. *Rodong Sinmun*, 29 May 1991.
26. *Renmin Ribao*, 5 June 1991.
27. Qian, *Waijiao shiji (Ten Episodes in China's Diplomacy)*, 153–154; *Renmin Ribao*, 18 June 1991.
28. *Renmin Ribao*, 1 October 1989; *Renmin Ribao*, 2 October 1989; *DXNP,1975–1997*, 1291; *Renmin Ribao*, 4 October 1989.
29. *Renmin Ribao*, 15 October 1989.
30. *DXNP*, 1294–1295; Zhonggong zhongyang duiwai lianluobu bangongting: *Zhonglianbu laobulingdao tan dangde duiwai gongzuo (Former Officials of the International Liaison Department of the Central Committee of the C.P.C on Foreign Affairs)*, 2004, 185.
31. Zhonggong zhongyang duiwai lianluobu bangongting: *Zhonglianbu laobulingdao tan dangde duiwai gongzuo (Former Officials of the International Liaison Department of the Central Committee of the C.P.C on Foreign Affairs)*, 180, 189; *Renmin Ribao (People's Daily)*, 13 November 1989.
32. *Renmin Ribao (People's Daily)*, 15 March 1990; 16 March 1990.
33. Zhonggong zhongyang duiwai lianluobu bangongting: *Zhonglianbu laobulingdao tan dangde duiwai gongzuo (Former Officials of the International Liaison Department of the Central Committee of the C.P.C on Foreign Affairs)*, 194.
34. Qian Qichen, *Waijiao shiji*, 152.
35. Zhonggong zhongyang duiwai lianluobu bangongting: *Zhonglianbu laobulingdao tan dangde duiwai gongzuo (Former Officials of the International Liaison Department of the Central Committee of the C.P.C on Foreign Affairs)*, 106–107.
36. Ibid., 187.
37. Ibid., 195.
38. In September 1990, the Foreign Minister of Soviet Union informed North Korea during his visit that Soviet Union would establish diplomatic relationship with South Korea. North Korea requested Soviet Union delay this by two years, so that North Korea would be in a better position on the discussion table of South–North prime minister talks. (Zhonggong zhongyang duiwai lianluobu bangongting: *Zhonglianbu laobulingdao tan dangde duiwai gongzuo (Former Officials of the International Liaison Department of the*

Central Committee of the C.P.C on Foreign Affairs), 193.) In April 1991, Chinese president Yang Shangkun visited Pyongyang to celebrate Kim Il–sung's birthday. During his visit, Yang informed North Korea that China was considering establishing diplomatic relationship with South Korea. Kim Il–sung also requested China delay it by another year. (Yanjing, "Lishi de xuanze," *Baogao Wenxue (Reportage)*, 2008(1).)

39. Armstrong, "Fraternal Socialism," 170.
40. Conversation briefing between Kunadze and the North Korea ambassador, 20 September 1991, ГАРФ, ф.10026, оп.4. д.2803, л.1–3.
41. Li Peng, *Heping Fazhan Hezuo: Lipeng waishi riji (Li Peng's Diary on Foreign Affairs)*, 349–350.
42. Zhonggong zhongyang duiwai lianluobu bangongting: *Zhonglianbu laobulingdao tan dangde duiwai gongzuo (Former Officials of the International Liaison Department of the Central Committee of the C.P.C on Foreign Affairs)*, 102–103.
43. Ibid., 195, 213.
44. *Renmin Ribao (People's Daily)*, 6 October 1990; 8 October 1990.
45. "Li Peng zongli huijian sulian waizhang riben waiwudachenshide tanhua qingkuang" (Prime minister Li Peng's Talks with Foreign Ministers of the Soviet union and Japan), 25 April 1991, People's Republic of China Foreign Ministry (PRCFM), *Waishi Dongtai (The Foreign Affairs Dynamic)*, 1991(5).
46. Zhonggong zhongyang duiwai lianluobu bangongting: *Zhonglianbu laobulingdao tan dangde duiwai gongzuo (Former Officials of the International Liaison Department of the Central Committee of the C.P.C on Foreign Affairs)*, 203.
47. Ibid., 204.
48. DXNP, 1332; Zhang Tingyan, "Deng xiaoping guanxin chaoxian bandao jushi," *Dangshibolan*, 2013(5).
49. Zhonggong zhongyang duiwai lianluobu bangongting: *Zhonglianbu laobulingdao tan dangde duiwai gongzuo (Former Officials of the International Liaison Department of the Central Committee of the C.P.C on Foreign Affairs)*, 210–211.
50. *Renmin Ribao (People's Daily)*, 17 October 1991.
51. Shen, *Zuihou de "tianchao,"* 705.

Bibliography

Periodicals
JoongAng Daily
Renmin Ribao
Rodong Sinmun
Xin Qingkusng

Other Sources
Armstrong, Charles. "Fraternal Socialism," *Cold War History*, Vol. 5, No. 2 (May 2005).
Cao, Liqin. "Beinan chaoxian jiaru lianheguo hou de chaoxian bandao tongyi wenti," *Shijie jingji yu zhengzhi [World Economics and Politics]*, 1993.

Deng Xiaoping Nianpu, 1975–1997 (Beijing: Zhongyang wenxian chubanshe, 2007). Cited as DXNP.

Jonsson, Gabriel. *South Korea in the United Nations: Global Governance, Inter-Korean Relations, and Peace Building* (New Jersey: World Scientific, 2017).

Kim Geun Sik. "bukhan ui UN gaib ijeon gwa ihu ui bigyoleur jungsimeuro," *Gukje jeongchi nonchong*, 2001(4), 91–103.

Kim Il-sung. "Guanyu zuguo tongyi wuda fangzhen," 25 June 1973, *Weile zuguode heping tongyi [For the Peaceful Reunification of Our Country]*, (Pyongyang: Waiguowen chubanshe, 1977).

Kim Nam Sik. "Bukhan ui UN gaib seoneon gaehyeok ui sijakingan—UN gaib gyeorjeong baegyeong gwa daenae byeonhwa jeonmang," *Tongil Hanguk*, 91, 1991, 86–89.

Lee Jong Seok. "bukhan ui UN gaib gyeoljeong gwa tongil ui jeonmang," *worgan sahoe pyeonglon*, 1991(7), 240–249.

Li Peng. *Heping Fazhan Hezuo: Lipeng waishi riji (LiPeng's Diary on Foreign Affairs)* (Beijing: Xinhua chubanshe, 2008).

Lin Xiaoguang. "chaoxian beinan shuangfang jiaru lianheguo de jiannan licheng," *Waiguo wenti yanjiu (Studies of Foreign Problems)*,1992 (4).

Pak, Chi Young. *Korea and the United Nations* (Boston Mass.: Kluwer Law International, 2000).

Qian Qichen. *Waijiao shiji [Ten Episodes in China's Diplomacy]*, (Beijing: Shijie zhishi chubanshe, 2003).

Shen Zhihua. "Miandui lishi jiyu: zhongmei guanxi hejie yu zhongchao guanxi(1971–1974) [Facing historical opportunities: Sino-US relations reconciliation and Sino-DPRK relations]," *Huadong shifan daxue xuebao (Journal of East China Normal University)*, 2014 (1).

Shen Zhihua. *Zuihou de "tianchao": Mao Zedong Jin Richeng yu Zhong Chao guanxi (1945–1976) [The Last "Celestial Empire": Mao Zedong, Kim Il Sung and Sino-North Korean Ralations,1945–1976]*, (Hong Kong, The Chinese University Press, 2017).

Zhonggong zhongyang duiwai lianluobu bangongting: *Zhonglianbu laobulingdao tan dangde duiwai gongzuo (Former Officials of the International Liaison Department of the Central Committee of the C.P.C on Foreign Affairs)*, 2004.

CHAPTER SIX

Explaining Economic Order in North Korea

Sheena Chestnut Greitens

Introduction

As North Korea's behavior leads the country to feature regularly in international news, the regime itself has been the subject of continued analysis in policy and academic communities. In the scholarly community, there is debate over the development of the North Korean economy and how best to characterize it. One characterization is of North Korea as a "criminal" or "mafia" state, with a "court economy" powered by the sale of drugs and weapons overseas and prone to importing cognac and yachts for its leadership.[1] A second characterization is of North Korea as a poverty-stricken and struggling society overtaken from below by the black market, a phenomenon often referred to as "marketization from below."[2]

This chapter argues that in fact, two distinct political-economic orders emerged inside North Korea beginning in the early 1990s. They developed in parallel and share a common point of origin: the surrounding international economic environment, which turned sharply negative in the late 1980s and early 1990s. These global changes forced inhabitants throughout North Korea to dramatically alter their economic survival strategies and precipitated domestic transformation at two levels: the level of high politics, and the level of "everyday politics." North Korea's economic trajectory thus proceeded upon two parallel tracks, each based on citizens' pursuit of economic survival and each reliant on illicit international networks to sustain them when domestic mechanisms failed. North Korean elites pioneered one set of transnational links to the outside world to further both their physical and political survival, while ordinary people adopted and created another set of illicit trans-border connections to survive—in this case physically more than politically.

In pursuing these parallel paths to survival, residents of North Korea from Pyongyang to North Hamgyung also created parallel economic orders *inside* the country. A reasonably extensive literature has focused on a number of different coping mechanisms that exist within the North Korean economy—the evolution of state trading networks abroad[3]; North Korea's participation in illicit activities to raise revenues[4]; and the gradual expansion of market mechanisms and lively black market (or "grey market") trade in goods, information, and people along the Chinese border.[5] As yet, however, none of these studies has linked back to a structured, comparative analysis of how these different transnational illicit networks have affected subnational variation in the organization of economic and political activity inside North Korea itself. That is the gap that this chapter aims to fill.

The chapter makes two interconnected arguments to substantiate its main claim. First, it argues that elite attempts to cope with economic crisis created a new subnational economic order that was geographically centered on Pyongyang and composed of regime elites who used their access to state resources, positions, and networks to make money. These elites found a comparative economic advantage in transnational illicit activities, such as drug production and counterfeiting, which they then used to generate income that entered North Korea at the top of the political system, similar to other personalist kleptocracies throughout the world. The second order that evolved was geographically centered in the country's northeast, where ordinary people developed bottom-up black-market coping mechanisms and smuggling networks that straddled the border with China to deal with the collapse of the centrally planned economy; these informal market networks have similarities with the shadow economies found in other post-socialist states. Although transnational illicit activity was also used to obtain money and goods in the northeast, the activity was primarily oriented around ensuring the physical survival of ordinary citizens, was conducted much more by women, and relied on social connections and geographic proximity to China rather than DPRK state resources and globally distributed facilities as the primary resources for initiating trade.

These two economic orders emerged in parallel, for a common reason, and both depended in fundamental ways on transnational illicit activity for their development and function. But it is also important to note their major differences, especially in terms of domestic organization and impact. The key actors involved, the type of resources employed, the specific type of transnational networks developed, and the social and political relationships that were constructed in these parallel pursuits of survival are all very different. For that reason, it is possible, even expected, that the political and social consequences of these two emerging orders will be different as well. More broadly, the emergence of these two parallel but distinct types of political-economic order inside North Korea helps to excavate and elucidate previously hidden interconnections between geopolitics, sub-state and intra-state transnational economic networks, and state-society relations inside North Korea in the post-Cold War period—and also offers some new suggestions on how these factors might interact to shape North Korea's future in the years ahead.

This chapter makes the above argument in three main sections. The first section explains the concept of economic order, and outlines its utility as a framework for understanding the potentially contradictory trends and developments in the North Korean economy that have been described by scholars and observers. The second section describes the emergence of an elite-centric, Pyongyang-based economic order, and links its development to the transnational survival strategies employed by members of the North Korean elite to confront economic crisis. The third section examines the alternative economic order that emerged among the ordinary citizens of the country's northeast, demonstrating that this order resulted from ordinary citizens' pursuit of physical and political survival under the same conditions of international economic strain and domestic commitment to continued authoritarian rule. Each of these middle sections chronicles the emergence of the specific form of economic order that has emerged, and clarifies the commonalities and differences that exist across the two. The fourth, concluding section examines what has resulted from the accumulation of these parallel strategies over time, and discusses implications for North Korea's likely future.

Economic Order: Understanding North Korea

What is "economic order"? Why do we use that term to describe and explain what's happening in North Korea? What is gained by employing this framework?

This chapter employs the term "economic order" following Rithmire (2014), who describes it as "the logic of economic decision-making and patterns of behavior" at the local level. Thinking in terms of economic order allows scholars to move beyond describing variation simply in terms of economic output—a difficult task in North Korea's case, given that the country doesn't release typical economic performance statistics, or even a regular census. Instead, employing the concept of economic order allows researchers and readers to look at the political structures and practices that make up leaders' and citizens' participation in and governance over the economy of a particular locality. Economic order is about whatever variations in relationships and practices structure a particular place's economic activity, whether these factors are local institutions, relationships with the center, long-standing political-historical practices and traditions, material incentive structures, or normative beliefs. Relationships and patterns of authority—whether these patterns are material, social, or political—are therefore central to characterizing economic order and its variation within a particular country.

Why is "economic order" a useful concept? First, because it allows us to look beyond more traditional but narrower indicators and areas of focus like industrial organization or provincial GDP growth, and to replace them with a "broader lens to analyze economic *practice* [emphasis mine]."[6] If we are interested not only in understanding economic performance or outputs, but the *political* rules, organization, and implications of economic activity in North Korea, then the concept of economic order is a useful place to start. It allows us to ask who the important economic players are, how their relationships are defined, what rules govern their interactions, and what the results—social, political, *and* economic—are, rather than taking these things for granted or assuming that the answers are the same in one locality versus another. In the case of North Korea, these are all questions about which some information already exists, and where scholars have focused on empirically establishing one piece or another of how things work on the ground—but where the field lacks an overall framework for organizing and theorizing the data that it possesses.

Second, employing the concept of economic order also provides a way to connect North Korea to some of the broader work on subnational variation that has emerged of late within comparative politics. It might seem odd to speak of regional economic orders within a country like North Korea, typically regarded as small and relatively homogenous or monolithic. In fact, as we show below, subnational variation in economic order has existed in North Korea for some time, but has never been explicitly identified, characterized, or explained as such. In the presence of subnational economic order, North Korea is surprisingly *not* different from other countries studied by comparative political scientists, including autocracies, where subnational analysis of political economic phenomena and even "subnational authoritarianism" have received increased attention of late.[7]

That comparative perspective helps us not only to place North Korea within a broader set of cases across the world, but to refract our analysis of those cases back to the Korean peninsula, to help us more fully understand developments in the DPRK itself. For example, one recent survey of North Korean defectors found roughly equal rates of participation in the informal economy when comparing North and South Hamkyung to other provinces in North Korea[8]; we show below that while many areas of North Korea participate in the informal economy, the type of informal economy they participate in, and the specific modes and patterns of engagement, are in fact quite different, and arguably bear more similarity to global comparative categories than to each other. The final section of this chapter leverages that comparative perspective to think through the implications of our findings for the future of North Korea.

Survival at the Top: Illicit Elite Networks and Personalist Kleptocracy in Pyongyang

This section discusses the elite-centered, Pyongyang-based economic order that arose as the North Korean regime attempted to navigate the economic crisis of the early 1990s. It shows that opportunistic elites, faced with crisis, leveraged access to what would normally be considered state resources—inside North Korea and abroad—to engage in business operations to generate revenue for themselves and for the regime in Pyongyang. Much (though not all) of this business was illicit, in part because of the comparative advantages derived from state-sanctioned illicit activity. The important players in this activity were individuals at high levels of the party, military, and government, typically senior and male, who had access to resources that could be exported for or leveraged to generate hard currency, both for Pyongyang and themselves. As a result, extensive links developed between the North Korean regime and illicit actors across the globe, including criminal organizations. These were concentrated around areas where the DPRK had a diplomatic-commercial presence, and provided revenue from a mix of constantly-evolving sources that flowed from abroad directly into the upper levels of the regime.

North Korea's elite-based survival strategies originated in behaviors that began prior to the economic collapse of the early 1990s. The involvement of DPRK officials, often diplomatic personnel at North Korean embassies abroad, in illicit smuggling operations dates back to the first recorded case in Scandinavia in 1976; elites posted abroad by the government had been accustomed to having to provide for themselves financially since North Korea's default in the middle of that decade.[9] The economic collapse that occurred at the end of the Cold War, however, catalyzed the employment of these techniques on a much broader scale, with long-term repercussions for the way that the elite economy was organized inside the DPRK.

Elite calculations and the permissiveness of the structure within which they operated both changed with the onset of economic crisis. Nicholas Eberstadt, Marcus Noland, and others have documented the ways in which the loss of Russian and Chinese subsidies in the early 1990s was compounded by natural disaster and agricultural problems that resulted in economic collapse, disintegration of the state-managed economic system including the Public Distribution System (PDS), and widespread famine.[10] Particularly disastrous was the decision of the post-Soviet Russian government to demand hard currency rather than barter payment for the oil that it had long supplied, which produced a steep drop in electricity output. Without fertilizer and electricity, agricultural and industrial output—for both domestic consumption and export—plummeted. Without products to sell, North Korea was unable to earn the hard currency necessary to get the imports to restart production and export processes, creating a downward slide.[11]

As part of its efforts to cope with the crisis, North Korea created a new system for foreign trade. The regime permitted—and often actively encouraged or required—certain institutions within the North Korean system to plan and engage in foreign trade in order to provide for their own survival.[12] As Byung-yeon Kim notes, North Korea's intent in allowing this latitude does not seem to have been liberalization, as ownership and coordination were never devolved or privatized, but rather "to allow these organizations and institutions to seek their own means of securing resources for operation and paying their workers," and to create a licensing process that would control who could engage in foreign trade, upon what terms.[13] This removed pressure from the center to supply inputs and consumer goods, but it also meant that firms semi-independently engaged in exports to earn the hard currency to obtain whatever imports they and their personnel required—and often, in a role reversal, to send funding home rather than receiving it from the center. It was, in essence, an expansion of the "embassy self-financing" system of the 1970s to organizations based inside North Korea itself.

This newly permissive environment, combined with increased economic stress, altered the calculations of those members of the elite with some sort of international access, whether that access was from being physically stationed abroad at a DPRK embassy, or having relational or logistical connections to various international networks. The Korean Workers' Party (KWP), the military, and various government ministries all appear to have established their own trading companies to engage in revenue-generating activities abroad, using whatever resources, relationships, or organizational assets they could.[14] For example, the Ministry of the People's Armed Forces established companies to engage in foreign trade, mining, and farming, drawing particularly on their transportation and infrastructural assets to move goods for export; the KWP, which had established the Daesong Trading Group under Office 39 in the 1970s, expanded these operations using its personnel stationed in the DPRK's diplomatic outposts around the world.[15]

Members of the North Korean elite therefore began to try to earn money in a variety of areas where they had access to something to sell or offer. Given the poor state of the North Korean economy, however, their options were generally limited. The production and distribution (usually wholesale) of illicit goods was one area in which the North Korean regime enjoyed—and leveraged—atypical comparative advantages.[16] In the early and mid-1990s, for example, North Korea was implicated both in distributing high-quality counterfeit U.S. $100 bills and in the production and distribution of unusually pure heroin and methamphetamines. The country has also been linked to the production of high-quality counterfeit cigarettes and pharmaceuticals. Official assessments from U.S. government agencies at the time and afterward concluded that this activity was likely state-sanctioned and officially encouraged, if not state-directed.[17]

Both currency counterfeiting and drug production, in particular, drew on clear comparative advantages for North Korea. For example, evasion of law enforcement authorities, or bribery of them, is often a major cost incurred by criminal enterprises worldwide. North Korean authorities, however, *were* the law enforcement—meaning that domestic production of illicit goods proceeded unhampered. In other cases, state support was not merely in lack of enforcement, but in the actual direction of the activity itself. State resources and production facilities, as well as high-level personnel, were the key actors in both drug and counterfeit currency production, according to numerous accounts from defectors and refugees in interviews with this author and others; the government established opium farms, repurposed otherwise nonoperational pharmaceutical factories in Hamhung and Chongjin for methamphetamine production, and reportedly ran a printing plant in Pyongsong responsible for generating counterfeit currency.[18] This kind of operational subsidization by the state, as well as reduced costs from evading law enforcement, provided clear comparative advantages to the North Korean government in engaging in certain forms of illicit activity.

State support also explains the high quality of the goods produced, improving their marketability and the profit margins obtained. Counterfeit currency linked to North Korea was so good that the Secret Service referred to it as "Supernote," and experts judged that no-one other than a government was capable of creating notes of that standard.[19] North Korean-made methamphetamine was chemically distinct from equivalent amphetamine-type stimulants produced elsewhere, perhaps because of the involvement of state laboratories and highly trained state chemists, and became known abroad for its unusually high purity and sophisticated packaging. North Korea's organizational assets—its diplomatic stations worldwide, and in some cases its military transportation inventory—were used to hand off products to distributors. North Korean military and merchant vessels were associated with drug drops at sea for Japanese criminal organizations to pick up, often with ethnic Koreans as intermediaries, and with transport of drugs directly to and from Japan; DPRK embassies were named in indictments related to currency distribution as well as drug seizures.[20] State support, in other words, provided the DPRK with a quality as well as a cost advantage.

Not all of North Korea's money-making operations were illegal, though some became so because of North Korea's frequent attempts to engage in the import and export of otherwise-legal goods without paying the requisite duties or customs fees. The director of the Zokwang Trading Company—a company that had been implicated in counterfeit currency distribution in Macau in the mid–1990s—described the company's operations as exporting herbal supplements for the Chinese market and textiles to other parts of the world.[21] Other North Korean companies were involved in exporting textiles, foodstuffs, natural resources, and other commodities.[22] North Korea's weapons trade was also a source of income—sometimes legal, sometimes covert, as with the diplomatic exchanges in 1993–1994 that culminated in a 1995 agreement for North Korea's (specifically, the Korean Mining and Development Corporation (KOMID) subsidiary company, Changgwang Sinyong) to provide Pakistan with missiles, missile components, and related training.[23]

The basic overseas trading system established at this point in North Korea's history remains in use. That system has been continually modified, and has evolved as sanctions have exerted intermittently-increased pressure on state-run trading networks. Over time, this has forced changes to lines of production/activity, partner organizations, the structure of collaborative arrangements with partners, and key markets.[24] Cyber-crime, for example, is a new area of revenue-generation activity for the DPRK: the Lazarus Group, believed to be affiliated either with Office 39 or with the Reconaissance General Bureau (North Korean intelligence), has been linked to cyber-crime operations ranging from a theft from the Bangladesh Central Bank to the Wannacry ransomeware attack in the UK to attempted bitcoin heists in as many as 18 different countries worldwide.[25] The use of front companies and other disguise mechanisms has also increased as US and international sanctions on DPRK-based entities have outstripped sanctions on the third-party actors that enable their continued transactions.[26] As it relates to the organization and function of the North Korean political-economic system, however, the basic structure of these operations—and, particularly relevant for this chapter, their relationship with the North Korean political system—appears to be essentially unchanged. A variety of organizations under state, party, and military auspices engage in entrepreneurial commercial activity abroad, sometimes licit and often illicit, using whatever state resources are most advantageous to leverage at that time, to generate revenues that flow back into elite coffers—either at home in Pyongyang, or in overseas bank accounts where they are more readily transferrable to wherever a purchase might be necessary.

This part of North Korea's international trading profile remains elite- and regime-dominated; money flows from the various sources described above into the top of the North Korean system, where it is used to further elite political survival. It helps explain, for example, why high-ranking officials have been consistently able to purchase consumer goods that were unavailable to ordinary people, at exclusive state shops that require political connections (or at least good political standing and access to Pyongyang).[27] These networks arose from elite efforts to continue to earn money in a changing global economic and enforcement environment. Faced with a deliberately permissive structure established by the center for its own benefit, opportunistic elites leveraged access to state resources and international networks to forge relatively long-standing patterns of economic activity that accrue benefits both personally and for the regime. Note that up to this point, this account of North Korea's economic coping strategies has left ordinary citizens virtually untouched; this is an ecosystem that involves members of the North Korean elite in Pyongyang and abroad, and one that is socially and geographically distinct from what ordinary citizens created to survive.

Elites, who earn the money to support themselves, also win political points by sending revenue home; the center benefits both from the direct revenue it obtains, and from having satisfied the material demands of a key group of supporters. In that sense, the system has maintained its equilibrium—a political equilibrium referring to the balance of power and alignment of incentives within the regime elite—since it first took shape in the 1990s. This part of North Korea's economic order, therefore, resembles a personalist kleptocracy, in which the ruler exploits national resources for personal and political benefit and obtains buy-in from politically critical actors by implicating them in that system and providing them with its spoils. Moreover, in North Korea's case, the state resources that are used are employed not just for lavish and narrowly distributed personal consumption—think Congolese dictator Denis Sassou-Ngesso's mansions in Paris—but to generate revenues abroad that flow back into the North Korean system at points controlled by the regime, to be shared amongst the elites as well as distributed downward in whatever way the regime sees fit. Literature in comparative politics suggests that this kind of equilibrium will, while it lasts, be conducive to regime survival; other states where regime leadership maintain access to and control over revenues generated abroad have proven to be more long-lasting and durable than ones in which elite fortunes depend upon domestic extraction of resources.[28] One of the key survival techniques that North Korea learned, therefore, was to harness foreign-earned income to prolong its rule, and to manage its own elites, in part, by embedding them into the processes that generate and distribute foreign income.

Finally, it is worth noting that these dynamics emerged from historical trends that form a recurring theme in this volume. North Korea's adoption of drug production was the result of opportunism by elite agents, but it also drew on historical legacies that were the unintended consequences of foreign intervention on the Korean peninsula: the fact that Japanese colonialism left Korea's chemical-industrial base in the northeast largely untouched allowed factories there to be repurposed decades later for production of drugs—many of which were then exported back to Japanese shores for consumption there—while Japan's own role in state development and use of methamphetamine provided important material for North Korea's elite opportunists to work from in their pursuit of survival forty years after the war's end.[29] North Korea's dramatic involvement in the drug trade, therefore, is also one part of a larger story about the history of drug production and drug use in Asia that spans multiple regions and links Asia's imperial experience with its postcolonial history and contemporary security challenges.

Coping by Ordinary Citizens: Cross-Border Smuggling, Black Markets, and the Birth of a Post-Socialist Shadow Economy Inside North Korea

As elites drew on official connections and leveraged state resources in their search for hard currency, ordinary citizens were left largely to their own devices to manage the challenges of the same period of economic hardship, often referred to as the Arduous March or March of Suffering (고난의 행군).³⁰ Ordinary citizen survival strategies during this time created a different economic order, one that was geographically centered in the country's northeast and made up of (largely female) citizens who were ordinary residents of North Korea, rather than privileged members of the elite.

This order bears some resemblances to the elite-based order. Like the elite order, the economic order that emerged among ordinary citizens relied on transnational links—although in this case, the links that mattered were interpersonal relationships across the Chinese border, including family connections to ethnic Koreans or other contacts in China's northeast, rather than the more globally-distributed, official relationships upon which the elite order evolved. Likewise, many of the citizens involved in illicit trade initially began by trying to leverage whatever assets they could obtain—though these were generally personal or smaller-scale assets like access to copper wire at one's workplace, rather than whole factories or diplomatic postings. Additionally, like the elite order, this citizen-based organization of the economy mixed trade in licit products with trade in illicit ones like drugs—although in this case, North Korea's own formal strictures on market activity during this period made transactions that otherwise would have been considered normal business into formally "illicit" operations.

Close scrutiny also reveals other important distinctions. First, the social identity of the actors involved was quite different: in contrast to the elite order, which was predominantly male and high in political-social class standing, a large percentage of the key players in this bottom-up economic order were middle-to-lower class and largely female. Second, this order pulled money into North Korea at the bottom of the social-political structure, rather than the top; it decoupled political status from economic resources and reordered social relationships at the local level as a result. Traders rose in socioeconomic status (and sometimes in political status), while bribery and corruption of lower-level officials became commonplace. Local officials responded by trying to exploit the illegality and profit structures of this new trade to extract resources for themselves, becoming more reliant on predation and extraction from below and changing the state-society relationship at the local level in ways that appear never to have been reversed. The two types of economic order, therefore, have important social and political differences, and may well have different implications for North Korea's future.

By now, the overall story of the famine's impact on ordinary citizens in North Korea is relatively well-known: that the southern half of the peninsula produced a majority of food and consumer goods prior to division; that the DPRK was not fully self-sufficient in food production before the crisis of the

1990s, relying instead on foreign subsidies; that the cessation of that external aid, combined with natural disasters, produced a crisis in both the agricultural and industrial sectors that further tanked the country's ability to export and earn hard currency; and that under these strains, the Public Distribution System that people relied on to obtain basic items—most importantly food—broke down.[31] Most accounts of the famine center either on estimations of the impact of these processes on total mortality, or on ethnographic accounts of how individuals and families living inside North Korea experienced the famine process and the social dislocations and personal tragedies that accompanied it.[32]

Extant work hints at, though does not fully explore, subnational variations in the famine and its impact inside North Korea. Only recently have scholars gained access to enough systematic data—quantitative economic statistics, historical documents, or interview evidence—to understand how differently various provinces in China experienced famine during the Great Leap Forward and afterward[33]; as yet, no such work appears to be possible for North Korea. Scholars attempting to calculate mortality have generally assumed that the northeastern provinces, mountainous and politically disfavored, were the "hardest hit" by famine. One well-known study, for example, estimated that around 12% of North Hamkyung's population died between 1995 and 1997.[34] Similarly, Sandra Fahy's ethnographic account of the famine notes that individuals in the northeast placed the start of hunger, death, and dislocation a year or several years earlier than those in Pyongyang or elsewhere in the country; her interviewees pointed to food shortages and problems with the PDS emerging as early as 1991-1992 in the northeast, but not until 1996 or so in Pyongyang.[35] In short, thanks to two factors—the regionally-specific experiences of famine and the availability of coping strategies—a new and different social-political order arose in that part of the country over time.

As food shortages worsened and hunger grew more acute, private citizens responded by engaging in trade.[36] According to witnesses and participants in North Korean life during this period, initially many people tried to barter or sell whatever resources, assets, and property they already possessed, in what they viewed as a short-term coping mechanism to get through a temporary crisis.[37] Informal markets arose in northeastern cities and towns, where famine hit residents the hardest (urban residents lacking access to fields and farms where they could access alternate food supply) and where a segment of the population had surplus cash and goods in sufficient quantities to make barter trading possible. Marketization, therefore, was a localized urban phenomenon in its origins in the northeast, but gradually spread beyond that.[38]

When their resources-on-hand ran low, people began to steal from others, or from their workplaces, to obtain items to sell. In some cases, citizens were allowed to trade whatever they could gather or otherwise procure, but in other cases they were punished for it. Lee Hye-jin recounts the first execution she witnessed during this period: two miners who had stolen wiring and attempted to sell it at Sinuiju, the border town across from Dandong, and farmers who'd stolen grain from the town's threshing floor.[39] As the PDS stopped supporting even local officials, those who had access to state resources that could be sold for a profit—for example, the manager of a factory whose equipment and supplies could be cannibalized after the factory stopped running—could look for a place to sell that equipment, even if it was for scrap metal (the usual destination was China). Families were also permitted—sometimes with the explicit encouragement of local officials—to forage or create informal plots to produce extra food to substitute for the PDS deliveries that had ceased.[40] Traditionally strict constraints on internal travel were relaxed or simply unenforced, and memoirs of that period commonly recount travel to a more urban location, a border crossing, or a relative's house in search of food.

North Hamkyung Province lies across the Tumen River from China's ethnically Korean Yanbian Ethnic Autonomous Prefecture (located in Jilin Province), and connections with China became a lifeline for citizens in the northeastern part of the country during this period. Account after account of the famine period includes statements like "those who had close family in China, who would send things from China, those people lived well," or "those who had something to eat had family or friends in China."[41] Individuals who lived close enough to China to be physically capable of making the trip to the border (not something to take for granted, as many inhabitants were physically depleted by the time they seriously considered a strenuous journey over difficult terrain), or who had kinship or other connections on the other side, began to cross into China to forage, find work, or appeal to relatives for help.[42] In some cases, these individuals ended up returning to North Korea; in many others, they stayed for extended periods or eventually defected to live in South Korea. In other cases, individuals who remained in North Korea began to take items to border towns or border checkpoints to trade, either bartering for food or bartering for money that they then could use to purchase food.

Thus the rise of North Korean markets was heavily intertwined with cross-border smuggling to and from China. Family members who lived inside

China, or family members who had crossed in search of work, provided goods and sometimes capital that flowed back into North Korea, carried by North Koreans who were voluntarily returning to their families or by a system of brokers and couriers. This trade mixed licit exports and trading with illicit activities. On the licit side, Sun-hi Bak recounts women using the term "doing the laundry" in the Amnok River near the border town of Hyesan as a euphemism for selling precious metals to China in order to buy food.[43]

On the illegal side, trade in methamphetamine (often referred to even in North Korea by its Chinese name, *bingdu*) blossomed.[44] Chinese suppliers provided precursor chemicals, most commonly ephedrine hydrochloride, to (increasingly local, smaller-scale) manufacturers in North Korea who then sent the finished product back across the river for export and resale by ethnically Korean Chinese middlemen. Other effect of this localization of the drug trade was a rise in the mid–2000s in domestic methamphetamine consumption in North Korea, again concentrated in North Hamkyung Province, with a spillover effect into China that was so strong that authorities in Jilin and elsewhere mounted law enforcement campaigns specifically targeted at it.[45]) Bribery was commonplace: North Koreans who crossed to seek work[46] or who needed to get goods across the river for sale bribed border guards to look the other way, and these same guards often assisted in moving goods covertly back into North Korea in exchange for a bribe or a cut of the profit. By sometime in the 2000s, a majority of consumer goods on the North Korean market had their origins in China. The restrictions on cell phone usage in North Korea during much of this period—and the availability of Chinese cell phones that worked within a certain range of the border—contributed to an increasingly deep set of connections between the two sides.[47]

One of the other effects of this concentrated cross-border trade was the increasing use of foreign (Chinese) currency rather than the North Korean one. Again, this development shows both similarity and difference when placed alongside the elite order in Pyongyang: both orders conducted transactions denominated in foreign currency, but the foreign currency in use was different in different parts of the country. Chris Green, in exploring the relationship between economic shocks, marketization, and foreign currency, observes that the dollar is "beloved by elites in Pyongyang," while the ordinary citizens of the border areas rely on Chinese renminbi.[48] Studies done in 2013 and 2017 corroborate his finding: they suggest that over $2 billion in foreign currency (in an economy worth $21.5 billion) was circulating inside North Korea, that individuals who had defected to South Korea reported storing as much as 90% of their assets in foreign currency, and that dollars were the preferred foreign currency in Pyongyang and "non-border areas,"

Explaining Economic Order in North Korea 143

while the Sino-North Korean border areas predominantly employed Chinese renminbi.⁴⁹ Differential use of foreign currency, then, is another indicator of regional variations in the organization and structure of illicit cross-border economic activity inside North Korea.

The identity of the actors who engaged in this cross-border activity was markedly different from the identity of those who were the key actors in the Pyongyang-based order, and their participation in trade began to revise typical understandings of socioeconomic class inside the DPRK. Traders in the northeast were predominantly the less privileged—in terms of pre-famine status—members of North Korea's social and political class system. Eunsun Kim, for example, recounts:

> My family paid dearly as a result of our "privileged" status and our blind loyalty to the state system. We never imagined that the regime would allow us to die of hunger. We depended entirely on government rations to feed us, and thus succumbed more quickly than others who had learned to develop alternative methods of survival.⁵⁰

Other accounts note the same correlation, though it was far from universal: loyalists were more likely to die waiting for food, rather than engage in "anti-socialist" market activity that was seen as political betrayal. Loyalty, in this context, meant an embrace of sacrificial suffering and a deferral of one's needs even to the point of death; death was loyal, market trading was political deviance. As one commented, "Who do you think would die first? People who worked the hardest [and] who were devoted to the Workers' Party... Why? Because the Worker's Party didn't distribute food. These good people who trusted the government still went to work hungry thinking, 'Eventually the Worker's Party will distribute.'"⁵¹

The economic survival and relative success of these "less privileged" citizens had long-term ramifications for North Korean social order. Because China was a source of both goods and capital, those who could obtain these items became economically and socially important. The emergence of cross-border trade, then, weakened—and over time, actually inverted—the tight link that had previously existed between political status and economic welfare. It created a new class of influential people whose power in North Korean society derived not from their loyalty to the regime's edicts, but from their willingness to interpret them flexibly—or defy them outright. Political deviance now meant survival.

Second, these market activities were pioneered by and largely conducted by women, though men also participated in the mechanics of cross-border trade and in the important permissive role played by border guards.[52] The predominance of women was largely due to previous labor and employment patterns that made women more flexible and available for market participation: women, who were less likely to be expected to appear for factory work, were relatively more able to trade during the day, and to travel if it was required, without their absence from home being detected.[53] One woman recounted:

> When they used to give the relief tickets, the men would get them and go stand in line to get the food, but that wasn't happening. Women were in the markets selling. Women knew how to talk to sell the stuff. Women did that. In North Korea, there is an expression that men are like daytime light bulbs. In the daytime you have no use for a light bulb, do you?[54]

The rise of this kind of trading activity—and the reliance of many families on it for sheer physical survival—also began to reorder social relations inside North Korea. As Sung Kyung Kim describes it, "North Korean women became the main agents for household economy."[55] Women became the primary breadwinners—one study found that they earned 70% of the household income in North Korea, the majority through trading—and also developed separate economic and social networks based on their participation in the market, while men were required to report to factories that sat idle. Their increased willingness to break from previous social norms around gender roles also were reflected in the decisions of some to cross the border into China, which sometimes was a strategic use of gender and marriage in search of a better life, but which also rendered them vulnerable to trafficking, exploitation, prostitution or forced marriage, and sexual violence.[56]

The rise of broader people-smuggling networks (not just those that trafficked women) likewise contributed to the reordering of economic and social relations inside North Korea. As the number of escapees who made it to South Korea rose, professional brokers began to arrange for the extraction and transmission of family members to the south, with key actors in the network typically located across the border in northeastern China. Because of China's view that North Koreans were "economic migrants" rather than refugees, the illegal status and consequent vulnerability of any North Korean who crossed into China created economic opportunity in the form of either bribery or outright profit from the sale of human beings, accruing resources to those on both sides of the border who were willing to participate in these activities.

But the rise of these cross-border networks had other effects within North Korea as well. In addition to the much-described role that some of these networks play in providing information to North Koreans,[57] there was a direct economic effect as well. In many cases, those who had family in the South, but had not yet decided or been able to physically leave North Korea, experienced an increase in their economic security and in many cases their social standing as well. An individual who had relatives sending remittance money from South Korea could joke about being well-off thanks to the "Halla-san line" (a play on the "Paektu-san line" that describes the Kim family).[58] The capital sent via the remittance process could be used to buy food, or even to start a small business, stabilizing entire families in the process. The majority of these remittances from the south (81%) travel through ethnic Koreans in China to family in North Hamkyung. The eventual *desirability* of a connection to individuals in the southern half of the peninsula, who had previously been a political liability, is yet another example of how citizens' search for survival along the Chinese-North Korean border, and the trans-national marketization processes that resulted from their survival strategies, reordered social relationships and re-patterned economic activity throughout the northeastern part of the country.

That reordering has continued as both state and society have adjusted to the partial marketization of the country, and as the regime has sought ways to manage that marketization without losing political control.[59] One of the key consequences of the economic order that arose in the country's northeast was that it created a way for money to enter North Korea at the bottom of the political hierarchy, produced by trading arrangements that are neither directed nor controlled by the regime. This is a fundamentally different political issue than the more controlled, even directive arrangements upon which the elite order relied, where income was captured abroad and brought in at the top to distribute downward. For the regime to benefit from—and not be challenged by—this ground-level, independently-created income, it had to find a way to extract that income and siphon it upward. The regime has tried to tap that income, usually via mechanisms that are more similar to rent-seeking than taxation.[60]

The regime's efforts to limit, control, and benefit from existing market activity have led local actors to respond strategically—with the effect again being an adjustment of state-society relations and of the political order that governs economic activity inside North Korea. The requirement that those engaging in market activity mitigate the risks of the legally grey areas in which they operate has helped to structure a new set of potentially consequential relationships between traders and local members of the North Korean political system.[61] To make the arrangements that arose in crisis sustainable and profitable for the long-term required a symbiosis between officials and individual holders of capital (or eventually, creators of private enterprises): political connections help business flourish, and business activities benefit political actors. As a result of private traders' self-protective efforts to co-opt lower-level local officials, those officials often now share stronger economic and social ties with market traders in their geographic area than vertical ties to political superiors in Pyongyang.[62] Even intermarriage between the two groups (traders and officials) is said to be on the rise.[63]

These partnerships take a variety of forms. Some involve the use of the black or grey market to prop up the formally state-controlled economy, as when government factories or farms rely on the market to obtain inputs (seed, fertilizer, parts) to operate effectively. More common, however, is the use of some state resource by private actors to engage in money-making activity where at least three actors benefit: the private entrepreneur or business, the government official (in their institutional capacity), and the government official (personally). A factory manager might, for example, "rent" their transportation equipment to someone who wants to send goods to the border, and accept a rental fee in exchange.

The most common variant seems to be not use of physical state resources, but monetization of government approval, which as the state has moved to reassert control over economic life has become a necessary condition for a business to survive and profit. Officials now issue foreign trading licenses, stamp travel permits for domestic or cross-border travel, approve permits for space in a sanctioned public market, or register private businesses as state ones—with a loyalty fee that benefits them as both an office-holder and an individual.[64] Many of these arrangements are more predatory than voluntary: bribery is common, and coercive power is used to force unwilling participants to play the game. Not for nothing, police are the most commonly-cited bribe-takers in North Korea today.[65] It is clear, however, that this diversity of arrangements centers around a fundamental fact that much of the economic activity in northeastern North Korea—illicit or otherwise—operates under a hybrid arrangement that benefits both private economic actors and government officials, and that may have begun to blur the distinction between the two.

In short, the economic order that has emerged in the northeastern provinces of North Korea developed in parallel to the elite economic order in Pyongyang, for a similar reason: the pursuit of economic survival in the face of crisis. Moreover, both orders depended on some form of trans-national illicit activity to generate that survival. In other ways, however, the two orders are very different: the class and gender of key actors, the locations and types of international networks they employ, and the financial mechanisms that they utilize are all different. Not surprisingly, the economic and political results have differed sharply as well: the black-market ordinary-citizen economic order of the northeast has more in common with the "shadow economies" of other post-socialist states than the personalist kleptocracy on display in Pyongyang.[66]

Conclusion

Precipitated by dramatic changes to North Korea's international economic environment and the crisis that the country experienced in the early 1990s, North Korean elites and ordinary citizens each attempted to survive by looking outside the country: finding connections abroad to facilitate their physical and sometimes political survival. Many of the activities that these transnational networks conducted were illicit, either as a result of North Korea's own legal restrictions on otherwise normal market activity, or because the operations were illegal in the countries where they occurred (such as drug trafficking and counterfeiting). As a result of sustained engagement in these activities over a period of years, two parallel but distinct economic orders emerged inside North Korea.

A Pyongyang-centered, elite-based order pioneered the use of largely illicit transnational activity, conducted by senior male diplomatic and state-trading personnel, to generate new sources of dollar-denominated hard currency from abroad. The income flowing in from these operations was used for the benefit of the small group of regime elites who kept the Kim family in power. At the same time, desperate lower-class citizens, many of them female, drew on social connections and geographic proximity to northeastern China to develop cross-border smuggling networks. These networks facilitated the survival of ordinary families inside North Korea and led over time to the emergence of a very different type of bottom-up, black-market (or, at various times, grey market) economic order centered in the country's northeastern provinces and denominated largely in Chinese renminbi. While these two economic orders shared common origins and developed in parallel over time, the key actors, practices, international networks, and social-political dynamics that constitute are in fact quite different.

This depiction of two parallel and separate economic orders is, of course, an oversimplification: the above depiction has been stylized to clarify the distinctiveness of the processes and structures that emerged. As the last paragraphs of the preceding section describe, these complementary economic orders increasingly appear to be moving toward symbiosis. In particular, North Korean elites appear increasingly—as sanctions have led to pressure on their external networks—to rely on domestic extraction of hard currency income to facilitate elite and regime survival, and to have decided to co-opt private capital rather than trying to banish it altogether.[67] As a result, today, the elite Pyongyang-based economy is less insulated from the citizen economy grounded in the northeast than it was for most of the period described in this article. North Korea increasingly looks like neither an all-powerful criminal totalitarian state nor a failed state whose desperate citizens smuggle with impunity across its borders, but a crony capitalist system: one in which economic and political power have become heavily intertwined. As the two orders become interdependent, the differences between them also become less pronounced.

North Korea's is an evolving and uncertain balance. Other researchers have noted previously that the mere presence of market mechanisms is unlikely to be sufficient in isolation to destabilize North Korea.[68] And the regime itself appears to be avoiding conscious overdependence on the trend toward domestic extraction; the export of human labor abroad and cyber-crime are both recent revenue-generating activities that could be seen as efforts to develop new lines of income that lessen this domestic dependence. The domestic effects of these new and still poorly-documented forms of illicit international economic engagement are far from understood. What the remaining presence of two somewhat contradictory forms of economic order inside an evolving crony-capitalist system does suggest, however, is that the sources of North Korea's political vulnerability may be somewhat misunderstood. North Korea, like the Soviet Union, may be most vulnerable not so much to revolution from below, or stalemate and defection at the top, but a hollowing out from within, based on individual opportunism.[69] If this chapter's assessments are correct, that opportunism is already well-developed inside North Korea, and the hollowing out process has already begun.

Identifying and understanding the development of these two parallel but distinct types of political-economic order inside North Korea, therefore, helps to excavate and elucidate previously hidden interconnections between geopolitics, sub-state transnational economic networks, and state-society relations inside North Korea in the post-Cold War period, and to suggest how these factors might interact to shape North Korea's future in the years ahead. One possible next step for researchers is to think about what this new understanding of the internal workings of North Korea, combined with what we know of the fate of other countries that have exhibited at least partly similar dynamics, tells us about North Korea's likely future. The challenge for policymakers, on the other hand, is to consider how this revised understanding of what's happening domestically inside North Korea might affect the policy options before the United States and the international community as they seek to address a continued national security challenge and human security tragedy.

Notes

1. Chestnut 2007 Greitens 2014; Kan, Bechtol, and Collins 2010; Kim 2011; Kelly 2016.
2. Haggard and Noland 2011; Smith 2015; Kim 2017; Sullivan and Kim 2017; for a somewhat different perspective on marketization, see Park 2016.
3. Park, 2009; Hastings 2016.
4. Chestnut 2007; Greitens 2014.
5. Haggard, Lee, and Noland, 2012.
6. Herrigel, 1996.
7. On subnational analysis, see Snyder 2001; Tsai 2007; Tsai and Ziblatt 2010. On subnational authoritarianism, see Gibson 2013; Giraudy 2015; Hiskey and Bowler 2005; Mickey 2015.
8. Kim 2017, 101.
9. Chestnut 2007.
10. Noland 2000; Eberstadt 1999.
11. Kim 2017, 47.
12. Author's interview, Seoul, summer 2013.
13. Kim 2017, p. 50; see also Hastings 2016.
14. For background on the organization of North Korean elites, see Oh Hassig et al. 2004.
15. On Office 39, see Chestnut 2007; Kan, Bechtol, and Collins 2010.
16. This paragraph and the section that follows draw on Chestnut 2007, Greitens 2014.
17. JIATFW 2000; DEA 1999.
18. For one of the latest defector interviews specifically on Office 39's role in illicit activity, see Carney 2018.
19. United States v. Sean Garland et al, 30 August 2004, http://www.mcclatchydc.com/latest-news/article24174742.ece/BINARY/Indictment%20against%20Garland,%20various%20persons%20for%20counterfeiting
20. JIATFW 2000; also discussed in Hastings 2016.
21. Lintner and Yoon 2001.
22. See, for example, Carney 2018.
23. Squassoni 2006; Bermudez 1999.
24. On the camouflaging effect of sanctions, see particularly the detailed analysis in C4ADS 2017.
25. Barker 2017; Bossert 2017; C4ADS 2017.
26. The best source on this evolving process is the series of reports issued by the UN Panel of Experts; for an analysis of the 2018 report, see Berger and Cotton 2018.
27. Lankov 2007, 2014.

28. Ahmed 2012.
29. Edstrom 2015.
30. For one of the best and most detailed accounts of how citizens perceived what was happening, see Fahy 2015.
31. Kim 2017.
32. Robinson et al., 1999; Fahy 2015.
33. On how death tolls varied by province, see Yang 2013; econ papers. On the way that Great Leap Forward and famine experiences shaped long-term economic trajectories, see Yang 1996.
34. The study noted that it lacked the data to systematically examine and compare other provinces. Robinson et al., 1999.
35. Fahy 2015, pp. 108–111, among others.
36. This section draws on interview research previously conducted by the author with North Korean refugees and defectors. Interviews were conducted in Seoul and the United States, from 2005 to 2017. Where other sources corroborate the author's accounts, I include a reference in the footnotes below.
37. Smith 2015, especially pp. 207–215.
38. My thanks to Yang Mun-su for making this point in conversation. It is also true that markets existed in North Korea before the economic crisis; for an English-language review of important work on this by Choi and Koo, see https://sinonk.com/2014/05/27/before-the-collapse-the-micro-foundations-of-marketization-in-north-korea/
39. Execution recounted in Fahy 2015, pp. 116–117; on toleration of this activity, see Haggard and Noland 2011; Smith 2015.
40. By the early 2000s, an estimated 60–70% of food and other consumer goods came from market sources. Smith 2015; Lankov 2007.
41. Fahy 2015, pp. 70, 75.
42. Greitens 2014; see also Smith 2005; Kim 2012, pp. 49–51.
43. Fahy 2015, p. 75.
44. Much of this paragraph is drawn from author's interviews, previously summarized in Greitens 2014, pp. 80–93.
45. Greitens 2014, pp. 92–93.
46. Eventually a legalized work permit system arose that allowed citizens to get approval to enter China for work purposes, but this happened later than the period I focus on here. Lankov 2007.
47. Greitens 2013; Greitens 2014.
48. Green 2016.
49. Mun and Jung 2017; SERI 2013.
50. Kim 2012, pp. 42–43.
51. Recounted in Fahy 2015, pp. 43–44.
52. Greitens 2014.
53. Lankov and Kim 2008; Lim 2005.
54. Quoted in Fahy 2015, p. 100.

55. Kim 2016.
56. Kim 2014; see also HRNK 2009.
57. Kretchun and Kim 2012.
58. Author's interview, Seoul, July 2013; also cited in Greitens 2014, pp. 58–61.
59. For a good series of reviews of work on how marketization has evolved since the period described here, see https://storify.com/SinoNK/peter–ward–s–north–korean–contemporary–economic–hi

60. I have elsewhere used the term "informal taxation" to describe these practices, because in some cases they are relatively institutionalized. The 2009 currency reform has been largely interpreted by economists as an unsuccessful attempt to cut back the power of the market; in the aftermath, the regime has sought less dramatic and less unpopular ways of regulating and benefitting from market activity. Kim 2017.

61. Greitens 2014.
62. Author's interviews, Seoul, summer 2013.
63. Ward 2013.
64. Lankov et al., 2017.
65. As one former trader recounted, "Officials can pick a fight over goods on sale or accuse traders of selling without the right permission. They pocket the fines for themselves. Those who can't pay the fines have their goods confiscated, and these are then sold off to other traders [by officials, for personal profit]." NFI 2013; on bribery, see Kim 2017, pp. 186–187.

66. For a slightly different disaggregation of "parallel economies" in North Korea in an earlier period, see Habib 2011.
67. Greitens 2013, 2014; for recent defector corroboration, see Carney 2018.
68. Kim 2017 examines the potential cross–cutting effects of bribery; for an examination of the shadow economy's potential contribution to either authoritarian resilience or corrosion, see Dukalskis 2016.
69. Solnick 1998.

Bibliography

Ahmed, Faisal Z. "The Perils of Unearned Foreign Income: Aid, Remittances, and Government Survival," *American Political Science Review*, Vol. 106, No. 1 (February 2012), pp. 146–165.

Barker, Anne. "Bitcoin Exchanges Targeted by North Korean Hackers, Analysts Say," *ABC Australia*, 20 December 2017, http://www.abc.net.au/news/2017-12-20/north-korean-hackers-raiding-bitcoin-exchanges/9277044.

Berger, Andrea, and Shea Cotton. "Walls and Ladders: The Latest UN Panel Report on North Korea Sanctions," *War on the Rocks*, 28 March 2018, https://warontherocks.com/2018/03/walls–and–ladders–the–latest–un–panel–of–experts–report–on–north–korea–sanctions/.

Bermudez, Joseph S. Jr. "A History of Ballistic Missile Development in the DPRK," Monterey Institute of International Studies Center for Nonproliferation Studies working paper, 1999.

Bossert, Thomas. "White House Press Briefing on the Attribution of the WannaCry Malware Attack to North Korea," 19 December 2017, https://www.whitehouse.gov/briefings–statements/press–briefing–on–the–attribution–of–the–wannacry–malware–attack–to–north–korea–121917/.

Carney, Matthew. "Defector Reveals Secrets of North Korea's Office 39," *ABC Australia*, 5 January 2018, http://www.abc.net.au/news/2018–01–06/north–korea–defector–reveals–secrets–of–office–39/9302308.

Chestnut, Sheena. "Illicit Activity and Proliferation: North Korean Smuggling Networks," *International Security*, Vol. 31, No. 1, pp. 80–111, Summer 2007.

Committee on Human Rights in North Korea [HRNK]. *Lives for Sale: Personal Accounts of Women Fleeing North Korea to China* (HRNK, 2009).

Drug Enforcement Administration [DEA]. Europe/Asia/Africa Unit Intelligence Section, "Major Incidents of Drug Traficking by North Koreans," in *North Korea Advisory Group Report to the Speaker of the U.S. House of Representatives*, November 1999.

Dukalskis, Alexander. "North Korea's Shadow Economy: A Force for Authoritarian Resilience or Corrosion?" *Europe-Asia Studies*, Vol. 68, No. 3 (2016), pp. 487–507.

Eberstadt, Nicholas. *The End of North Korea* (American Enterprise Institute Press, 1999).

Edstrom, Bert. "The forgotten success story: Japan and the methamphetamine problem," *Japan Forum*, Vol. 27, No. 4 (2015).

Fahy, Sandra. *Marching Through Suffering: Loss and Survival in North Korea* (Columbia University Press, 2015).

Gibson, Edward. *Boundary Control: Subnational Authoritarianism in Federal Democracies* (Cambridge, 2013).

Giraudy, Agustina. *Democrats and Autocrats. Pathways of Subnational Undemocratic Regime Continuity Within Democratic Countries* (Oxford, 2015).

Green, Christopher. "The Sino-North Korean Border Economy: Money and Power Relations in North Korea," *Asian Perspective*, Vol. 40, No. 3: (July–September 2016), pp. 415–434.

Greitens, Sheena Chestnut. "Authoritarianism Online: What Can We Learn From Internet Data in Non-Democracies?" *PS: Political Science & Politics*, Vol. 46 No. 02, (April), pp. 262–270.

Greitens, Sheena. *Illicit: North Korea's Evolving Operations to Earn Hard Currency* (Washington, DC: Committee for Human Rights in North Korea, 2014).

Habib, Benjamin. "North Korea's parallel economies: Systemic disaggregation following the Soviet collapse," *Communist and Post-Communist Studies*, Vol. 44, No. 2 (2011), pp. 149–159.

Haggard, Stephan, and Marcus Noland. *Witness to Transformation: Refugee Insights into North Korea* (Peterson Institute, 2011).

Haggard, Stephan, Jennifer Lee, and Marcus Noland. "Integration in the Absence of Institutions: China-North Korea Cross-Border Trade," *Journal of Asian Economics*, Vol. 23, No. 2 (2012), pp. 130–145.

Hastings, Justin. *A Most Enterprising Country: North Korea in the Global Economy* (Cornell University Press, 2016).

Herrigel, Gary. *Industrial Constructions: The Sources of German Industrial Power* (New York: Cambridge University Press, 1996).

Hiskey, Jonathan, and Shaun Bowler. "Local Context and Democratization in Mexico," *American Journal of Political Science*, Vol. 49, No. 1: (2005), pp. 57–71.

Joint Interagency Task Force West [JIATFW]. "North Korean Drug Trafficking," Department of Defense, May 2000.

Kan, Paul, Bruce Bechtol, and Robert Collins. *Criminal Sovereignty: Understanding North Korea's Illicit International Activities*, (Strategic Studies Institute 2010).

Kelly, Robert. "North Korea as a Mafia State," *Lowy Interpreter*, 16 March 2016, https://www.lowyinstitute.org/the-interpreter/north-korea-mafia-state.

Kim, Eunsun. *A Thousand Miles to Freedom: My Escape from North Korea* (New York: St. Martin's Griffin, 2012).

Kim, Kwang Jin. "The Defector's Tale: Inside North Korea's Secret Economy," *World Affairs Journal*, September 2011, http://www.worldaffairsjournal.org/article/defector%E2%80%99s-tale-inside-north-korea%E2%80%99s-secret-economy.

Kim, Byung-yeon. *Unveiling the North Korean Economy: Collapse and Transition* (Cambridge 2017).

Kim, Sung Kyung. "Mobile North Korean women and their places in the Sino-North Korea borderland," *Asian Anthropology*, Vol. 15 (2016), pp. 116–131.

Kim, Sung Kyung. "I am well-cooked food: survival strategies of North Korean female border crossers and possibilities for empowerment," *Inter-Asia Cultural Studies*, Vol. 15, No. 4: (2014), pp. 553–571.

Nathaniel Kretchun and Jane Kim. *A Quiet Opening: North Koreans in a Changing Media Environment* (Intermedia, 2012).

Lankov, Andrei. *North of the DMZ: Everyday Life in North Korea* (McFarland Press, 2007).

———. *The Real North Korea: Life and Politics in the Failed Stalinist Utopia* (Oxford, 2014).

———, and Seok-hyang Kim. "North Korean Market Vendors: The Rise of Grassroots Capitalists in a Post-Stalinist Society," *Pacific Affairs*, Vol. 81, No. 1 (2008), pp. 53–72.

———, Peter Ward, Ho-yeol Yoo, and Ji-young Kim. "Making Money in the State: North Korea's Pseudo-State Enterprises in the Early 2000s," *Journal of East Asian Studies*, Vol. 17, No. 1 (2017), pp. 51–67.

Lim, Soon-hee. "The Food Crisis and Life of Women in North Korea," Korea Institute for National Unification working paper, 2005.

Lintner, Bertil, and Suh-kyung Yoon. "North Korea: Coming in from the Cold," *Far Eastern Economic Review*, 25 October 2001.

Mickey, Robert. *Paths Out of Dixie: Democratization of Authoritarian Enclaves in America's Deep South, 1944–72* (Princeton, 2015).

Mun, Sungmin, and Seungho Jung. "Dollarization in North Korea," *East Asian Economic Review*, Vol. 21, No. 1 (March 2017), pp. 81–100.

New Focus International (NFI). "Setting Up a Market Stall in North Korea," 8 May 2013, http://newfocusintl.com/setting–up–a–market–stallin–north–korea/.

Noland, Marcus. *Avoiding the Apocalypse: The Future of the Two Koreas* (Peterson Institute, 2000).

Hassig, Kongdan Oh, Joseph S. Bermudez Jr., Kenneth E. Gause, Ralph C. Hassig, Alexandre Y. Mansourov, and David J. Smith. "North Korean Policy Elites," IDA Paper P–3903 (Washington, D.C.: Institute for Defense Analyses, June 2004).

Park, John. "North Korea, Inc.: Gaining Insights into North Korean Regime Stability from Recent Commercial Activities," USIP working paper, 15 May 2009, https://www.usip.org/publications/2009/05/north–korea–inc–gaining–insights–north–korean–regime–stability–recent.

Park, Phillip. *Rebuilding North Korea's Economy: Politics and Policy* (Kyungnam University Press, 2016).

Rithmire, Meg E. "China's 'New Regionalism': Subnational Analysis in Chinese Political Economy," *World Politics*, Vol. 66, No. 1 (January 2014), pp. 165–94.

Robinson, W. Courtland, M. Lee, K. Hill, and G. Burnham. "Mortality in North Korean migrant households," *Lancet*, No. 3542 (1999), pp. 91–95.

Samsung Economic Research Institute (SERI). "Use of Foreign Currencies in North Korea," *SERI Quarterly* (April 2013), pp. 106–109.

Smith, Hazel. "North Koreans in China: Separating Fact from Fiction," in *Crossing National Borders: Human Migration Issues in Northeast Asia*, Tsuneo Akaha and Anna Vassilieva (Tokyo: United Nations Press, 2005).

Smith, Hazel. *North Korea: Markets and Military Rule* (Cambridge University Press, 2015).

Snyder, Richard. "Scaling Down: The Subnational Comparative Method," *Studies in Comparative International Development*, Vol. 36, No. 1 (Spring 2001).

Solnick, Steven L. *Stealing the State: Control and Collapse in Soviet Institutions* (Harvard University Press, 1998).

Squassoni, Sharon. "Weapons of Mass Destruction: Trade Between North Korea and Pakistan," *Congressional Research Service*, November 2006.

Sullivan, Tim, and Hyung-Jin Kim. "Rough Times for Smugglers Who Knitted North Korea to the Outside World," *Associated Press/ABC News*, 24 December 2017, http://abcnews.go.com/International/wireStory/rough–times–smugglers–knitted–korea–world–51975907.

Tsai, Lily. "Solidary Groups, Informal Accountability, and Local Public Goods Provision in Rural China," *American Political Science Review*, Vol. 101, No. 2 (May 2007), pp. 355–372.

Tsai, Lily, and Daniel Ziblatt. "The Rise of Subnational and Multilevel Comparative Politics," *Annual Review of Political Science* (2010).

Ward, Peter. "Reining in Rent-Seeking: How North Korea Can Survive," *SinoNK.com*, 2 July 2013, http://sinonk.com/2013/07/02/reining-in-rent-seeking-how-north-korea-can-survive/.

Yang, Dali. *Calamity and Reform in China: State, Rural Society, and Institutional Change since the Great Leap Famine* (Stanford University Press, 1996).

Yang, Jisheng. *Tombstone: The Great Chinese Famine 1958–62* (Farrar, Straus and Giroux, 2013).

CHAPTER SEVEN

~

Multiculturalism as State Developmental Policy in Global Korea

Darcie Draudt

Introduction

South Korea, by some accounts, might be read as a textbook account of an ethnically homogeneous, modernizing project.[1] However, from the early 2000s, the country saw a late but sudden state-controlled opening to ethnically dissimilar migrants. After maintaining an official national narrative that emphasized common descent and monocultural heritage, why did the government seemingly change tack? This puzzle is all the more striking given that Korea *resisted* immigration for decades following rapid industrialization, only to swiftly implement some of the most progressive policies from the early 2000s due to demographic changes that have affected the workforce size and content. The result meant Korea has shifted from a country of emigration to one of immigration, and the slowly diversifying residents are finding new and contested spaces in official policy and social practices.

To explain these changes, I turn the focus to two types of national membership in South Korea. In addition to the ethnocultural field of national membership that has been the traditional target of national membership literature, I emphasize here economic membership as key to the state view of members of its national project. Rather than citizenship, which tends to focus on the contestation for rights acquisition, the Korean case demonstrates theoretical value in analyzing hierarchized membership (rather than only the terms and practices of legal citizenship) in the national project and state goals. This paper focuses on the latter field by examining the state motivations and policies what the South Korean government calls "multiculturalism" (*damunhwaju-ui*) as a strategy for development. In the next section, I discuss the South Korean state's developmental project, which has privileged economic development as a key part of becoming a "Global Korea." I then parse the development and trajectory of South Korea's multiculturalism (or multiculturalism policy, *damunhwaju-ui jeongchaek*) found in the Basic Plans for Immigration. I am here concerned with official, national-level motivation and formulation of immigration and incorporation policy, not its implementation or practice—a task which warrants further investigation elsewhere but is outside the scope of this chapter. I put the state plans in conversation with its larger goal to achieve a "Global Korea" to demonstrate how multiculturalism is a state policy for continued economic development. I conclude with a discussion of the theoretical implications, as well as with suggestions for future research.

Global Korea as State-Led Development Project

Global Korea is not about integrating or assimilating into a global political economy or global political culture, but a form of nation-bounded globalization.[2] Global Korea has often privileged national economic development over attention to political development.[3] Compared to "international," "global" emphasizes the bounded rather than transnational nature of the state's vision of its roles on the global stage. It also evokes a new vision for Koreanness, one based on the foundation of national growth from the era of rapid development that also evolves its national project for renewed and revised international competitiveness.

Historical Roots of Global Korea

South Korea's variety of a "global vision" draws from its experience as a late industrializing, postcolonial nation that emerged into a context of Cold War competition. While the Japanese Empire has often been credited with facilitating the opening and modernization of Korea,[4] the ideational foundations for—in Schmid's (2002) words—"globalizing the national and nationalizing the global" in fact precedes Japanese rule.[5] In the final decade of the 19th century, the crown and academy—in addition to the nascent merchant classes—woke up to the call to "globalize" and latched onto a message of "civilization and enlightenment" (*munmyeong gaehwa*), which Schmid describes as a "conceptual framework in which various groups could come to terms with their recent integration into the global capitalist system."[6]

Rather than a primordial ethnic community, the Japanese colonial experience reformed how the state and people in Korea formed a community.

J. Kim (2016) convincingly writes how bureaucratic infrastructures and state goals created the very category of Korean itself. Migration—forced or voluntary—meant transterritorial membership and the imperial desire to register and regulate necessarily called for new linguistic, legal, and practical categories of membership (based on horizontal and vertical relations).[7] Dealing with this transterritorial regulation, both the Japanese colonial state and anticolonial nationalism broadened the scope of the Korean nation.[8] As J. Kim writes: "As migrants engaged with various state practices that regularly sorted, re-sorted, and treated them as 'Koreans,' they also came to experience their Korean identity as tangible and consequential."[9]

After liberation from Japanese rule in 1945, Korea was subsumed into a larger international competition as the Soviet Union and the United States divided the peninsula and focused on rebuilding the country into the international political economic project of each side of the Cold War. For South Korea, that first came via a state-led development project.[10] The autonomous state colluded with large business conglomerates (*chaebol*) in a public-private arrangement since theorized as the *developmental state*, defined by its capacity to direct national industrial policy while the modes of production were in the hands of private actors.[11] Counter the designs of the patron U.S. government, the South Korean state's early development mode was not to focus on export-led growth, but to pursue a path of import-substitution industrialization so that Korea could elevate itself in the East Asian economy on its own terms, rather than as a peripheral supply station and market for Japanese growth.[12]

Contemporary Global Visions

Though Korea may be more connected with the rest of the world, scholars such as S. Kim and Shin, separately, have suggested that Korea's form of "globalization" has been informed by ethnic nationalism and its experience of national development.[13] After its democratization in the late 1980s (which also coincided with the thawing of Cold War battle lines), Koreans first began greater opening to the world with measured skepticism and hesitance, based on the fear that the structural changes globalization would bring would alter the Korean core of individual identity and social relations.[14]

With the introduction of various political and economic liberalization in the 1990s, the South Korean state has found new tactics to serve the goal of national development even as those goals are reshaped by the evolving international and domestic context. Prior to democratization, the goal of national development was both international (in the context of Cold War competition on the global scale) and parochial (in terms of its diplomatic competition with North Korea and the material concerns of late development). Following the ending of the Cold War, South Korea has emerged as a "middle power" (a diplomatic identity) with an internationally competitive economy (currently ranked the 11th-largest economy in terms of national GDP as of 2016).[15]

The Kim Young-sam progressive administration's (1993–1998) *segyehwa* (globalization) strategy sought increase competitiveness in *global* terms. Rather than explicitly receive international norms or uncritically join international flows of people, ideas, services, and goods, *segyehwa* sought to export Korea's successes to the world. Han Sung-joo, foreign minister under Kim Young-sam, characterized Korea's *segyehwa* as globalism, diversification, and a future-looking orientation—aspects which were framed as "commensurate with [Korea's] standing in the international community."[16] Thus *segyehwa* (as a type of nationalistic globalization) was about South Korea finding its own space in a larger arena.

Another push for a global (re)positioning of Korea came under the conservative Lee Myung-bak administration (2008–2013), whose national slogan "Global Korea" took on a variety of substantive forms, including through "hosting diplomacy" by serving as host for such high-profile multilateral meetings as the G20 Summit (2010), the OECD Development Assistance Committee meeting (2011), the Nuclear Security Summit (2012), and the Green Climate Fund (since 2012).[17] This move echoed Seoul's initial entrée onto the global stage as host for the 1988 Summer Olympics, which the government at the time saw as key to showcase South Korea's rapid economic develop and recent moves toward democratic reform.[18] The government has also increasingly latched on to the popularity of Korean cultural products (music, television shows, movies, food, and fashion) and has actively funded efforts to strengthen and amplify the Korean Wave (*hallyu*) phenomenon to augment its soft power and economic gain.[19]

Rather than a recent phenomenon, the conceptual and practical interactions between global and national in Korea had been in conversation with each other for nearly a century by the time Korea started to open to more immigrants in the 1990s. Globalization literature tends to assume nations as fenced-off, parochial wholes of national projects, when in fact the interaction with the global in material *and ideational* ways is much more complex. From the state perspective, Global Korea is not only about a cultural regulation of society, but rather a regulation of a national developmental project, which has been largely measured in terms of economic competitiveness and growth on an international scale.

Membership in Nationalistic Globalization

The liberalization of markets of goods, finance, and labor have meant, from the perspective of the state, *membership*—instead of citizenship—in the national political economy may be a more useful category by which to discuss inclusion. Through regulated immigration, the state can grow its workforce while withholding full citizenship. The state is not merely a *political* project, but a *political economic* one that has the power to adjudicate among and prioritize political, social, security, and economic goals. What is of concern here, for the developmental state, is what Scott articulates as the "transformative" effects of state simplification in its orientations toward national goals that produce inscribe subjects with a productive place.[20]

Immigrant incorporation literature has turned past constructed but dichotomous categories of citizen and non-citizen determined along constructed identity lines. Discussion of citizenship as a legal category may necessarily need to focus on the acquisition of (civil, political, social) rights[21] and (active) practice of political participation.[22] Citizenship may indeed have implications for the stability of residence and access to rights.[23] However, the democratic and liberal contexts from which these theories are often derived might not extend to a newly democratized environment in which work is not a right but a duty to the nation-state.

Nominally, the category of "Korean citizen" seems ascriptive, limited, and relatively homogeneous, and extant work examining the role of "Korean identity" in "Korean citizenship" largely focuses on possession of ethnic and civic markers.[24] Recent scholarship has sought to further dissect the politics and contingencies of the ethnic constructions of Korea's national boundary.[25] J. Kim warns against giving too much explanatory power to the role of ethnic nationalism (or even civic nationalism) for terms of belonging and membership to cases like South Korea.[26] Whereas these focus on the ethnic politics of belonging, I here take a step to focus on fields of national membership and roles in the *political economy* of the nation-state.

Global Korea as Nationally-Bounded Globalization

Membership in the political economic trajectory of the developmental state is markedly different from membership in more liberal contexts. The nation-building project of mid-century South Korea laid the foundations for a new narrative of South Koreanness (based on the constructed community of an ethnically homogeneous and monocultural *minjok*); the state simultaneously cited economic and security competition with North Korea to foster an allegiant and productive workforce committed to national development. Developmental states have had the political capacity to impress upon society the state's developmentalist logic in order to successfully carry out their project.[27] Whether the academic literature on the developmental state still accurately describes contemporary states is up for debate. Wong, for example, describes the "adaptive developmental state" as a resilient and "maturing" mode of governance that retains the developmental nature while utilizing targeted neoliberal and/or welfare policies for the best possible economic effects.[28]

Chang has offered the concept of *developmental citizenship* to suggest how the developmental state's strong and pervasive capacity constructed contemporary citizenship in Korea.[29] To achieve national economic goals, the nation-state project coerced individuals to sacrifice certain individual rights. Chang argues that this "trade" of rights for economic assurance—to benefit as private individuals as the national economy grows—is the basis for national membership in Korea. Despite the memory of repressive authoritarianism during the era of rapid economic growth, many Korean citizens desire a return to developmental citizenship in the face of material hardship and economic insecurity.[30] The social contract in the developmental state is predicated on participation in a growing economy.

Multiculturalism in South Korea

Global Korea is not only about a cultural regulation of society but is also focused on regulation of a national developmental project. National development is measured in terms of economic competitiveness and growth on an international scale. As will be discussed below, the state has framed immigration and the inward movement of people (Korean or foreign) as an economic solution to demographic and workforce limitations. As N. H. J. Kim has argued, pursuing *damunhwa*—Korean multiculturalism—is "a means to improve Korea's reputation."[31] The state now selectively evokes or minimizes ethnonational boundaries to control and shape the influx of new persons participating in the Korean economy and society.

In the Korean case, the multiculturalism issue is not the same debate as in much more diverse nations that focus on claims for nationalism or cosmopolitanism, liberal or otherwise.[32] In general, multiculturalism is an ambiguous and confusing term, and can be employed to describe multinational states, polyethnic societies, and immigrant phenomena; this ambiguity leads to confusion among the populace as well as a fragmented and likely ineffective government policy for managing changes in the ethnic profile of a populace.[33] N. Kim suggests how multiculturalism in contemporary South Korea has been framed as "a means, end, and object of national development."[34] N. Kim is particularly focused here on Korea's national standing. Compared to the experience of Eastern and Central European countries—where liberal and inclusive minority group policies were required for membership in the European Union and were met with popular movements against incoming residents—multiculturalism in South Korea has served as a policy for a desirable and attainable "developed-nation ideal," rather than a policy for explicitly national economic development (N. Kim 2015).

I build off N. Kim's understanding of multiculturalism as a policy and norm for national development in South Korea, but my approach reframes the issue, as I seek to demonstrate how a hierarchy of various "Global Koreans" play different productive roles in the national economy. In Europe, states were generally transformed from "passive labor importers" into "countries of immigration" where immigrant-related diversity "assists in and serves as the catalyst for defining criteria for national membership and belonging."[35] South Korea—which until recently has been a country of *emigration*—has sought to attract foreign labor and productive residents while retaining its nationally-bounded developmental nature.

Multiculturalism as a Strategy for Economic Development

In the eyes of the Korean developmental state, membership has been and continues to be predicated on contribution to the national development project. South Korean society may not be comfortable with the creation of categories for "minorities."[36] But, the state seems to have created *functional* minorities of Global Koreans even as it neglects racial and ethnic categorization. A recent mode of development for Korea is the introduction of an official multiculturalism—a global orientation that includes native Koreans and a variety of immigrants—which is, I argue, at its core based on economic logics.

This section examines the motivations, conditions, and policies and programs that target a variety of Global Koreans as outlined in the two successive Basic Plans for Immigration (2007–2012, 2013–2017). The First Basic Plan targeted several areas for policy improvement: boosting the competitiveness of the workforce, assisting multicultural families, carrying out immigration laws and border control, protecting human rights of immigrants, and working against discrimination. Ushering in this "multicultural era," proponents of the reforms said, would "strengthen the economic power of the country" (*gukka gyeongjaeng-nyeok ganghwa*).[37] The Second Basic Plan reviewed implementation of the first, and then created five main goals: support economic stimulus and recruit overseas human resources, promote social integration while keeping "shared Korean

Table 1. Conditions of Economic Opportunity and Residence for "Global Koreans"

	LIMITS ON SOJOURN	SOJOURN CONDITION	ECONOMIC OPPORTUNITY	EMPLOYMENT CONDITION	STATE RECRUITMENT
NATIVE KOREAN NATIONAL	□ none	□ none	□ can work full time in any area (unless regulated, like law or medicine) □ can work part time	□ none	□ n/a
CO-ETHNIC FOREIGN NATIONAL	— up to 2 years (F4 visa) — can be renewed	— previously had Korean citizenship or has at least one parent or grandparent who has or had Korean citizenship — differentiated by sending country	— can work full time in any area (unless regulated, like law or medicine) — can work part time	— F4 visa	— preferential treatment in employment compared to other foreigners
HIGH-SKILLED RESIDENT	□ can be renewed annually □ can change into long-term (F2) residence status (3-year) after which time can apply for F5 permanent residence visa	□ employment or points system	□ must work full time □ can change workplaces □ can start businesses with minimum investment (100M won→unless F2 no minimum needed)	□ points-based system for highly skilled foreigners allows residence without employment contract □ can change workplace	□ new visas start-up visa, job-seeker visa, investment condition □ "Contact Korea" program, including overseas job fairs overseas offices help with recruitment, liaise with Korean companies
MARRIAGE MIGRANT & FAMILIES	— depends on marriage to Korean national; can apply for naturalization after 2 years of residence	— marriage to Korean national (F6 visa, formerly F2)	— can work full time in any area (unless regulated, like law or medicine) — can work part time	— n/a	— First wave (1990s): informal and ad hoc through local governments, assemblies and agriculture associations — Second wave (2000s-present): private brokers in Korea
MIGRANT WORKER	□ 1-year (renewable for up to 5 years in one-year terms) □ Employment Permit System (EPS) started in 2004	□ Based on employment condition	□ Must work full time □ Can only work for one employer	□ Must be in employment or training program □ To convert to long-term residence visa (F2); either 4-year employment and certain skills, annual wage minimum, or 2-year college degree	□ workers signed via agreements with labor-sending country (quota for each), through private employment brokers in South Korea

values" at the fore, follow human rights norms by preventing discrimination, ensuring safety and security, and "promote co-prosperity with the international community."[38] Immigration experts—including the IOM Migration Research and Training Center (which was consulted in the review process)—heralded the plan as a marked improvement over the first plan, lauding its "whole-of-government" approach to focus on integration without overlapping programs.[39]

Conditions of Membership for Global Korea(ns)

Rather than seeing one type belonging in a cohesive Global Korea, we might be served better, analytically and conceptually, by differentiating between different types of these purportedly cosmopolitan and/or transnational persons that contribute to the national economic development project. Here, I turn to a brief characterization of five types of "Global Koreans" (Table 1) and demonstrate how, from the state perspective, they variously play into a strategy for national development defined in economic terms.

Native Korean National

The ethnic Korean has Korean citizenship, ethnic Korean parents, and has mostly resided in Korea. This Global Korean citizen might fill this role in several ways. First and foremost, the Global Korean citizen participates in the Korean economy, thus aiding with the developmental goals of the nation-state to maintain and increase its position in the global economy. The native Korean national faces no limits or conditions on sojourn or workforce participation. Their membership is conditioned by participation in a neoliberalized workforce.[40] The mandate of "global" can also be seen in the pursuit of education, particularly language education or study abroad. English—the "global" language—is a marker of employability in Korea, with scores on tests of English proficiency used to evaluate applicants for employment.[41] The Immigration Plan views high-skilled native Korean nationals as a group to be recruited to *grow* and *stay* in Korea. The First Basic Plan discusses the implications of Korea's poor performance in terms of "brain drain."[42] One key policy motivation indicated in the Second Basic Plan was to "[p]ursue comprehensive measures at the governmental level to aggressively bring back Korean students who went to study abroad."[43]

With legal citizenship, in-group ethnic status, and no legal barriers to residence and employment, this group of "Global Koreans" are the benchmark against which other Global Koreans are placed. Despite their core role in a Global Korea, this group is also not homogeneous, particularly in the economic field of membership. Class divisions and economic inequality are a contentious issue in Korean social politics.[44] Despite some introduction of neoliberal reforms, changes to domestic labor and welfare policy have been made in an ad hoc way to placate constituent concerns, not to reform the developmental state; these reforms seem to have paved the way for relaxed restrictions on temporary contract labor and unemployment and underemployment.[45] The result of this means greater heterogenization along class and workforce participation lines among these native Koreans, meaning that the purportedly "core group" of Global Koreans are themselves diverse and hierarchized when it comes to participation in the national economic project.

Co-Ethnic Foreign National
According to the First Basic Plan for Immigration, this group is to be given preferential treatment in employment compared to other foreigners.[46] This is mainly carried out through the low barriers to entry according to the visa regime. As Lee and Chien demonstrate, the Korean state is able to control the flow of migrants through "gates of temporariness," and privileged migration status can be conferred depending on ethnicity and citizenship as well as "its position in the global hierarchy."[47] Several explanations for differentiation among co-ethnic return policies have been proffered, such as the political value of ties or the relationship between state and nation-building or the foreign policy goals of the state.[48] The strongest factor determining ease of entry of co-ethnics in South Korea is how these countries can be seen as developing co-ethnics who contribute to the national economy. This can be seen in the state's differentiation among co-ethnics in the Second Basic Plan, which extended overseas Korean status to Koreans in China and the Commonwealth of Independent States only to those "who are unlikely to be engaged in unskilled jobs."[49] Such a provision does not exist for *jae-oe dongpo* ("overseas brethren") from other countries—mainly western Europe and North America.

High-Skilled Resident
The South Korean state sees high-skilled residents as particularly desirable. The First Basic Plan focused on recruiting foreign talent to "enhance national competitiveness" and the guidelines and criteria were created "on the basis of national interest through cost-benefit analysis."[50] To reduce hurdles to entering the country, new visas—including a start-up visa, a job-seeker visa, and investment visa—were offered to attract potential employees as a way to "satisfy corporate needs."[51] The Second Basic Plan extended more policies to contribute to this latter motivation by opening Korea Business Centers "in countries where corporate demand is high allows them to provide 'one-stop services,' from headhunting and academic and career record verification to arranging interviews and requiting candidates."[52]

The job-seeking visa is only available for those seeking employment in professional careers, has been employed at a Fortune 300 company, or graduated from a top 200 university.[53] In order to recruit high-skilled residents, the First Basic Plan established the "Contact Korea" program that included overseas job fairs.[54] Once in Korea, high-skilled residents can find support through the Korea Trade-Investment Promotion Agency (KOTRA) support center to help with settlement.[55] Additionally, the First Basic Plan sought to promote naturalization of high-skilled residents. The review period for naturalization was shortened and written test component of the application process was abolished.[56] This group of residents are, as the policy explicitly outlines, key to the future economic development of South Korea.

Marriage Migrants and Multicultural Families
Over the past twenty years, the number of international marriages has grown in South Korea. As more Korean women have moved to the city to work and marry, men in rural areas find fewer options for partners.[57] The first wave of marriage migrants were connected informally and on an ad hoc basis through local governments and agricultural associations.[58] Since the 2000s, many migrant brides arrive through the support of a private marriage brokering agency. Marriage migrants can apply for naturalization after two years of residence. They can legally work full time or part time in any area if they have the necessary qualifications.

There are practical and social barriers to their entering the workforce and, despite interest, marriage migrants have low participation in the workforce.[59] The First Basic Plan surveyed marriage migrants and identified limited childcare services, lack of job-seeking help, and lack of language training as major barriers.[60] It also set aspirations for "immigrants through marriage to achieve financial independence by either getting a job or by starting up a business of their own" and even suggested the creation of new jobs specifically tailored to marriage migrants, such as multicultural teachers, instructors, interpreters, and translators.[61] The Second Basic Plan set out to expand employment services targeting marriage migrants, including circulating a list of spouses seeking employment to job centers and a job program to expand opportunities.[62]

The children of these families are also targeted as participating in the economy adequately due to familial, social, and educational barriers. The First Basic Plan indicated that the children of multicultural families need "nurturing occupational and social adaptability and for enhancing employability."[63] The Second Basic Plan augmented this goal with programs to improve vocational training and career and educational counseling for these youth.[64] The children of these multicultural families (*damunhwa gajeong*) are targets for Korea's development-focused multiculturalism because they possess Korean citizenship, have access to Korean familial-social networks, and can go through the national education system. The limitations on their participation in the workforce are structural and social, not legal at the level of the national multiculturalism policies, which are gradually seeking to address discrimination nominally.[65]

Foreign Worker

Currently, labor visas are given in one-year terms and are renewable each year for up to five years as part of the Employment Permit System, which was started in 2004 and replaced an earlier program that allowed only up to two years' sojourn. Workers (migrant labor) are signed based on agreements by each labor-sending country through employment brokers in South Korea with other countries at the state level.[66] The First Basic Plan sought to attract "manpower for the balanced development of the national economy."[67] The state specifically wants unskilled labor "to reflect corporate demand and social costs."[68] Responding to labor shortage due to low birth rate, rapid aging, and increase in higher education, the migrant workers will make up for the shrinking and unbalanced native-born workforce.

Foreign workers in this category may apply for a long-term residence visa if they have accrued skills as determined by examination by the Human Resources Development Service of Korea.[69] Lim has suggested this means the Korean state has already recognized foreign workers' right to permanent residence.[70] The point emphasized here, though, is that those rights are contingent upon an integration which also includes economic contribution and independence. Despite their importance to filling out the workforce, the foreign worker is the Global Korean with the greatest limitations on residence or employment within Global Korea.

Development, Multiculturalism, and Globalization

Rather than distinct phenomenon, I suggest that citizenship, national membership, immigration, and multiculturalism are neither linear processes of rights attainment nor dichotomized as membership/non-membership to the nation-state. Instead, these phenomena are *overlapping* and *co-constituted* facets of a "Global Korea" development strategy with a much longer history that has gone by a variety of names but have consistently focused on economic development and international competitiveness. The economically-focused developmental bent of the contemporary immigration policy is discernable in the motivations and policies of national-level multiculturalism policies that involve a variety of residents from different categories of membership in different spaces of membership. The focus on prioritizing long-term or permanent residence for high-skilled residents and marriage migrants, as seen explicitly in the Second Basic Plan, is based on recognition that temporary foreign labor (unskilled or temporary migrant workers) will not improve the demographic decline and, by extension, will not help build a sufficient workforce for continued economic growth.[71]

I argue that rather than a process of *assimilation*, the state multiculturalism policy is in fact the extension of a larger globalization drive that infuses nationalistic elements with developmental goals. Instead of access to rights or status, from the state's perspective national membership might instead be conceived as performance of membership duties. Marshall had framed the "right to work" as a civil right,[72] but work could also be a duty or condition of national membership. Here, residents and workers are *incorporated* or *placed* into hierarchized spaces of the national project by virtue of their varying functions in the political economy and to varying degrees of visibility, but all are ascribed a role in the official multiculturalism plans of this Global Korea.

Racial and ethnocultural differences are downplayed in the official policy, and "antidiscrimination" policies in the plans target societal behavior and overlook the question of whether the visa and other regulatory mechanisms by which immigrants are sought out and permitted residence and employment may in fact structure and maintain the conditions of that discrimination. In this sense, the state sees the productive roles of the Global Koreans in its development-focused multiculturalism, and works to downplay the ethnic or racial categorization.

Conclusion

This paper analyzed how multiculturalism, defined in developmental terms, creates diverse and hierarchized memberships in a contemporary nation-state project. The "Global Korea" development strategy involves a variety of residents from different categories of membership. I have looked at the conditions by which different potential Global Koreans are sought out by the state to play a role in the political economy of the nation. From the perspective of the state, to be a Global Korean is not limited to Korean citizenship (a legal status) or ethnic status, but rather participation in a larger Korean development project. Inclusion in that project does not mean membership is socially and everywhere recognized, nor that the roles and rights and pathways to inclusion are linear and overlapping. As the multiculturalism policy shows, membership in this project is hierarchized, diverse, and contingent.

This paper examined how the shape of government policy and state aspirations limits and supports hierarchies of national membership through a "globally-oriented" but still "nationally bound" development-focused multiculturalism that finds spaces for varieties of residents in the economic sphere. Working against reified notions of national identity that focus on ethnic and/or civic homogeneity, I instead consider several types of Global Koreans, all of whom contribute to the national development goal of becoming a Global Korea. Making this move shows the diversity and hierarchies of membership in this imagined national community: membership in the Korean developmental project is predicated not only on ethnic but also economic participation. The state has turned to create new members of the national economic development project to fill gaps in the workforce.

Future research might further dissect and problematize hierarchies of national membership in terms of development-focused multiculturalism. For potential and current members, *belonging* matters. The processes of belonging, then, are a variety of boundary crossings, boundary blurrings, and boundary shiftings.[73] These processes and the successes and failures of finding new desired places within the fields of hierarchized memberships might vary subnationally.[74] Such research can then be used to relate the community belonging to de facto *hierarchized membership*, which is practiced through the social effects of racialization, class, and gender.[75] Interesting approaches to the construction of citizenship as a national membership category have invoked discussion of identity as public and relational and constructed from ties to a community.[76] By contrasting at how different residents are limited and sought out by the state with how the varieties of Global Koreans participate in the political economy and contribute to the developmentalist goal, we might uncover a variety of unrecognized populations who perform duties of the citizen and who access various (and often limited) rights and privileges of membership to the national project.

Notes

1. Em, *Nationalist Discourse in Modern Korea*.
2. In fact, "Global Korea" was the slogan for the Lee Myung-bak administration's (2008–2013) foreign policy vision that sought greater activity on the global scale and to leave behind the narrow focus on peninsular affairs. For more discussion on the foreign policy aims of the Lee administration's "Global Korea," see Hermanns, "National Role Conceptions in the 'Global Korea' Foreign Policy Strategy," 55–82.
3. Kim, "State and Nation Building in South Korea," 121–50.
4. The Korean Peninsula, previously a dynastic, agrarian monarchy, became a Japanese protectorate via a coerced treaty in 1905 and eventually annexed in 1915

as part of Japanese empire-building. Under Japanese rule, the narrative goes, the Korean peninsula was thrust into the global political economy as part of a chain of international production and consumption.

   5. Schmid, *Korea Between Empires, 1895–1919*.
   6. Ibid.
   7. Kim, *Contested Embrace*, 36–7.
   8. Ibid., 30.
   9. Ibid.
   10. Woo, *Race to the Swift*.
   11. Evans, *Embedded Autonomy*; Johnson, *MITI and the Japanese Miracle*; Woo-Cumings, ed., *The Developmental State*.
   12. Woo, *Race to the Swift*, 7
   13. Kim, *Korea's Globalization*; Gi Wook Shin, *Ethnic Nationalism in Korea: Genealogy, Politics, and Legacy* (Stanford, CA: Stanford University Press, 2006).
   14. Alford, *Think No Evil*.
   15. IMF, "World Economic Outlook: October, 2016," http://www.imf.org/external/pubs/ft/weo/2016/02/index.htm
   16. Han Sung-joo, "Segyehwa diae ui Hanguk oegyo: Han Sung-joo jeon oemunhanggwan yeonseol kigomun-jip" [Korean Diplomacy in an Era of Globalization: Collection of Speeches and Essays by Former Foreign Minister Han Sung-joo], 73–103, quoted in B.C. Koh, Segyehwa, the Republic of Korea, and the United Nations, in Korea's Globalization, Samuel S. Kim, eds. Cambridge: Cambridge University Press (2000), 198–9.
   17. Scott Snyder, "Introduction," in *Middle-Power Korea*, ed. Snyder, 1–7.
   18. Park Seh-Jik President SLOOC to Samaranch, 18 April 1987, IOC Archives, 1988 Olympic Games Organizing Committee File and SLOOC, Official Souvenir (Seoul: SLOOC, 1964), 56.2. Quoted in Sandra Collins, "Asian Soft Power: Globalization and Regionalism in the East Asia Olympic Games," in Rethinking Matters Olympic: Investigations into the Socio-Cultural Study of the Modern Olympic Movement. Tenth International Symposium for Olympic Research, the International Centre for Olympic Studies at The University of Western Ontario (2010), 169.
   19. Park, "The Korean Wave: Transnational Cultural Flows in East Asia," in *Korea at the Center*.
   20. James C. Scott, Seeing Like a State.New Haven CT: Yale University Press (1998).
   21. Lipset, "Introduction," in *Class, Citizenship and Social Development*, v–xxii.
   22. T.H. Marshall, *Class, Citizenship and Social Development*.
   23. Howard, "Comparative Citizenship: An Agenda for Cross-National Research," 443–55.
   24. Shin, *Ethnic Nationalism in Korea*.
   25. Seol and Skrentny, "Ethnic Return Migration and Hierarchical Nationhood: Korean Chinese Foreign Workers in South Korea," 147–74; Seol and Seo, "Dynamics of Ethnic Nationalism and Hierarchical Nationhood: Korean Nation and Its

Othernesss since the Late 1980s," 5–33; Timothy Lim, "Rethinking Belongingness in Korea: Transnational Migration, "Migrant Marriages," and the Politics of Multiculturalism," 83, no. 1 (2015): 51–71.

26. J. Kim, *Contested Embrace*.

27. Castells, "Four Asian Tigers with a Dragon Head," in *States and Development in the Asian Pacific Rim*, 33–70.

28. Wong, "The Adaptive Developmental State in East Asia," 345–62.

29. Chang, "Economic Development, Democracy and Citizenship Politics in South Korea: The Predicament of Developmental Citizenship," 29–47.

30. Ibid., 39.

31. Kim, "Developmental Multiculturalism and Articulation of Korean Nationalism in the Age of Diversity," *Reimagining Nation and Nationalism in Multicultural East Asia*. Sungmoon Kim and Hsin-Wen Lee, eds., 153.

32. Kymlicka, *Politics in the Vernacular*.

33. Kymlicka, *Multicultural Citizenship*, 14–5.

34. Kim, "The Retreat of Multiculturalism? Explaining the South Korean Exception," 727–46.

35. Goodman, "Fortifying Citizenship: Policy Strategies for Civic Integration in Western Europe," 659.

36. Lee, "Review of Multiethnic Korea: Multiculturalism, Migration, and Peoplehood Diversity in Contemporary South Korea."

37. Hahm, "The Multicultural Era and South Korea's Capacity" (in Korean), Munhwa ilbo, December 20, 2008, http://www.munhwa.com/news/view.html?no=20081220010323371910020, accessed July 24, 2015.

38. Immigration Policy Commission, "The Second Basic Plan for Immigration Policy (2013–2017)," 2012, http://www.immigration.go.kr/HP/COM/bbs_03/ShowData.do

39. Lee, "Migration Policy Development in the Republic of Korea: Progress Qualified," 22–3.

40. Chang, "Economic Development, Democracy and Citizenship Politics in South Korea: The Predicament of Developmental Citizenship."

41. Shin, *Ethnic Nationalism in Korea*, 206–7.

42. First Basic Plan, 7. Demographers project the economically active population of South Korea to peak in 2020, with a 9 percent decline in the working-age population from 2005 to 2030 and an addition decline of 26 percent from 2030 to 2050. Hayutin, "Critical Demographics: Rapid Aging and the Shape of the Future in China, South Korea, and Japan," 2009, http://longevity3.stanford.edu/wp-content/uploads/2012/10/Critical-Demographics-Asia-Briefing-China-South-Korea-Japan-02-25-09-for-printing.pdf, 13.

43. Immigration Policy Commission, "The Second Basic Plan for Immigration Policy (2013–2017)," 28.

44. Pirie, *The Korean Developmental State*.

45. Suh and Kwon, "Whither the Developmental State in South Korea? Balancing Welfare and Neoliberalism."

46. Korea Immigration Service, "The First Basic Plan for Immigration Policy (2008–2012)," (2008) 11. Available at http://immigration.go.kr/HP/IMM/icc/basic plan.pdf, accessed April 15, 2017.

47. Lee and Yi-Chun Chien, "The Making of 'Skilled' Overseas Koreans: Transformation of Visa Policies for Co-Ethnic Migrants in South Korea," 12.

48. Brubaker, "Migrations of Ethnic Unmixing in the 'New Europe,'" 1,047–65; Joppke, "Citizenship between De- and Re- Ethnicization," 429–58; Mylonas, *The Politics of Nation-Building*.

49. Immigration Policy Commission, "The Second Basic Plan for Immigration Policy (2013–2017)," 101.

50. First Basic Plan, 11, 16.

51. First Basic Plan, 18.

52. Second Basic Plan, 35.

53. "D-10 (Job Seeking) Visa," Korean Embassy in Great Britain, Ministry of Foreign Affairs. November 30, 2015, http://gbr.mofa.go.kr/webmodule/htsboard/template/read/new_legengreadboard.jsp?typeID=16&boardid=13402&seqno=669262&c=TITLE&t=&pagenum=2&tableName=TYPE_ENGLEGATIO&pc=&dc=&wc=&lu=&vu=&iu=&du=, accessed May 7, 2017.

54. Korea Immigration Service, "The First Basic Plan for Immigration Policy (2008–2012)," 20–1.

55. First Basic Plan, 20.

56. First Basic Plan, 20.

57. International marriages between a Korean man and non-Korean woman reached its peak at 14 percent of all marriages in 2005, and continues to hover around 10 percent of marriages per annum. Chung and Kim, "Citizenship and Marriage in a Globalizing World: Multicultural Families and Monocultural Nationality Laws in Korea and," 195–219.

58. Ibid., 209.

59. Lee, "Political Economy of Cross-Border Marriage: Economic Development and Social Reproduction in Korea," 190.

60. First Basic Plan, 47, 53–4.

61. First Basic Plan, 53.

62. Immigration Policy Commission, "The Second Basic Plan for Immigration Policy (2013–2017)," 54.

63. Korea Immigration Service, "The First Basic Plan for Immigration Policy (2008–2012)," 64.

64. Immigration Policy Commission, "The Second Basic Plan for Immigration Policy (2013–2017)," 58.

65. Historically, by leaving out the category of race and instead focusing on national membership (via legal citizenship), "mixed-race" people in Korea have been

placed in conditions of "social illegitimacy." See Lee, "Mixed Race Peoples in the Korean National Imaginary and Family," 56–85.

66. Ministry of Employment and Labor, "Employee Permit System," 2010, https://www.eps.go.kr/en/duty/duty_03.jsp

67. First Basic Plan, 25.

68. First Basic Plan, 30.

69. This includes Korean language proficiency as demonstrated by performance on the national examination, and financial independence, among other criteria. Korea Immigration Service, "The Sojourn Guide for Foreigners," 182–3.

70. Timothy Lim, "South Korea as an 'Ordinary' Country: A Comparative Inquiry into the Prospects for 'Permanent' Immigration to Korea," 525.

71. Lee, "Migration Policy Development in the Republic of Korea: Progress Qualified," 24.

72. Marshall, *Class, Citizenship and Social Development*, 82.

73. Zolberg and Long Litt Woon, "Why Islam Is Like Spanish: Cultural Incorporation in Europe and the United States," 5–38.

74. Abbas, "Internal Migration and Citizenship in India," 158–68.

75. Chung, "Citizenship in Non-Western Contexts," in *Oxford Handbook of Citizenship*. Ayelet Shachar, Rainer Baubock, Irene Bloeraad, and Maarten Vink, eds. 431–542.

76. Tilly, "Citizenship, Identity, and Social History," 236.

Bibliography

Abbas, Rameez. "Internal Migration and Citizenship in India," *Journal of Ethnic and Migration Studies* 42, no. 1 (2015)

Alford, C. Fred. *Think No Evil: Korean Values in the Age of Globalization* (Ithaca, NY: Cornell University Press, 1999).

Brubaker, Rogers. "Migrations of Ethnic Unmixing in the 'New Europe,'" *The International Migration Review* 32, no. 4 (1998).

Castells, Manuel. "Four Asian Tigers with a Dragon Head," in *States and Development in the Asian Pacific Rim*, ed. Richard P. Appelbaum and Jeffrey Henderson (London: Sage Publications, 1992), 33–70.

Chang, Kyung-sup. "Economic Development, Democracy and Citizenship Politics in South Korea: The Predicament of Developmental Citizenship," *Citizenship Studies* 16, no. 1 (2012): 29–47.

Chung, Erin Aeran, and Daisy Kim. "Citizenship and Marriage in a Globalizing World: Multicultural Families and Monocultural Nationality Laws in Korea and," *Indiana Journal of Global Legal Studies* 19, no. 1 (2012).

Chung, Erin Aeran. "Citizenship in Non-Western Contexts," in *Oxford Handbook of Citizenship*. Ayelet Shachar, Rainer Baubock, Irene Bloeraad, and Maarten Vink, eds. (Oxford: Oxford University Press, 2017).

Em, Henry H. *Nationalist Discourse in Modern Korea: Minjok As a Democratic Imaginary* (Dissertation, University of Chicago, 1995).

Evans, Peter. *Embedded Autonomy: States and Industrial Transformation* (Princeton University Press, 1995).

Goodman, Sara Wallace. "Fortifying Citizenship: Policy Strategies for Civic Integration in Western Europe," *World Politics* 64 (2012).

Hahm, In-hui. "The Multicultural Era and South Korea's Capacity" (in Korean), Munhwa ilbo, December 20, 2008, http://www.munhwa.com/news/view.html?no=20081220010323371910020, accessed July 24, 2015.

Han, Sung-joo. "Segyehwa diae ui Hanguk oegyo: Han Sung-joo jeon oemunhanggwan yeonseol kigomun-jip" [Korean Diplomacy in an Era of Globalization: Collection of Speeches and Essays by Former Foreign Minister Han Sung-joo], Seoul: Chisik Sanposa (1995).

Hayutin, Adele. "Critical Demographics: Rapid Aging and the Shape of the Future in China, South Korea, and Japan," 2009, http://longevity3.stanford.edu/wp-content/uploads/2012/10/Critical-Demographics-Asia-Briefing-China-South-Korea-Japan-02-25-09-for-printing.pdf

Hermanns, Heike. "National Role Conceptions in the 'Global Korea' Foreign Policy Strategy," *The Korean Journal of International Studies* 11, no. 1 (2013): 55–82.

Howard, Marc Morjé. "Comparative Citizenship: An Agenda for Cross-National Research," *Perspectives on Politics* 4, no. 3 (2006): 443–455.

Immigration Policy Commission. "The Second Basic Plan for Immigration Policy (2013–2017)," 2012, http://www.immigration.go.kr/HP/COM/bbs_03/ShowDatado

Johnson, Chalmers. *MITI and the Japanese Miracle: The Growth of Industrial Policy, 1925–1975* (Stanford, CA: Stanford University Press, 1982).

Joppke, Christian. "Citizenship between De- and Re- Ethnicization," *European Journal of Sociolgy* 44, no. 3 (2003).

Kim, Choong Nam. "State and Nation Building in South Korea: A Comparative Historical Perspective," *The Review of Korean Studies* 12, no. 1 (2009): 121–50.

Kim, Jaeeun. *Contested Embrace: Transborder Membership Politics in 20th-Century Korea* (Stanford, CA: Stanford University Press, 2016).

Kim, Samuel S. *Korea's Globalization* (Cambridge: Cambridge University Press, 2000).

Kim, Nora Hui-Jung. "Developmental Multiculturalism and Articulation of Korean Nationalism in the Age of Diversity," *Reimagining Nation and Nationalism in Multicultural East Asia*. Claire Lee, Seungeun, "Review of Multiethnic Korea: Multiculturalism, Migration, and Peoplehood Diversity in Contemporary South Korea," *Asian Ethnology* 75, no. 2 (2016).

Kim, Sungmoon, and Hsin-Wen Lee, eds. (Abingdon, Oxon: Routledge, 2018).

Kim, Nora Hui-Jung. "The Retreat of Multiculturalism? Explaining the South Korean Exception," *American Behavioral Scientist* 59, no. 6 (2015): 727–46.

Korea Immigration Service. "The First Basic Plan for Immigration Policy (2008–2012)," (2008), 11. Available at http://immigration.go.kr/HP/IMM/icc/basicplan.pdf, accessed April 15, 2017.

Korea Immigration Service. "The Sojourn Guide for Foreigners" (Seoul, South Korea, August 17, 2015).

Kymlicka, Will. *Politics in the Vernacular: Nationalism, Multiculturalism and Citizenship* (Oxford: Oxford University Press, 2001).

———. *Multicultural Citizenship: A Liberal Theory of Minority Rights* (Oxford: Oxford University Press, 1995).

Lee, June. "Migration Policy Development in the Republic of Korea: Progress Qualified," *Migration Policy Practice* 3, no. 5 (2013): 22–3.

Lee, Sohoon, and Yi-Chun Chien. "The Making of 'Skilled' Overseas Koreans: Transformation of Visa Policies for Co-Ethnic Migrants in South Korea," *Journal of Ethnic and Migration Studies* (2016): 12.

Lee, Hyunok. "Political Economy of Cross-Border Marriage: Economic Development and Social Reproduction in Korea," *Feminist Economics* 18, no. April (2012).

Lee, Mary. "Mixed Race Peoples in the Korean National Imaginary and Family," *Korean Studies* 32, no. May (2008).

Lim, Timothy. "South Korea as an 'Ordinary' Country: A Comparative Inquiry into the Prospects for 'Permanent' Immigration to Korea," *Journal of Ethnic & Migration Studies* 38, no. 3 (2012).

Lipset, Seymour Martin. "Introduction," in *Class, Citizenship and Social Development* (Chicago: University of Chicago Press, 1964).

Marshall, T.H. *Class, Citizenship and Social Development* (Chicago: University of Chicago Press, 1964).

Ministry of Employment and Labor, "Employee Permit System," 2010, https://www.eps.go.kr/en/duty/duty_03.jsp

Mylonas, Harris. *The Politics of Nation-Building: Making Co-Nationals, Refugees, and Minorities* (Cambridge: Cambridge University Press, 2012).

Park, Jung-Sun. "The Korean Wave: Transnational Cultural Flows in East Asia," in *Korea at the Center: Dynamics of Regionalism in Northeast Asia* (Armonk, New York: M.E. Sharpe, 2006).

Pirie, Iain. *The Korean Developmental State: From Dirigisme to Neo-Liberalism* (Abingdon, Oxon: Routledge, 2008).

Schmid, Andre. *Korea Between Empires, 1895–1919* (New York: Columbia University Press, 2002).

Seol, Dong-hoon, and John D. Skrentny. "Ethnic Return Migration and Hierarchical Nationhood: Korean Chinese Foreign Workers in South Korea," *Ethnicities* 9, no. 2 (2009): 147–74.

Seol, Dong-hoon, and Jungmin Seo. "Dynamics of Ethnic Nationalism and Hierarchical Nationhood: Korean Nation and Its Othernesss since the Late 1980s," *Korea Journal* 54, no. 2 (2014): 5–33.

Shin, Gi Wook. *Ethnic Nationalism in Korea: Genealogy, Politics, and Legacy* (Stanford, CA: Stanford University Press, 2006).
Snyder, Scott, ed. *Middle-Power Korea: Contributions to the Global Agenda* (Washington, DC: Council on Foreign Relations, 2015).
Tilly, Charles. "Citizenship, Identity, and Social History," *International Review of Social History* 18, no. 1991 (1996).
Wong, Joseph. "The Adaptive Developmental State in East Asia," *Journal of East Asian Studies* 4, no. 3 (2004): 345–62.
Woo-Cumings, Meredith, ed. *The Developmental State* (Ithaca, NY: Cornell University Press, 1999).
Woo, Jung-en. *Race to the Swift: State and Finance in Korean Industrialization* (New York: Oxford University Press, 1991).
Zolberg, Aristide R., and Long Litt Woon. "Why Islam Is Like Spanish: Cultural Incorporation in Europe and the United States," *Politics & Society* 27, no. 1 (1999).

CHAPTER EIGHT

Democratic Support and Generational Change in South Korea

Steven Denney

New research suggests a downward trend in support for a democratic political order among younger age cohorts in consolidated Western democracies. What about newly consolidated democracies in East Asia? Using a research design similar to that employed in studies of post-Communist societies, this research investigates how democratic transition and consolidation in South Korea has affected the political opinions of Korean citizens by comparing support for democracy and political norms across generations and by levels of economic satisfaction. Generational analysis measures the impact of formative years' experiences on political attitudes and orientations, while testing an economic theory of democratic support considers whether preferences are constantly updated over the course of the life-cycle. Overall, this research finds that younger South Koreans—those from the democratic generation—are, like their Western counterparts, more critical (i.e., less supportive) of democracy in the abstract, but hold values congruent with a democratic order. The research findings provide both comparative and case-specific insights into democratic support, generational analysis, and political culture.

Whither Democracy?
Democratic Support and Global Trends

It has been long argued that citizens socialized in democratic political systems internalize democratic values and show supportive attitudes towards democratic regimes, even if they show signs of dissatisfaction with democratic governments. Indeed, "critical citizens" is a trademark feature of democratic societies.[1] New research suggests a downward trend in support for a democratic political order. Amid worsening inequality and diminishing expectations for upward mobility and a better life, some find support for democratic rule among younger age cohorts in long-consolidated democracies is waning. In the July 2016 edition of the *Journal of Democracy*, Roberto Stefan Foa and Yascha Mounk sound the alarm:

> Even as democracy has come to be the only form of government widely viewed as legitimate, it has lost the trust of many citizens who no longer believe that democracy can deliver on their most pressing needs and preferences. The optimistic view that this decline in confidence merely represents a temporary downturn is no more than a pleasing assumption, based in part on a reluctance to call into question the vaunted stability of affluent democracies.[2]

Comparing data from two waves of World Values Survey data collected between 2005–2014 for the United States and Western Europe, Foa and Mounk examine responses to relevant measure of democratic support. The authors fix their attention on one particular question, which reads: "How important is it for you to live in a country that is governed democratically?" This is seen as the most direct and reasonable measure of one's support of a democratic regime. Respondents are asked to answer on a scale of 1 ("not at all important") to 10 ("absolutely important"). The authors look specifically at the number of respondents who answered 10/10, or those who think it is essential to live in a democracy. They find significant variation across birth cohorts. Seventy-two percent of those born before World War II in the United States thought it essential to live in a democracy; only 30 percent of those born in 1980 or earlier agreed. The same cohorts for Europe show a similar downward trend across cohorts, although support has never been as high as in America or, currently, as low (e.g., in the Netherlands, the authors find that 55 percent of the interwar generation answered 10 and 33 percent of those born in 1980 or after).[3] Foa and Munk dismiss the idea that this discrepancy is due to young people being more "critical," or because of life-cycle effects. To the authors, the differences in opinion are due to a cohort effect rather than a life-cycle effect.[4] In other words, the decline in support for democracy is part of a new generational predisposition[5] and reflective of a downward trending democratic support—the beginnings of democratic deconsolidation. The authors' claims challenge the long-held belief that once democracies consolidate, they never go back. In a time of rising populist-authoritarianism,[6] Foa and Munk's finding could be seen as the proverbial canary in the coal mine.

Not everyone, however, is convinced that there is an anti-democratic wave sweeping the West. Pippa Norris and Erik Voeten, for instance, do not think Foa and Munk's findings are necessarily supported by the data. Their main criticism is that, without data going back further than the 2000s (additional measure considered by Foa and Munk go back to the mid–1990s), one cannot conclude that the variation in opinion across birth cohorts are due to generational differences and not simply a predisposition of young people.[7] In other words, the differences in opinions might be due to life-cycle effects, something which the authors cannot so easily dismiss. There is also exception taken to Foa and Munk's measurement of democratic support. To take only those who answered 10/10 to questions about democratic support as constituting those who support democracy conflates those who answered 9 and those who answered 1 as *the same*. As Voeten points out, "In reality, almost no one (less than 1 percent [of the samples used]) said that democracy is 'not at all important.'"[8]

Criticism of interpretation and measurement aside, the data do show significant variation in opinion in the United States and Western Europe. But what about in newly consolidated democracies elsewhere? The debate about democratic deconsolidation has focused mainly on Western countries, but there is no reason to limit the scope to only these democracies. There is much to learn comparatively about democratic political culture by expanding the scope of the investigation to the newly consolidated democracies of East Asia, specifically South Korea. Do differences in historical sequencing and the timing of democratic transitions make any difference? As a newly consolidated democracy, is there a difference in values between the pre-democratic and post-transition generations? This research adds to the ongoing debate by considering the extent of democratic support among generations in South Korea. Similar studies of post-autocratic political cultures haven't rendered definitive answers.[9] This paper won't forward unequivocal evidence either, but it will contribute to the ongoing conversation on democratic political cultures and support for democracy in the current era.[10]

Consolidation Among the Third Wave Democracies: South Korea as a Case Study

Most research into democratic values centers on Western Europe and North America. This is not surprising. Most of the world's democracies are found there, and they have been there the longest. However, the universe of possible cases has expanded as the number of democracies have grown. With the maturation of some "Third Wave" democracies,[11] there are new cases from which to choose and data to use. Recent political developments in South Korea have also attracted more attention to its relatively young democratic political system. On March 10, 2017 then-president Park Geun-hye was removed from office by the Constitutional Court following an impeachment process started by the country's legislature after the revelation of a corruption scandal and the severe abrogation of presidential duties. The lead-up to the impeachment vote on December 9, 2016 saw large-scale, peaceful protests by an engaged citizenry in the capital Seoul and throughout the country. The videos and images of protestors dancing, chanting, and marching are impressive, and repeatedly went viral. For a country with a history of military intervention during times of government instability, what happened is no small feat—even if the peacefulness with which it took place wasn't all that surprising.[12]

However, not everyone in South Korea agreed that the president should have been impeached. A number of pro-Park Geun-hye rallies are evidence that at least some in South Korean society did not agree that the president should have been removed from office.[13] They may not have been as large as the anti-Park rallies, but these counter-protests, which were made up largely of elder members of society, indicate that not all Koreans agree on what it means to be a democracy. One organization that rallied in support of Park Geun-hye—the "National Coalition of Martial Law Implementation"—publicly called for the re-implementation of martial law, citing threats from communists and anti-state elements.[14] Anti-communism may seem like a strange and antiquated remnant of the Cold War, but the message is better received than some might otherwise think. Survey data indicates that many South Koreans, and a vast majority of elderly South Koreans, find value in anti-Communist ideology.[15] It's also worth noting that the main conservative candidate in the latest presidential election, Hong Jun-pyo, ran on an anti-Communist platform. Hong publicly accused the current President Moon Jae-in of being a "pro-North Korean leftist" during his election campaign.[16] His message did not resonate with the 20–40 year-old crowd, but it did succeed in capturing the older, more conservative base. Among older age groups, Hong received either a plurality or majority of the vote. By stark contrast, with those 30–39, he received effectively no votes![17]

On the day of the Constitutional Court, the institutional body with authority to remove presidents, voted in favor of upholding the impeachment motion, many pro-Park protestors marched to the location of the court, demanding its dissolution.[18] They may not have been calling for the reinstatement of a dictator, but democracy means something different for these citizens than it does for their younger compatriots. This is worth further consideration. Are there any differences in political attitudes and orientations between those who came of age prior to South Korea's transition to democracy in 1987 and those who "grew up democratic?" If there is indeed a downward trend in support for a democratic political system, then we should expect to see some evidence of this in South Korea. To orient our empirical expectations, we will turn briefly to existing theoretical explanations regarding the legitimacy of democratic regimes and the foundation of democratic norms.

Basis of Democratic Support: Existing Explanations

Why do citizens support democracy? There are many ways to answer this question, but this research draws from two bodies of research: that which looks at the role of political socialization and regime legitimacy (1) and performance-based theories of political support (2). The first body of literature focuses on the theoretical relationship between late adolescent and early adult life experiences (the "formative years") and support for political systems. It argues that early life experiences shape political predispositions over the course of the life-cycle. The second body of research sees regime legitimacy as rooted in things like economic performance; predispositions towards a particular regime, then, are not enduring but are constantly updating over the course of one's life.

Socialization and Political Generations
Political culture has long been understood as reflective of deeply ingrained norms, values, and behavior. Early research into this subject stressed the importance of early-life family and educational experiences in cultivating democratic norms.[19] The importance of early life experiences has been repeatedly confirmed in the political culture literature.[20] The theoretical expectation established by this literature is that learning in the early years is conditioned by the socialization process within the family, at school, and from the broader structure of society.

Socialization theory suggests that citizens internalize values of the political systems into which they are socialized, forming concrete political values in late adolescent and early adult years.[21] The assumption here is that political attitudes and values broadly supportive of the extant political system will be cultivated during the formative years and that these predispositions will endure over time. In short, the *type* of political system in which one comes of age will determine what kind of system they are more likely to support. Those coming of age under democratic conditions, then, will show political values more in align with democratic principles. By contrast, older generations—those who came of age under autocratic or distinctively non-democratic conditions—will find it more difficult to adjust to a new, democratic political system.[22] The theory is congruent with the story told above of older South Korean citizens, upset at the conditions created by mass protests and impeachment, calling for the restoration of order, even if it means acting in a manner not befitting a consolidated democracy (i.e., dissolving a court).

According to socialization theory, we should expect to find those socialized under democratic conditions show greater support for democratic rule and have values congruent with a democratic political order. Inversely, we can expect to find those socialized under alternative political systems to show relatively less support and have values less congruent with democracy.

Economic Performance
Research exploring the relationship between economic conditions and political order shows that support for a given political system is a function of economic performance.[23] Economic theories of democratic support posit that attitudes towards democratic political systems stem mainly from the successful implementation of a market economy, in addition to continuous economic growth.[24] This approach, tucked within the folk of revised modernization theory, specifies political culture as a crucial intermediary variable between economic performance and regime type, arguing sustained growth and development creates and maintains cultural conditions supportive of democracy.[25] Studies in post-Communist countries finds the same effect at play. Those who perceived themselves as beneficiaries of the democratic transition were more likely to positively evaluate the new democratic system.[26]

An economic theory of political support suggests legitimacy of a democratic regime has little to do with political socialization; it is a function of economic satisfaction. Assessments are, in other words, performance-based. There is a constant updating of institutional preferences over the course of the life-cycle with adult experiences mattering just as much, if not more than, early-life experiences. Theoretically, then, we should expect to find that the more satisfied one is economically, the more support they will show for a democratic political system and the more oriented their values will be towards democratic rule.

Methods, Variables, and Data
This research looks at whether there are any generational differences in South Korea on two dimensions: regime support for democracy (regime legitimacy) and political orientations (norms). It also considers whether

Table 8.1. Generations by Historical Period

Historical Period		Birth Year	N (2005)	N (2010)
Democratic	1988–	1970–	500	549
	Transition in 1987; successful turnover in rule (party-opposition in 1997 and again in 2006). Increasing political (and social) pluralism coupled with post-industrial social and economic changes.			
Transition	1980–1987	1962–1969	267	269
	Political instability and military coup (1979–1980); oppressive authoritarian rule (e.g., Gwangju massacre); social unrest notable, with large-scale opposition and protests.			
Authoritarian	1971–1979	1953–1961	203	188
	Heavy industrial push coupled with centralized and highly authoritarian control under the Yushin Constitution (promulgated in 1972, ended in 1979).			
Older Authoritarian	Before 1968	Before 1953	230	194
	Late colonial rule followed by contentious state-society relations (esp. under First Republic) and economic malaise; modest economic recovery and social stability in the 1960s following a military coup lead by Park Chung-hee.			

opinions vary according to economic performance. Data for this research come from the World Values Survey (WVS) longitudinal dataset (survey years 2005 and 2010). The WVS is a cross-national survey project that collects nationally representative samples on values, beliefs, and attitudes using a common questionnaire. In addition to collecting demographic and socioeconomic data, the WVS tracks support for democracy and attitudes towards religion, political leadership, and the military, among many other variables.[27]

South Korea by Generations
Defining a generation is as much a work of art as it is a science. Generally, the age range of 18–25 is understood as the pre-adolescent formative years when political predispositions are formed. Following closely previous examples in generational analysis[28] five generations are identified. Each generation is defined by the historical period under which individuals turned 18 (i.e., "came of age"). Due to the space and scope constraints of this paper, it isn't possible to go into great detail regarding the conditions which define each generation. Table 1 provides a description of each generation by the historical period under which they came of age.

Economic Performance
While measurements for economic performance aren't as difficult as that for generations, there is some debate as to whether people's opinion of the economy as a whole (sociotropic) or egocentric measures (individual or household) should be used. This research uses egocentric evaluations of financial well-being, which measures how satisfied people are with their household's financial situation, as a measure of economic performance. Respondents are asked to rate on a scale of one-to-ten how satisfied they are with their household's financial situation, with ten being "completely satisfied." While alternative measures may capture a similar sentiment (and perhaps do so better than the one chosen here), it is in the opinion of the researcher that an egocentric measure of financial well-being is a suitable measure for economic performance for this research.

Regime Legitimacy and Political Values
There are many ways to measure support for democracy. No one way will best capture the desired concept. What questions are used is in part determined by what the researcher is interested in measuring. This research is concerned first in regime legitimacy—whether people think living in a

democracy is important—and second in the political orientation or norms of citizens. The former is a relatively straight-forward and admittedly abstract gauge of democratic support, while the latter is a deeper, more substantive measure.

To measure regime legitimacy, we look at the importance South Korean citizens place on living in a democratic political system. Respondents were asked to rate how "important" it is "to live in a country that is governed democratically" on a ten-point scale. The distribution of responses for the entire sample is shown in Figure 1.

It is clear that most South Koreans think it is important to live in a democracy, with most of the variation taking place between seven and ten. Rather than consider scores across the entire index, this research looks instead at those who score at or above the median for the sample (a score of nine). Accordingly, a new binary variable is created with those responding with nine or greater categorized as "strongly supporting democracy." The research by Foa and Mounk (cited above) measured only those answering 10/10 as strongly supportive—that is, those who think it is "absolutely important" to live in a democracy. As discussed above, it is problematic counting those who answered nine and one as the same. The same could be said for counting those who answered eight and one as the same, but the point here is to set a high threshold for regime legitimacy.

However, to consider only whether people think it is important to live in a democracy doesn't give us a full appreciation of what people think about democracy. We need to look at a more substantive measure of democratic support. To do this, a battery of questions from the WVS that

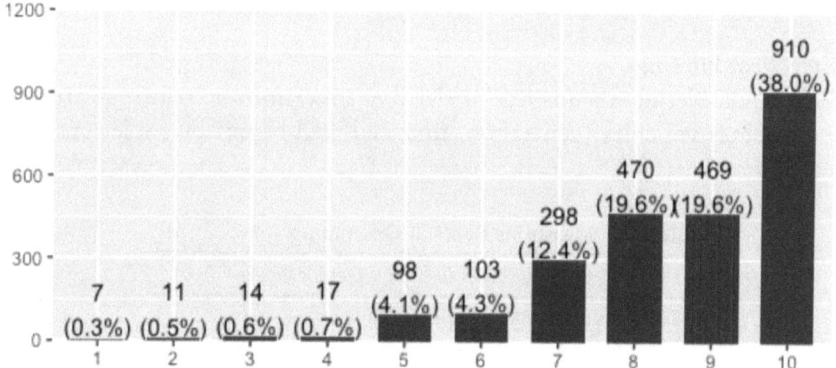

Figure 8.1. Importance of living in a democracy (10 = absolutely important)
Source: World Values Survey (2005 and 2010); missing variables (n=3) excluded

examine what people think is "essential" in a democratic political system are assessed. Respondents are asked to indicate, for instance, if the army taking over when the government is incompetent is desirable in a democracy and whether obedience to rulers is an essential trait of democratic rule. Answers range along a ten-point scale, with 10 indicating the respondent thinks the quality is essential to a democracy and 1 indicating the inverse (not essential). The most relevant items were identified using a data reduction technique on a dimension relevant to this research.[29] The items used are shown in Table 2.

Together these questions represent a close measure of respondents' orientation towards democratic and authoritarian norms. Scoring higher on the items selected will indicate values more congruent with an authoritarian political system than a democratic one. Rather than examine responses to all questions individually, a new variable was created by averaging the total scores of all items on the authoritarian/democratic dimension. The higher the score, on a scale of zero to one, indicates a stronger preference for authoritarian norms. The distribution of responses for the sample is shown in Figure 2.

Unsurprisingly, scores are skewed towards zero. Strong orientations towards authoritarian norms isn't to be expected in a consolidated democracy. This doesn't mean, however, that there isn't notable variation in the data. The question is whether one generation or another scores relatively higher (or lower), and why. As with the previous measure, a binary variable is created using the median score. This sets a higher threshold for what constitutes firmly entrenched democratic values. The democratic/authoritarian scale is divided by the median score (.375); those scoring lower than this central point are counted as demonstrating "strong democratic norms."

Empirical Findings

Before considering a statistical model that takes into account our primary explanatory variables (generation, financial well-being) plus relevant con-

Table 8.2. Measuring Political Orientation

What is "Essential" to a Democracy?
1. Religious authorities interpret the laws.
2. The army takes over when the government is incompetent.
3. The state makes people's incomes equal.
4. People obey their rulers.

(authoritarian/democratic norms)

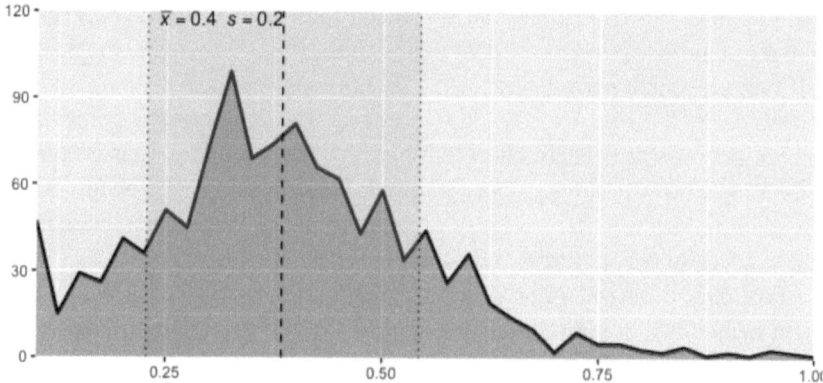

Figure 8.2. Political orientation scores (higher score means more authoritarian)
Source: World Values Survey (2010). N=1136 (no missing variables reported)

trols, we can look at descriptive statistics to get an idea of whether there is any meaningful variation. Table 3 shows the percentage of each generation showing strong support for democracy with a control for economic evaluation.

The immediate takeaway is that there isn't a great deal of variation across generations for regime legtimacy. A closer look, however, indicates some small but notable differences. Specifically, the authoritarian generation scores highest, with 61 percent indicating strong support for democracy. It is only three percentage points higher than the average (58%), but five points higher than the democratic generation (55%)—who we expect to score highest—and six points higher than the older authoritarian generation (55%). It would appear that having experienced autocracy—these are citizens who came of age during Park Chung-hee's highly repressive Yushin regime—makes one modestly more supportive of a democratic regime. These findings run somewhat contrary to theoretical expectations. Socialization theory, as it is understood in the context of regime legitimacy, suggests that regimes cultivate supportive attitudes through various mechanisms (education, propaganda). Political culture, in other words, is tilted in favor of the

Table 8.3. Strong Support for Democracy by Generation and Economic Evaluation

	Democratic	Transition	Authoritarian	Older Authoritarian
Positive Economic Evaluation	57%	62%	66%	61%
Negative Economic Evaluation	54%	58%	56%	49%
Overall	56%	60%	61%	55%

Data: World Values Survey (2005 and 2010). N = 2397 • x̄ = 0.58 • σ = 0.49

ruling regime. It is thus somewhat surprising that those from the authoritarian era are more supportive of democracy than those of the democratic era.

When economic performance—that is, life-long learning effects—is taken into account, there is a clear additive effect. Regardless of the generation, support increases or decreases according to how one evaluates their economic well-being. The only thing of note is that the performance effect seems strongest among older cohorts. This is not unexpected, as younger people are more able to adapt to new political and economic conditions.

As discussed above, only looking at eagerness to live in a democracy (ergo, democratic support) may not give us the full picture. Looking at political orientation might uncover differences in an understanding of the way democracy works, and what it means, to citizens. Table 4 shows the percentage of those showing strong democratic values, as measured by the selection of items from a battery of questions that measure democratic/authoritarian orientation (see Table 2).

Results for strong democratic norms show significant generational differences. Those coming of age under democracy score highest (54%). This is seven percentage points higher than the average and 19 points higher than older authoritarians. Notably, the authoritarian generation scores closer to the democratic generation (48%, or a six-point difference) than the historically closer older authoritarian generation (15-point difference). The closeness between the democratic and authoritarian generations suggests they are the most similar generations—norms-wise—in South Korea. The effect of economic performance is less clear on norms than it is for general support for democracy. For two of the generations (democratic and authoritarian), those with positive economic outlooks score lower. For older authoritarians, however, the effect is reversed. There is no effect for the transition generation.

There are other notable findings from our descriptive statistics. Comparing results from Tables 3 and 4, we see that those from the democratic gener-

Table 8.4. Strong Democratic Values by Generation and Economic Evaluation

	Democratic	Transition	Authoritarian	Older Authoritarian
Positive Economic Evaluation	52%	40%	43%	38%
Negative Economic Evaluation	58%	40%	53%	31%
Overall	54%	40%	48%	35%

Data: World Values Survey (2010). N = 1136 • x̄ = 0.47 • σ = 0.50

ation and older authoritarian both put a relatively lower level of importance on living in a democracy compared to other generations, but only the latter shows any indication of holding values incompatible with established democratic norms and practices. It would appear that the democratic generation might be simply more critical than other generations, a finding consistent with the existing literature.

These descriptive statistics reveal some interesting differences between generations, but they are merely suggestive of what the relationships are between our variables of interest. Not yet considered is whether outcomes are influenced or confounded by relevant socioeconomic, political, or geographic variables. Subject to our preliminary findings to greater rigor, probit regression models are estimated (see Appendix for control variable construction and description). These models let us consider the independent effects of our two main explanatory variables, in addition to controlling for the effects of other relevant variables.

One model is specified for each of the response variables (democratic support and political orientation). The probit regression output (coefficient estimates, corresponding standard errors, and odds ratios) are produced in Table 5. For the generational variable, the democratic generation is used as the reference category against which all other generations are compared. In model 1 (democratic support), we find that the transition generation and authoritarian generations are statistically significant predictors of democratic support. Those from the authoritarian generation are, in fact, 1.48 times more likely than the democratic generation to show strong support for democracy. Economic evaluation also has a strong and independent effect. As expected, the better one assesses their economic well-being, the more supportive they are of a democratic political system.

Model 2, which regresses generation and economic valuation on a measure of political orientation, adds much needed nuance to the story. Compared to the democratic generation the coefficients for transition and older authoritarian generations (negative) indicate that the democratic generation is more strongly oriented towards democratic norms than the older cohorts. The older authoritarian generation is .50 times more likely than those from the democratic generation to show *authoritarian* values.

Probit estimates aren't intuitive to read and while odds ratios are certainly useful, predictive probabilities—which tells us the likelihood that any one of our four generations either strongly support democracy or have strong democratic orientations—provide a better reading of our regression output. Figure 3 shows predictive probabilities for democratic support (showing gen-

Table 8.5. Logit Regressions (Standard Errors in Parentheses)

	Model 1 Democratic Support	Model 2 Political Orientation
Generations		
Democratic (ref.)		
Transition	0.28**	−0.55***
	(0.12)	(0.17)
Authoritarian	0.39***	−0.22
	(0.13)	(0.19)
Older Authoritarian	0.16	−0.69***
	(0.13)	(0.19)
Economic evaluation	0.08***	−0.08**
	(0.02)	(0.03)
Controls		
University degree	0.19*	0.13
	(0.10)	(0.15)
Female	0.11	−0.07
	(0.09)	(0.12)
Unemployed	−0.16	−0.46
	(0.22)	(0.33)
Urban dweller	0.04	−0.15
	(0.10)	(0.15)
Rural dweller	0.03	−0.10
	(0.13)	(0.18)
Progressive	0.48***	0.48***
	(0.12)	(0.17)
Conservative	0.14	0.39**
	(0.11)	(0.16)
Survey Year 2010	−0.12	
	(0.09)	
Constant	−0.65***	0.32
	(0.19)	(0.29)
N	2349	1136
Log Likelihood	−1576.95	−762.71
Pseudo-R^2	R^2_N = .063	R^2_N = .051
X^2 deviance	p = .000	p = .000
AIC	3179.89	1549.42

***p < .01; **p < .05; *p < .1

Notes: Reference for year dummy in Model 1 is 2005. Model two uses responses from 2010 WVS survey wave only. R^2 is Nagelkerke's pseudo R-squared.

erations only). The authoritarian generation is most likely to show strong support for a democratic political system. The probability of someone from the authoritarian generation showing a strong preference for democracy is relatively high at 65 percent. Those from the democratic generation come

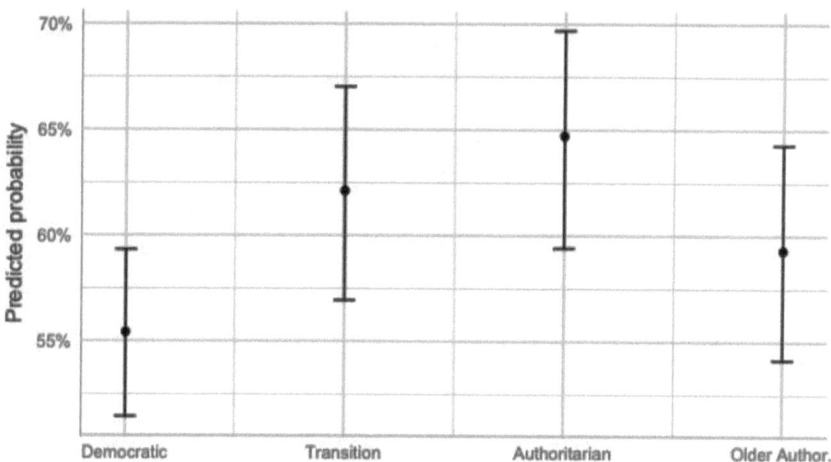

Figure 8.3. Democratic support model (Generations Only)
Source: Author, based on World Values Survey 2005 and 2010.

in at 55 percent, noticeably lower, as the descriptive statistics originally suggested. These probabilities are calculated holding the effects of economic satisfaction constant. How do the predicted probabilities differ according to the level of one's economic satisfaction?

Figure 4 shows predictive probabilities across different levels of economic satisfaction for each generation. The additive effect described above can be clearly observed. The more well-to-do one perceives their household to be doing, the more likely they are to approve of democracy *regardless* of the period during which they came of age. The democratic generation has the lowest probability of showing strong democratic support relative to older cohorts (especially the authoritarian generation, which has the highest probability), no matter the level of economic satisfaction.

If the analysis stopped here, we might conclude that South Koreans growing up democratic aren't fashioning opinions supportive of a democratic order, similar to what Foa and Mounk did for the United States and Western Europe. In the South Korean case, this means that democrats and older authoritarians think similarly. As suggested in our preliminary findings above, this conclusion might be wrong. Predictive probabilities for political orientation are shown in Figure 5. They confirm the descriptive statistics: the democratic generation is more likely to show values oriented towards democratic norms. In fact, it is the only generation that has a predicted probability above 50 percent. The most similar generation based on the regime legitimacy dimension (older authoritarian) is, on the norms dimension, *the*

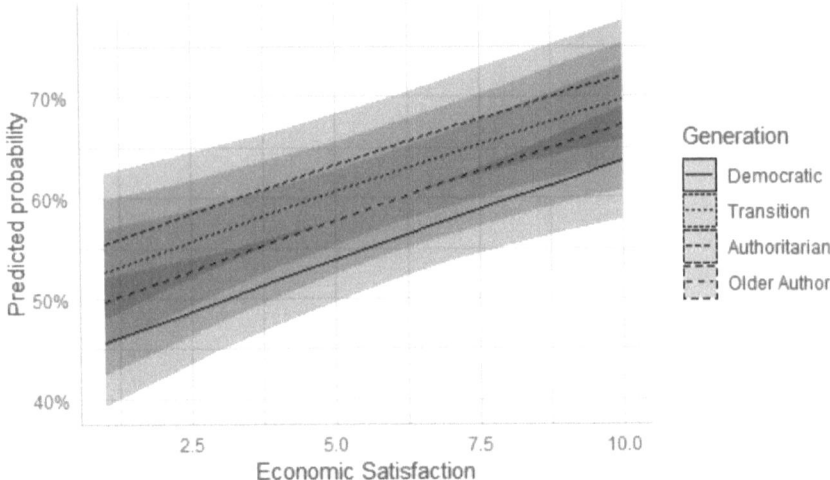

Figure 8.4. Democratic support model (Generations & Economic Evaluation)
Source: Author, based on World Values Survey 2005 and 2010

most dissimilar. The oldest cohort has a predicted probability of 36 percent. The implications of this findings are discussed more below.

An interesting thing happens when we look at predictive probabilities at differing levels of economic satisfaction. There is a similar additive effect for democratic support, but in the opposite direction (Figure 6). It appears that the more positive one's evaluation is of the economy, the more likely they are

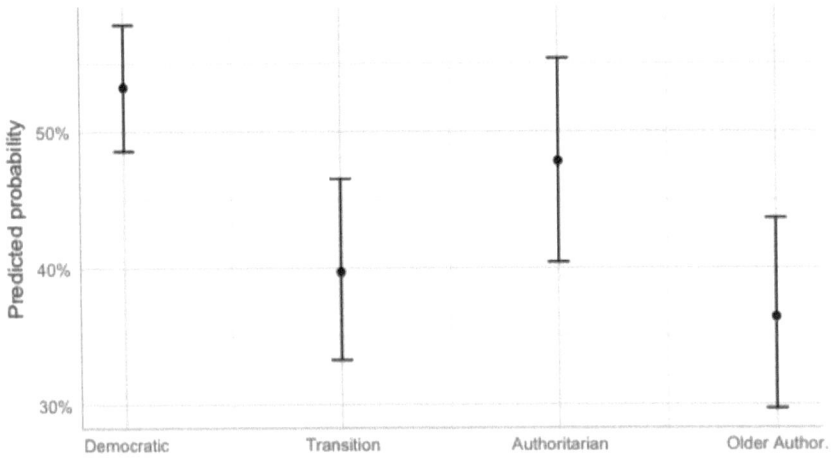

Figure 8.5. Political orientation model (Generations only)
Source: Author, based on World Values Survey 2010

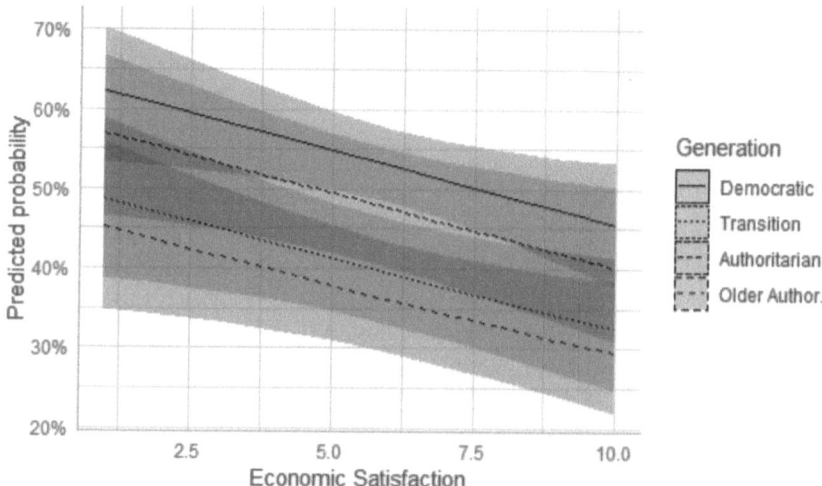

Figure 8.6. Political orientation model (Generations & Economic Evaluation)
Source: Author, based on World Values Survey 2011

to lean authoritarian. Contrary to our theoretical expectations, this somewhat surprising finding is discussed further in the conclusion and discussion.

Conclusion and Discussion

Several findings have been presented in this paper. They speak to both the comparative literature on democratic consolidation and norms, including the ongoing debate about democratic (de)consolidation, and to research specifically about South Korea.

First, like in the United States and Western Europe, there are notable cohort/generational differences in South Korea regarding attitudes towards democracy. Younger South Koreans—those who spent their formative years under democratic rule—are less enthusiastic about living in a democracy than those who came of age under an oppressive autocratic regime. In fact, in the South Korean case, the oldest and youngest (democratic and older authoritarian generations) think alike. However, a more substantive measure of political norms shows a significant gap in what these two groups think democracy really means. Those who came of age prior to the highly oppressive Yushin years but well before the period of democratic consolidation exhibit a significantly greater orientation towards authoritarian values than those who came of age later, and especially those who came of age under a democratic regime.

Second, the findings for South Korea suggest that democratic regime legitimacy may not be a function of the life-cycle. The inverted U shape for democratic support (Figure 3) indicates that responses may be a function of generational experiences. Furthermore, that the authoritarian generation shows a greater support for democracy suggests an alternative reading of the data for Western democracies. Older cohorts and South Koreans from the authoritarian era may show greater support for democracy because they understand, in a deeper sense, what is at stake.[30] In South Korea, those from pre-democratic generations (namely, those from the authoritarian generation) directly experienced political oppression; their formative experiences included assaults on political rights and freedoms. Similar to this, the older age cohorts in Western democracies either came of age at a time when autocracy was perceived to be a global threat. Those many decades divorced from the World War eras and the threat of oppressive Communist regimes during the Cold War era may have little appreciation for alternative political systems. This doesn't, however, mean they favor an alternative political system, as has been suggested. This interpretation of the data is far from definitive, but the findings presented here suggest it might be right.

Lastly, the findings of this research lend additional support to the economic theory of democratic support. Independent of generational effects, institutional preferences are constantly adjusted over the course of the life-cycle. Regarding political legitimacy, the causal claims is simple: regime legitimacy is a function of economic performance. The better one perceives their economic well-being, the higher is their approval of the political system in which they live. Democratic support, in other words, is dependent upon its economic performance. This finding is entirely in line with our empirical expectations, as defined by extant theories on the relationship between economic performance and regime support, but not everything is as expected.

There is an interesting, perhaps even puzzling, outcome for the relationship between economic performance and political orientation. As shown above (see Figure 6), the better one perceives themselves to be doing, the more likely they are to show authoritarian values. At first glance, this seems counterintuitive. Theory, after all, suggests that regime approval and, by extension, supportive norms are a function of economic performance. Then why would citizens lean authoritarian the better off they become? There are at least two possible explanations. One, a simple explanation, might be stated as such: If the system isn't broken, then let those in positions of power maintain course. A deference model of political support, it might be called. Authoritarianism in this context isn't *necessarily* a bad thing.

The second interpretation is less optimistic. It reads: economic well-being and support for authoritarianism are positively correlated, because those well-to-do are concerned about redistributive claims by the less well-to-do. Foa and Mounk see similar patterns in both Europe and the United States. They write, "If we widen the historical lens, we see that, with the expectation of a brief period in the late twentieth century, democracy has usually been associated with redistributive demands by the poor and therefore regarded with skepticism by elites."[31] The better off one is materially-speaking, the more they have to lose. Authoritarianism in the second case is contra to the democratic ideal of economic and social inclusion. It isn't clear, based on the data presented here, which interpretation is best (they needn't be mutually exclusive either). Either, or both, interpretation might be correct.

Is democracy undergoing de-consolidation? The answer, at least in the South Korean case, is probably not. While citizens being socialized under democratic conditions may show critical attitudes towards the idea of a living in a democracy (as do their younger compatriots in other consolidated democracies), they simultaneously hold values congruent with a democratic political system. There is a reason, after all, that young people weren't at the forefront of *pro*-Park Geun-hye rallies. They, and indeed much of society, demanded the slate be wiped clean of corruption and a leader, befitting from a consolidated democratic order, be elected. The findings here should not be taken as a guarantee of democracy's success. Discontent at the lack of upward mobility and job prospects has many young people genuinely concerned about their financial futures. Will critical attitudes develop into something more—say, a preference for an alternative to democracy? The findings here suggest that is possible, however unlikely. The future of democracy in South Korea and beyond seems safe for now, but that doesn't mean forever.

Appendix

Additional Variable Construction (controls) from World Values Survey (WVS) Pooled Data.

University Degree

Dummy variable. Those who have finished a four-year university coded as 1, else 0.

Unemployed

Dummy variable. Those answering "unemployed" for employment status coded as 1, else 0.

Female
Dummy variable. Those answering "female" for gender coded as 1, else 0.

Urban dweller
Dummy variable. For size of town, those answering "Urban industrial area," "Urban commercial area," or "Urban residence" coded as 1, else 0.

Rural dweller
Dummy variable. Those answering "Rural area" coded as 1, else 0.

Progressive
On political scale, those who self-identify between 1 (far left) and 4 are coded as 1 (progressive), else 0.

Conservative
On political scale, those who self-identify between 6 and 10 (far right) are coded as 1 (conservative), else 0.

Notes

1. Norris, *Critical Citizens*.
2. Fou and Mounk. 2016. "The Democratic Disconnect," 16.
3. Foa and Mounk, "The Democratic Disconnect," 8–9.
4. Life–cycle effects refer to changes that take place over the course of one's life. If variation on some variable of interest is a function of age (or the process of aging), then one can expect similar attitudinal or behavioral changes at certain points in the life–cycle regardless of, say, when one was born or what they experienced growing up. Changes due to the life–cycle are different from cohort effects, which emphasizes the importance of period–specific experiences and their life–long effect on attitudes or behavior. Methodologically speaking, it is difficult to determine what is a life–cycle effect and what is a cohort effect, or possible a temporary period effect. See: Glenn, *Cohort Analysis*.
5. Cohort and generation are often used interchangeably and will be done so in this paper.
6. Ronald Inglehart and Norris, "Trump and the Populist Authoritarian Parties: *The Silent Revolution* in Reverse," 443–454.
7. Norris, "Is Western Democracy Backsliding? Diagnosing the Risks"; and Voeten, "Are people really turning away from democracy?"
8. Voeten, "That viral graph about millennials' declining support for democracy? It's very misleading."
9. Shin and Dalton, "Growing up Democratic: Generational Change in East Asian Democracies," 345–372; and Denemark, Mattes, and Niemi, *Growing Up Democratic*.

10. This paper centers its focus on political culture and South Korean citizens' attitudes towards their political system. It is not concerned with elite statements or sentiment, or the formal political process. Of course, democratic orders depend in large part on political elites and other relevant political groups (e.g., political parties) accepting a democratic political order. However, democracy's long-term viability depends upon a supportive populace. In other words, democracy fails if the political system and political culture are incongruent. See, among many others: Ronald Inglehart and Welzel, *Modernization, Cultural Change and Democracy*.

11. Frist first coined by political scientist Samuel Huntington in 1991, the third wave of democracy refers to the countries which transitioned from autocratic to democratic rule between the mid–1970s through the early 1990s in Latin America, Asia Pacific, and Latin America. The failed or troubled transitions rule in many of these countries to consolidated democratic has given rise to the study of "hybrid regimes" and "competitive authoritarianism"—regimes that are democratic in name, but either partially or effectively autocratic. See Diamond, "Thinking About Hybrid Regimes," 21–35 and Way and Levitsky, *Competitive Authoritarianism*.

12. On May 16, 1961 Park Chung–hee (a Major–General in the army), with support from the Military Revolutionary Committee, overthrew the democratically elected—but unconsolidated rule—of the Yun Bo–seon government. General Chun Doo–hwan would lead two more coups (one in late 1979 and another in 1980) to secure and consolidate his rule in the power vacuum that followed the assassination of Park Chung–hee in 1979. Chun's consolidation of power included his violent suppression of the democratic uprising in Gwangju.

13. Aljazeera, "Rival protests in Seoul over Park Geun–hye impeachment."

14. JoongAng Daily, "Pro–Park rally calls for the imposition of martial law."

15. Denney, "Anti–Communism Endures: Political Implications of ROK Political Culture."

16. Kim, "North Korea the first question at first all–candidates presidential debate."

17. Denney, "South Korea's 19th Presidential Election: Lessons Learned."

18. Yonhap, "Two die as pro–Park protest turns violent."

19. Almond and Verba, *The Civic Culture*.

20. Niemi and Sobieszek, "Political Socialization," 209–233; and Pye, *Asian Power and Politics*.

21. Mishler and Rose, "Trajectories of Fear and Hope: Support for Democracy in Post–Communist Europe," 553–581; and Shin and Dalton, "Growing up Democratic."

22. Jennings and Richard Niemi, *Generations and Politics*; Jennings, "The Crystallization of Orientations," in *Continuities in Political Action*, eds. Samuel H. Barnes, Jan van Deth, and M. Kent Jennings (Berlin and New York: De Gruyter, 1989), 313–348; Sears and Nicholas A. Valentino, "Politics Matters: Political Events as Catalysts for Preadult Socialization," 45–65; and Neundorf, "Democracy in Transition: A Micro perspective on System Change in Post–Socialist Societies," 1096–1108.

23. Lewis–Beck, *Economics and Elections*; and Clarke, Nitish Dutt, and Allan Kornberg, "The Political Economy of Attitudes toward Polity and Society in Western European Democracies,'" 998–1021.

24. Lipset, Seymore M. 1959. "Some Social Requisites of Democracy: Economic Development and Political Legitimacy." American Political Science Review 53 (1): 69–105; and Przeworski and Fernando Limongi, "Modernization: Theories and Facts," 155–183.

25. The list is long, but revised modernization theory, from which this paper draws, is best summarized in a 2005 book by Inglehart and Welzel, Chapter 1, "A Revised Theory of Modernization, 15–47.

26. Mishler and Richard Rose, "Trajectories of Fear and Hope: Support for Democracy in Post–Communist Europe," 553–581; and Ekman and Jonas Linde, "Communist Nostalgia and the Consolidation of Democracy in Central and Eastern Europe," 354–374.

27. For more, see: http://www.worldvaluessurvey.org/wvs.jsp.

28. See Shin and Dalton, "Growing up Democratic" and Neundorf, "Democracy in Transition."

29. Using the latest survey wave (2010), there are nine questions from which to choose. Principal component analysis, a data reduction technique which identifies correlated variables within a dataset, shows two dimensions. The second dimension incorporates four of the original nine items and represents a dimension relevant for this research: democratic and authoritarian values.

30. As was suggested by social commentator Ezra Klein in an interview with Yascha Mounk, the reason older age cohorts may show greater support for democracy is because of their direct or indirect experiences with autocracy and oppression. See the interview, from the Ezra Klein Podcast, at: https://soundcloud.com/ezra–klein–show/yascha–mounk–is–trumps–incompetence–saving–us–from–his–illiberalism.

31. Foa and Mounk, "The Democratic Disconnect," 14.

Bibliography

Aljazeera. "Rival protests in Seoul over Park Geun-hye impeachment," February 26, 2017, http://www.aljazeera.com/news/2017/02/rival-protests-seoul-park-geun-hye-impeachment-170225135031979.html.

Almond, Gabriel, and Sindey Verba. *The Civic Culture: Political Attitudes and Democracy in Five Nations* (Princeton, NJ: Princeton University Press, 1963).

Clarke, Harold D., Nitish Dutt, and Allan Kornberg. "The Political Economy of Attitudes toward Polity and Society in Western European Democracies,'" *Journal of Politics*, 55 no. 4 (1993): 998–1021.

Denemark, David, Robert Mattes, and Richard G. Niemi. *Growing Up Democratic: Does It Make a Difference?* (Boulder, CO: Lynne Rienner, 2017).

Denney, Steven. "Anti-Communism Endures: Political Implications of ROK Political Culture," *Sino-NK*, May 8, 2017, https://sinonk.com/2017/05/08/anti-communist-ideology-endures-political-implications-of-rok-conservative-political-culture/.

Denney, Steven. "South Korea's 19th Presidential Election: Lessons Learned," *The Diplomat*, May 13, 2017, https://thediplomat.com/2017/05/south-koreas-19th-presidential-election-lessons-learned/.

Diamond, Larry. "Thinking About Hybrid Regimes," *Journal of Democracy*, 13 no. 2 (2002): 21–35.

Ekman, Joakim, and Jonas Linde. "Communist Nostalgia and the Consolidation of Democracy in Central and Eastern Europe," *Journal of Communist Studies and Transition Politics*, 21 no. 3 (2005): 354–374.

Fou, Roberto Stefan, and Yascha Mounk. "The Democratic Disconnect," *Journal of Democracy*, 27 no. 3 (2017): 5–17

Glenn, Norval D. *Cohort Analysis, 2nd Edition* (Thousand Oaks, CA: Sage Publications, 2005).

Jennings, M. Kent, and Richard Niemi. *Generations and Politics: A Panel Study of Young Adults and their Parents* (Princeton, NJ: Princeton University Press, 1981).

Jennings, M. Kent. "The Crystallization of Orientations," in *Continuities in Political Action*, eds. Samuel H. Barnes, Jan van Deth, and M. Kent Jennings (Berlin and New York: De Gruyter, 1989), 313–348.

JoongAng Daily. "Pro-Park rally calls for the imposition of martial law," January 23, 2017, http://mengnews.joins.com/view.aspx?aid=3028996.

Kim, Nam-il. "North Korea the first question at first all-candidates presidential debate," *Hankyoreh*, April 14, 2017, http://www.hani.co.kr/arti/english_edition/e_national/790762.html.

Lewis-Beck, Michael. *Economics and Elections: The Major Western Democracies* (Ann Arbor: University of Michigan Press, 1988).

Mishler, William, and Richard Rose. "Trajectories of Fear and Hope: Support for Democracy in Post-Communist Europe," *Comparative Political Studies*, 28 no. 4 (1996): 553–581.

Neundorf, Anja, "Democracy in Transition: A Micro perspective on System Change in Post-Socialist Societies," *Journal of Politics*, 72 no. 4 (2015): 1096–1108.

Niemi, Richard G., and Barbara I. Sobieszek. "Political Socialization," *Annual Review of Sociology*, 3 (1977): 209–233.

Norris, Pippa. *Critical Citizens: Global Support for Democratic Government* (Oxford: Oxford University Press, 1999).

———. "Trump and the Populist Authoritarian Parties: *The Silent Revolution* in Reverse," *Perspective on Politics*, 15 no. 2 (2017): 443–454.

———. "Is Western Democracy Backsliding? Diagnosing the Risks," *Journal of Democracy* (Web Exchange), April 28, 2017 (Updated June 2017).

Przeworski, Adam, and Fernando Limongi, "Modernization: Theories and Facts," *World Politics*, 49 no. 2 (1997): 155–183.

Pye, Lucian W. *Asian Power and Politics: The Cultural Dimensions of Authority* (Cambridge, MA: Harvard University Press, 1985).

Sears, David O., and Nicholas A. Valentino. "Politics Matters: Political Events as Catalysts for Preadult Socialization," *American Political Science Review*, 91 no. 1 (1997): 45–65.

Shin, Doh Chull, and Russel Dalton. "Growing up Democratic: Generational Change in East Asian Democracies," *Japanese Journal of Political Science*, 15 no. 3 (2014): 345–372.

Voeten, Erik. "Are people really turning away from democracy?," *Journal of Democracy* (Web Exchange), April 28, 2017 (Updated June 2017).

Voeten, Erik. "That viral graph about millennials' declining support for democracy? It's very misleading," *Monkey Cage*, December 5, 2016, https://www.washingtonpost.com/news/monkey-cage/wp/2016/12/05/that-viral-graph-about-millennials-declining-support-for-democracy-its-very-misleading/?utm_term=.3c4f449a59bc#comments.

Welzel, Christian. *Modernization, Cultural Change and Democracy: The Human Development Sequence* (Cambridge: Cambridge University Press, 2005).

Way, Lucan, and Steven Levitsky. *Competitive Authoritarianism: Hybrid Regimes after the Cold War* (Cambridge: Cambridge University Press, 2010).

Yonhap. "Two die as pro-Park protest turns violent." March 10, 2017, http://english.yonhapnews.co.kr/news/2017/03/10/0200000000AEN20170310009452315.html.

Index

American Korean Foundation (AFK), 42, 51, 52

Brzezinski, Zbigniew, 72, 75–76, 78–82
Busan, 1, 4, 13–28; railways in, 13, 19, 24

Carter, Jimmy: attempts at reviving inter-Korean dialogue, 81; plans towards Korean peninsula, 70–75; trilateral talks and, 81–83
Ceausescu, Nicolae, 76
Central Intelligence Agency (CIA), 47, 72–73, 77, 79
China, People's Republic of (PRC), 22, 40, 44, 69, 96–97, 111–12, 115, 130, 139, 140–45, 147, 166; policy towards North Korea, 116–23; in U.S. policy towards Korea, 71–84
China, Republic of (ROC), 42, 44, 79, 98
Chun, Doo Hwan, 83
citizenship, 157, 161–62, 165–66, 168–69

Cooperative for American Remittance Everywhere (CARE), 40, 49, 52
Cuba, 69, 70, 73, 83

democracy, 4, 8, 9–10, 179–196; consolidation in South Korea, 181–183;
global trends in support for, 180–181; support for among different generations, 189–191
Deng, Xiaoping, 73, 76, 79, 80, 83, 118, 119, 120, 121, 122
development, 13–27, 40–47; in a fishing village, 51–53

economic growth, 2, 168–69, 184
Egypt, 45, 82
Eisenhower, Dwight, 42, 43

food aid, 39–60
Food for Peace, 5, 39, 40, 43–52, 54–58

Germany, 43, 76, 77
Gleysteen, William, 81
global engagement, 3, 9

Index

globalization, 2, 3, 158–161, 168–69
Gukjesijang (Ode to My Father), 1–2

Honecker, Erich, 77
Hong, Jun-pyo, 182
Hua, Guofeng, 77, 78
Huang, Hua, 76, 78
human rights, 70, 82, 163, Hyundai Corporation, 13, 26–27

India, 40, 42, 45
inter-Korean relations, 80, 81, 93–94, 97, 99–100, 102–103, 105
International Cooperation Administration (ICA), 44, 45
Iran, 6, 83, 93–97, 100–105

Japan, 71, 73, 74, 116, 117, 121–23, 136, 138;
and colonial period of Korea, 14–22, 51, 53, 158–59
Jiang, Zemin, 118, 119, 120, 122
Johnson, Lyndon, 45, 59

Khamenei, Sayed Ali, 104
Kim, Il-sung, 40, 71–74, 76, 77–78, 80–81, 99, 104, 113, 116–22
Kim, Jong Il, 83
Kim, Young-nam, 118
Kim, Young-sam, 160
Korea, Democratic People's Republic of (DPRK), 1, 5–8, 19, 24, 26, 40, 42–43, 49, 58, 69–71, 76–84, 160–62; black markets in, 138–147; in Carter's foreign policy, 72–75; economic order in, 131–3; elite-centered economy in, 133–38; relations with China, 118–23; relations with Iran, 95–7, 104–105; smuggling between China and, 141–46; students at the Tehran Foreign School, 101–102; UN membership of, 112–18; Korea, North. *See* Korea, Democratic People's Republic of
Korea, Republic of (ROK), 13, 15, 16, 19, 23, 26, 43–46, 89, 69–77, 79–84, 111, 119–23, 141–2, 144–5, 157–60, 166–68, 179; democratic support in, 181–83, 186–97; economic development in, 163–65; immigration to, 166–68; multiculturalism in, 161–63; politics of, 8–9, 161, 165; relations with Iran, 97, 105; students at the Tehran Foreign School, 97–104; village self-help program in, 39–42, 49–57; UN membership of, 112–18
Korea, South. *See* Korea, Republic of (ROK)
Korean War, 14, 15, 18, 25–27, 42, 49, 51, 98, 112, 114
Korean Worker's Party (KWP), 134–35
Kunayev, Dinmukhamed Akhmedovich, 77

Li, Peng, 116, 119, 121–22

MacArthur, Douglas, 20, 22
Mexico, 42
Moon, Jae-in, 182
multiculturalism, 8, 157–59, 162–63, 168–70
Munam-Ri, 51–53

Nakamura, Masanao, 48
National Construction Services (NCS), 49
nationalism, 7, 159, 161–62

Park, Chung Hee, 15, 41, 44, 47, 51, 58–59, 70, 72, 76, 78, 113, 189
Park, Geun-hye, 182, 197
Philippines, 42, 44
propaganda, 44, 58, 98–100, 115

Qian, Qichen, 117, 119

Rhee, Syngman, 44, 52
Rodong Sinmun, 111, 115–17, 122
Rostow, Walt W., 41

self-help, 3, 39–41, 43, 45–58
South Chungcheong Province, 52–54
Soviet Union. *See* USSR

Taiwan. *See* China, Republic of
Tehran Foreign School, 6, 93–94, 97–104
Tito, Josip Broz, 76
trade, 9, 14, 17, 77, 80, 93, 119–22, 134–36, 138, 139; between North Korea and Iran, 95–96; North Korean illicit practices, 142–46
Trivellato, Francesca, 94

Union of Soviet Socialist Republics (USSR), 43, 71, 73, 77, 79–80, 112, 114–16, 118–21, 123, 148, 159
United Arab Republic, 45
United Nations, 7, 46, 70, 73, 111–23

United Nations Development Program (UNDP), 46
United States (U.S.), 39, 40–41, 46, 49–50, 51, 52, 54–55, 57–59, 69, 76–84, 112, 115, 117, 121, 135, 159; food relief program, 42–47; logistics during the Korean War, 19–26; plans to withdraw troops from South Korea, 70–75
United States Operations Mission (USOM), 39–42, 44–47, 51–52, 57–58

Vance, Cyrus, 70–71, 73–4, 76, 82
Vietnam, 27, 69, 70–71, 73, 75–76, 78–79, 81, 83–84
Vietnam War, 27

World Food Program (WFP), 40, 46–47
World War II, 13, 16, 18–19, 180

yushin, 189, 195

Zhao, Ziyang, 120

About the Author and Contributors

Gregg A. Brazinsky is professor of History and International Affairs at The George Washington University. He is the author of *Winning the Third World: Sino–American Rivalry during the Cold War* and *Nation Building in South Korea: Koreans, Americans, and the Making of a Democracy*. His current research focuses on the role of empathy in Sino–North Korean relations and American nation building in Asia.

Patrick Chung is assistant professor of history at the University of Maryland, College Park. His current research focuses on the relationship between the growth of the military–industrial complex in the United States and the industrialization of East Asia during the Cold War. He is working on a book (*Making Korea Global*) that traces the impact of the U.S. military on the "miraculous" growth of the South Korean economy.

Dajeong Chung is an independent scholar. She served as visiting assistant professor of history at the College of William and Mary from 2015–2017 and earned a PhD from Columbia in 2015. She wrote her dissertation on U.S. food aid to South Korea.

Khue Dieu Do (Đỗ Diệu Khuê) is a PhD candidate at Seoul National University's Graduate School of International Studies and was a visiting researcher at the George Washington University's Department of History. She has published in the *Journal of Social Sciences and Humanities* (JSSH) and *Journal of International and Area Studies* (JIAS). Her research interests include U.S. foreign policy, modern Korean history, U.S. relations with East and Southeast Asia during the Cold War and the Vietnam War.

Benjamin R. Young, PhD, is a postdoctoral fellow at the U.S. Naval War College. He graduated in 2018 with a PhD in East Asian history from George Washington University where he wrote his dissertation on the history of North Korea's foreign relations with the Third World. He is currently working on his book, tentatively titled *Guns, Guerillas, and the Great Leader: North Korea and the Third World, 1956–1989*.

Jie Dong is an associate professor of the Department of Party History at the Party School of the Central Committee of the CCP. Her research focuses on Sino–DPRK relations and diplomatic history. She is the author of *The USA, the USSR and the 38th Parallel* (Zhonghua Book Company, 2016). She has also published over a dozen articles in leading historical journals in China.

Sheena Chestnut Greitens is an assistant professor of political science at the University of Missouri and an adjunct fellow at the Korea Chair at the Center for Strategic and International Studies. Her work focuses on security studies, East Asia, and the politics of authoritarian regimes. Her first book, *Dictators and Their Secret Police* (Cambridge University Press, 2016), won the best book award from the International Studies Association and several awards from the American Political Science Association.

Darcie Draudt is currently a PhD candidate in the Department of Political Science at the Johns Hopkins University. She is also a non–resident James A. Kelly Korean Studies fellow at Pacific Forum.

Steven Denney is a PhD candidate in the Department of Political Science at the University of Toronto and an Asian Institute doctoral fellow at the Munk School of Public Policy and Global Affairs. His research examines the political culture of new democracies and transitioning societies, with a focus on the Korean peninsula.

www.ingramcontent.com/pod-product-compliance
Lightning Source LLC
Chambersburg PA
CBHW050904300426
44111CB00010B/1378